PRIVATE INVESTIGATOR
MY YEARS UNDERCOVER

SHIRLEY SLEATOR

Gill & Macmillan

This book is dedicated to the memory of my Mum and Dad.
Though always supportive of all I did or wanted to do, they
managed to keep my feet planted firmly on the ground.

Every time I saw them during my years as a private investigator,
Dad always greeted me the same way, irrespective of who was
around at the time: 'Are you on a mission?' I think it was his way
of discreetly asking me, 'What are you working on at the moment?'

Well, Dad, if you can hear me, 'Mission accomplished!'

Gill & Macmillan Ltd
Hume Avenue, Park West, Dublin 12
with associated companies throughout the world
www.gillmacmillan.ie

Typography design by Make Communication
Print origination by TypeIT, Dublin
Printed in the UK by CPI Mackays, Chatham

This book is typeset in 10pt Minion on 12.5pt.

The paper used in this book comes from the wood pulp of
managed forests. For every tree felled, at least one tree is
planted, thereby renewing natural resources.

A CIP catalogue record for this book is available from the
British Library.

5 4 3 2 1

Names, locations and other details in this book have
been changed to protect privacy.

CONTENTS

ACKNOWLEDGMENTS

A special thanks to Sam Carroll, my closest friend and former business partner. We have known each other since we were children and worked side by side for over twenty years. We still talk or meet up practically every day. Without him, I would not have continued in the investigation business, nor completed this book.

To Sarah Liddy, my editor, and all the team at Gill & Macmillan, and to my agent Jonathan Williams, thank you guys for having the confidence in me and for taking on board this, my first book.

Last, and by no means least, a big thank you to all those people who worked in state, semi-state and utility bodies, and all my contacts, who helped me or pointed me in the right direction in the course of my various investigations. For obvious reasons, I can't mention anyone by name. Without your help, I couldn't have done my job.

Shirley Sleator
December 2008

INTRODUCTION

Private investigators generally operate in a vacuum, a twilight zone, caught somewhere between the 'authorities' and the general public. The gardaí and state security services have statutory protection and, by definition, backup support from and mutual co-operation with a network of state agencies. The PI, on the other hand, is out there working without the benefit of automatic support and has to rely on the goodwill of others, including gardaí and state agencies, in order to do their work. If they get into serious difficulty during the course of a job, then just like any other member of the public, they call 999 and hope assistance arrives in time.

Apart from contacts and sources, which can take many years to build up, a private investigator's greatest resources are their wits, curiosity, a filing-cabinet memory, a knack for talking and listening, a hard neck, hard work and a bit of luck.

During the twenty years I worked as a private investigator, I seldom got into scrapes or found myself in dangerous situations, though during one of my early investigations I was trapped by a subject wielding a heavy garden spade. I was in a cul-de-sac watching him digging his garden and a neighbour spotted me taking photographs and tipped him off. He stood in the middle of the road grasping the spade in front of his body in a very threatening manner. The problem was, I had to drive past him to get out of the cul-de-sac. As soon as I moved my car forward, he walked out in front of me, forcing me to stop. I talked to the guy, maintaining eye contact, and tried to spoof him with some story about being a trainee estate agent, hoping he would think I was photographing houses, and not him. Looking at him, I knew that he knew, or suspected, my real reason for being there. He never uttered a word; he just moved to one side and let me pass. Maybe it was because I am a woman; perhaps the outcome would have been different if it had been a male PI – who knows? I learned a very valuable lesson that day: always check your observation position and plan your exit or escape route before starting any surveillance operation. And never position yourself at the bottom of a cul-de-sac.

I very much enjoyed the investigation business and, strange as it may seem, I had great craic on some of the jobs. My associate, Sam Carroll, and I occasionally came up with some really hare-brained ideas in our efforts to obtain information. Sometimes my two operatives, Michael, a retired garda sergeant, and David, who started working for me as a trainee investigator, had to implement my unorthodox ideas. It usually started with 'What if we were to . . . ?' An example of one of these ideas is related in the story of Stanley in Chapter 3, when we decided we would 'help' the local council with their bin collections.

I came up with the idea of doing 'pretext surveys' when I had a problem identifying a subject who lived in a flat in one of the Ballymun tower blocks. As you will see in Chapter 5, Face to Face, on that occasion it didn't go quite according to plan, but I hung on to the survey idea and put it to use in other investigations. I would prepare survey questions to suit a particular case and, with pen and clipboard in hand, I would boldly knock on doors and put all the usual questions – name, age, occupation, leisure activities, etc. – to people who were generally very chatty. I varied the 'free samples' according to the circumstances of the investigation I was working on and usually it worked a treat. It is amazing how some people open up to strangers when they're getting something for nothing.

No two days are exactly the same in a PI's life. Apart from occasions when I was attending court hearings, when I left home in the morning I had no idea where I would end up, what time I would get home or if I would get home at all that night. For me, it wasn't just a job: it was a way of life. The downside was that it was not conducive to maintaining personal relationships. I often wondered how some of my colleagues managed to stay married.

My work was extremely varied, from finding stolen tractors (nicked off a building site on Grafton Street) to finding birth mothers of adoptees, investigating accidents, fires, frauds, thefts, medical negligence and bad back merchants, and just a few matrimonials.

I have investigated people from all walks of life: artists, consultants, gurriers, gardaí; people with high public profiles and Mr or Mrs Joe Public. The socio-economic status of a subject never influenced me, one way or the other.

I have related some of these stories here. The names and locations have been changed, for obvious reasons. I hope you enjoy reading them.

01 | UNDERCOVER

On my way to meet with a garda superintendent in Store Street Garda Station, I stopped off at a landmark hotel in Dublin city centre, just to do some background research. I wanted to get a feel for the place, its guests, and the routine of the front-of-house staff. I had visited the hotel on a number of occasions, but never in the course of my job, so I paid particular attention to the layout, clients, staffing levels and front-of-house activities.

I noted that the main hubs of activity were the reception desk, which was to the left as I entered the hotel, and the concierge's desk, which was located at the centre left of the foyer. I took a seat at the rear of the lobby area facing the front door and ordered coffee. I wanted to get a feel for the place. I knew that I would be back, most probably working undercover. So I sat and watched.

———

I was shown into the superintendent's office at three o'clock that afternoon. Apart from the superintendent, there were two detectives, a representative from the hotel's parent company, and Brian, the claims manager of the insurance company who was my client.

The background to the case was that the hotel was losing up to £20,000 per month as a result of theft from guests' bedrooms. Whilst the hotel's policy was that guests were responsible for loss of property from their rooms if they did not avail of the safety deposit facilities, the reality was that the hotel was compensating the guests for their losses to avoid bad publicity. They in turn were claiming from my client, the insurance company.

The hotel had consulted with the gardaí and, as it was clearly an inside job, it had been agreed that local management at the hotel would not be informed that the gardaí were looking into the thefts.

The garda investigation had not been successful. They had tried a number of methods. A couple of detectives from Harcourt Square Detective Unit had gone to the hotel posing as guests, but one of them had been recognised as a garda.

Then they tried covert cameras. They had taken two adjoining rooms with the intention of videoing the activities in one of the rooms. The video equipment was to be used by an officer in one room while one of their colleagues, posing as a hotel guest, left the adjoining room empty. They had drilled a pinhole through the wall, inserted a mini lens attached to recording equipment, which they had set up on a tripod. That attempt hadn't worked either. They had left the room with the video equipment unmanned while they went off for something to eat. They hadn't even thought of hanging the 'do not disturb' tag on the outside of the door when they left. Sod's law was in operation that day, and one of the housekeeping staff entered the room, saw the equipment and immediately reported it to the duty manager.

I tried to hide my smile as the superintendent continued with the story. The duty manager assumed that someone was intending to take a compromising video of the occupants of the adjoining room and telephoned the local garda station.

'It was an embarrassing debacle,' the superintendent declared.

I avoided making eye contact with Brian. I wanted to keep a

straight face. Brian's sense of humour was very similar to mine, and I knew if I looked at him, I'd crack up.

Brian had already told the superintendent that he wanted to get me involved to try and resolve the case. It was clear that the gardaí were not enamoured by the idea of a civilian, a private investigator and (probably worst of all from their point of view) a female private investigator getting involved in their territory. I didn't take their hostility personally. I had had no previous dealings with any of the three officers, so they couldn't know of my professionalism or my dogged determination. Both the hotel and my client were adamant: they wanted me in. Now my stubborn streak, my 'I'll show them what a bloody amateur can do' attitude kicked in. I was determined to succeed where they had failed.

Following a lengthy discussion, it was agreed that I would stay at the hotel, posing as a guest, at a date to be agreed, and that there would be two detectives in the hotel to cover my room if I left the hotel for any period of time.

My planning for this job was meticulous. My client gave me details of the previous thefts and arranged for the hotel to provide me with the staff rosters for the times when these thefts had occurred. By cross checking both sets of information, I was able to identify four possible suspects. At least two of the four had been working on each occasion. Two were brothers and worked as night porters, and a third was a member of their extended family. One of the two night porters was rostered for work the following weekend. So far so good!

I wanted a good cover story, so I got a contact in London to make the hotel reservation in order to provide me with an address abroad. Another contact obtained an Aer Lingus bag tag and a couple of Heathrow duty free carrier bags, complete with duty free cigarettes and wine, to complete the image I wished to convey at the hotel. I checked the Friday afternoon incoming flights from Heathrow so that I could time my arrival at the hotel.

I met the superintendent again and outlined the arrangements I had made. He seemed suitably impressed, and though I am sure he still thought of me as an amateur, maybe now he felt I was at least an enthusiastic and determined amateur.

It was arranged that I would call in to the garda station the following Thursday with some currency to be marked. I brought with me £300 in Irish notes, some sterling and some other foreign currency I had lying around. The money-marking process was fascinating. The powder used is not visible to the naked eye, but it leaves indelible indigo marks on contact with skin. The marked money was carefully placed inside a bright blue pouch-type wallet, which in turn was put in a plastic bag. The last thing I wanted was to arrive at the hotel with blue hands.

The usual feeling of anticipation and excitement started to grow. It happens every time at a certain point in an investigation – this is it, we've passed a critical point, let's go for it!

I decided to time my arrival to coincide with the Aer Lingus flight from Heathrow that arrived in Dublin Airport at 3.40p.m. This would give me the opportunity to deal with general admin work on the Friday morning. It was the end of the month so my VAT returns needed to be prepared, bills had to be paid and jobs for the following week allocated to my two 'lads', Michael, a former garda sergeant who had taken early retirement, and David, my apprentice or trainee PI.

I worked solidly from 8a.m. to 1p.m., then left the office and went home. I needed time to focus on the job in hand. I turned on the TV and switched to an English channel to get an overview of current UK news, which could come in handy for general conversation purposes. Over three cups of coffee, to get the adrenaline going, I visualised what I needed to do to get the job done, what could go wrong and how I would handle any unexpected events. I guess this process is similar to what I imagine an actor goes through when preparing for a character role. I had to be ready to 'live', to 'be', the character I was going to portray.

I was as ready as I could possibly be when Sam, my associate, collected me at two thirty. We drove to the airport and waited in the arrivals hall for my chosen flight from London. Flight EI165 landed at 3.35p.m. and the first of its passengers emerged into the arrivals area just before four. Sam and I walked to the taxi rank outside and I joined the queue. Having lived in London for fourteen years, I could summon up a passable English accent quite easily. I found that, quite unconsciously, I had begun to speak in my 'English' accent; I was now in character.

The journey to Dublin was uneventful. I practised my character on the taxi driver. By the time we reached the city centre, I was really ready. When I got out of the taxi, a porter came out of the hotel and took charge of my suitcase. I checked in and was shown to my room.

I looked around the room. After the quality decor and layout of the main public areas of the hotel, it was a bit of a disappointment. The view from the window was of a brick wall, the furniture was basic but functional, the decor faded and dated. I noticed some cracked tiles in the bathroom. If I had been paying for the room myself, frankly I would have asked to be moved. But I was here to do a job, not to admire my surroundings.

I put on some rubber gloves and removed the wallet from the plastic bag, carefully wiping the outside with a tissue to make sure that there had been no leakage of the marking powder. To make doubly sure, I removed a sock from my suitcase and ran it all over the surface. So far so good: no blue dye to be seen anywhere.

After a quick shower, I pulled on a pair of cream trousers, cream shirt, black loafers and black jacket. I had borrowed some very expensive jewellery from my sister Barbara; diamond stud earrings and a large diamond solitaire ring. If anything happened to her jewellery, I couldn't go home. Checking my appearance in the mirror, I was happy enough. The jewellery in particular suggested wealth. The bright blue wallet really did clash with the outfit, but I wanted it to be noticed.

Carrying the wallet, I returned to the lobby and mooched around picking up information leaflets and a city centre street map. There were two employees on duty at the concierge's desk. I waited until some guests, Americans judging by their accent, approached the desk and engaged the two porters in conversation. I needed to identify which of the two porters – let's call him Paddy – was my subject.

I identified Paddy from his staff name tag. I settled myself in a large comfy armchair and watched. I wanted to imprint his description firmly in my mind. It's no good just obtaining a general description of someone. People can change clothes and therefore their overall appearance. Apart from any distinguishing marks, you have to look for things that cannot be easily or quickly changed, such as their general build and height; the shape of their head, hairline and hair colour; skin colour and tone; facial hair, if any; colour of eyes, shape of nose and, last but not least, their ears – whether big, small, flat or sticking out. It is always a good idea to check out their footwear; jackets and outdoor clothes can be changed very quickly, which can throw you off, but as a general rule – unless the person is going from a work environment to, say, a social activity – the footwear remains the same.

It was time for me to contact my detective friends. I left the hotel and telephoned Store Street. I gave a full description of Paddy, the number and the location of my room. Detective Sergeant W was going to make his way to my room while Detective Inspector F would take up his position in the bar. We agreed to meet at seven.

When I returned to the hotel, Paddy was alone at the desk. Taking a deep breath, I approached, grinning broadly, and in my best English accent, and doing my helpless female routine, I asked for his help. I plonked my room key down on the desk, making sure that the room number on the key tag was clearly visible.

'I wonder if you can help me,' I asked.

'Certainly, madam,' he replied.

I told him I had an appointment in a place called Santry and enquired what was the best way to get there. As I was speaking, I opened the wallet to extract a piece of paper where I had written an address. The marked money was in a zippered compartment, which I had unzipped earlier, and the wad of notes was clearly visible. The piece of paper with the address written on it was in a separate compartment.

As I extracted the paper, my only thought was, God, please don't let my hands turn blue. They didn't.

As Paddy checked the address he said, 'That's not a good area.

Don't go by bus; come back to me when you're ready and I'll get you a taxi.'

Bloody nerve, coming from a suspected thief, I thought. I had grown up in Santry and thought it was a very nice area. I had chosen to ask him about an address in that area because it had been my old stomping ground and felt like a comfort zone. Still, I smiled nicely and thanked him for his help. As I turned away from the desk I came face to face with a barrister with whom I had worked on a number of cases.

'Shirley,' he said in his loud barrister's baritone, with a big smile on his face, 'How are you?'

Bloody hell, I thought, what am I going to do now? Paddy was at his desk, no further than five feet from me. I had considered the possibility that I could bump into someone who knew me. I had hoped it wouldn't happen, but if it did, I would just have to deal with it as best I could. I reminded myself not to be so smug next time I saw the superintendent.

'David!' I said, in my best English accent.

He looked at me as if to say, 'What's with the accent?'

'What are you doing in Dublin?' I said. I hoped my smile was still fixed in place. I gave him a big hug and at the same time whispered, 'I'm working!' I grasped his elbow and pinched hard. I swung him around and, still grasping his elbow, practically dragged him back towards the entrance to the bar. I turned to face him, so that I could keep Paddy in my line of sight. Paddy was looking in our direction.

'David,' I said, 'don't look round, I'm on a job. Act as if we're old friends.'

I guess barristers could be described as actors in a way; some of them certainly seem to enjoy developing drama and suspense in a courtroom. David behaved admirably, and I could see that Paddy had apparently lost interest. But the whole incident had unnerved me somewhat.

Allowing a suitable time to elapse, I returned to my room and paced until W arrived, bang on seven o'clock. I filled him in on what had happened in the lobby and on the last part of my plan. We agreed to keep to my plan and hoped that my chance meeting with David had not unsettled Paddy to any great extent.

My plan was very simple. I had already displayed the wad of notes in the blue wallet to Paddy. Now I would leave the hotel as planned, leaving the wallet openly on display on top of the bureau.

The layout of the room was critical. It was basically square. The door was hinged on the left and opened flush to the left-hand wall. A bureau/dressing table, complete with mirror, was positioned against this wall and opposite the door was the window. Opposite the bureau was the bed and to the right of the bed was the ensuite bathroom.

The immediate problem was to find somewhere for W to conceal himself. He was about five foot ten, of trim build, and appeared very fit. We ruled out the wardrobe because if Paddy were to visit the room in my absence, he just might take a quick look inside it. W wriggled under the bed. I checked, and he couldn't be seen from the door, but unfortunately he had no line of vision to the top of the bureau. That left the bathroom as the only option.

W climbed into the bath and pulled the shower curtain across. The gap between the open door and the door frame afforded a good clear view into the room but the bureau wasn't quite in the right place. It took three attempts to shift the bureau to the optimum position. I closed the curtains, turned on the table lamp and positioned the wallet at the centre of the bureau top. We turned off all the other lights.

W got back in the bath and tried to manoeuvre himself into a comfortable position. I sat on the closed toilet seat and looked on. He lay belly down, elbows bent, with his face cupped in his hands, but he was too tall to stretch out so he had to bend his legs at the knees. He looked so comical that I had to bite hard on my bottom lip to stop a grin forming. As he wriggled around trying to get comfortable, I suggested that he might try another position – he might find it difficult to extricate himself from the bath in a hurry. I helped him up and he then tried sitting cross-legged in the bath. It wasn't wide enough to sit face on, so he had to sit sideways, looking over his left shoulder. He looked over at me. His stare seemed to ask a silent question – 'Well?' I couldn't keep the grin off my face.

I said, 'Well, just imagine if this comes to a court hearing and defence counsel asks you to describe exactly where you were positioned in the room.' We both got a fit of the giggles. I helped him up.

He eventually decided that alternating between standing upright and sitting on the edge of the bath would be the best option.

We did a couple of test runs, and W was happy that from his vantage point in the bath he could see and clearly identify anyone entering the room and, more important, he had a clear and uninterrupted view of the wallet.

We agreed that I would go back to see Paddy at eight. W called F on his mobile and filled him in on the finer details of the plan. F would take up an observation position in the front lobby to await my arrival and would then monitor Paddy's movements.

With fifteen minutes to go, I got the jitters – was the scene too well staged? Too bloody obvious? Paddy and his team had been involved in this scam for nearly three months by now. Would he smell a rat when he went into the room? Leaving the wallet and the lamp in exactly the same position, I put my make-up case at the other end of the bureau; I mussed up the bed a bit and left my open suitcase on top of the bed. Three minutes to go. I took my bottle of perfume, did a quick spray and replaced it in my bag. W was looking at me oddly. 'Morale booster,' I muttered, and walked out of the room.

Taking a deep breath, I went down to the lobby. Out of the corner of my eye, I saw F lounging in one of the armchairs. He was wearing jeans, white T-shirt and leather jacket.

For God's sake don't make eye contact with him, I thought. I admit another thought did cross my mind: he looks good – just as well he wasn't assigned to the room duties! Mentally giving myself a good sharp kick in the arse, I approached the desk.

Paddy was all smiles, as was I. He asked me for the address to give to the taxi driver. This time I was carrying a small clutch bag. As I rooted in the bag, I made sure that Paddy could see its contents – no big wad of notes this time. I handed him the piece of paper with the address on it and, at the front steps, Paddy whistled. A taxi from a nearby rank pulled over. He gave the address to the driver and handed me back the slip of paper. He cautioned me again about the Santry area, telling me to make sure that I took a taxi back to the hotel. Get stuffed, I thought, as I smilingly handed over a ten-pound note as a tip.

Mam and Dad were having a cup of tea in the kitchen when I arrived home in Santry just after eight forty-five. Sam, as arranged, had left my car in the driveway. Dad's greeting was the same as usual,

'You on a mission?' he asked as I entered the kitchen through the back door.

I had just settled down with a mug of tea when my mobile bleeped. It was F. 'Can you get back down to the station as soon as you can?'

'Did he bite?' I asked.

One word – 'yep' – and he hung up. Sourpuss, I thought.

Dad and Mam knew from my expression that whatever I had been working on had paid off. Their questions were coming thick and fast, but I just kept smiling and promised them I would call in tomorrow to fill them in. I made Store Street Garda Station in record time and left my car in one of the spaces reserved for garda cars. Sod it, I thought, I'm an honorary cop for the night.

F was waiting in the general office. I told the desk garda about my car and left him the keys in case they needed to move it.

We went upstairs to the detective unit. Superintendent J and Officer W were in the office. F arrived with four mugs of coffee on a tray.

'Sugar?' F asked as he handed me a bowl containing lumpy discoloured crystals and a number of foreign blackish bodies that certainly hadn't come from the original bag of sugar. I was glad I'd remembered my usual supply of sweeteners. We sat down around a large table and they told me what had happened after I left the hotel earlier that evening.

F started the story. From his vantage point in the front lobby, he had moved outside. He observed Paddy standing on the top step of the hotel entrance, watching my taxi drive away until it turned left and out of sight. Paddy returned inside, followed by F. Paddy stayed standing just inside the front door for ten minutes, and F felt he was making sure that I wasn't going to come back unexpectedly. Then he disappeared from view and F alerted W to be on standby.

As W picked up the story at this point, someone mentioned that they were hungry, which reminded me that I hadn't eaten since breakfast. Apart from the superintendent, the others hadn't eaten all day either, and we were all starving. We ordered pizzas. I was really enjoying myself. I wondered if this was routine for the others – the camaraderie, the sense of being part of a team, was exhilarating.

While we waited for the pizza delivery, W recounted events as he had seen them from his vantage point. Having received the alert from F, he prepared himself, checked his line of vision and, having satisfied himself that he was in the best position, he waited. There was a knock on the door and after a couple of seconds he heard a key turning in the lock. From his position in the bathroom, W clearly saw Paddy enter the room.

Paddy stood just inside the open door and glanced around. The room was so quiet that W could hear him breathing. Paddy slowly approached the bureau and glanced around again. He opened the flap of the wallet and stuck his hand inside. As he removed his hand from the wallet, W identified himself and as he was extracting himself from the bath, Paddy took off at a gallop.

The pizzas arrived at this point. The lads were keen to tuck in, but I wanted to know more – I wasn't interested in food, I really wanted W to continue with his report, but the detectives were happy to take their time.

Between mouthfuls of pizza, W continued, by now discretion didn't matter any more; W contacted F on his radio and a chase ensued. Following a pursuit through the back stairs of the hotel (obviously the guys had pre-checked the floor plans of the building), Paddy was eventually cornered in the hotel kitchen, where he was handcuffed.

As they left the building, Paddy volunteered the information that he had entered my room by mistake. He said he had to move a guest from one room to another (totally untrue); on entering my room he wasn't sure if he was in the right room so he had opened my wallet to look for some form of identification to reassure himself that he was in the right room. Paddy was now down in the cell area.

Although I still felt exhilarated, a wave of tiredness suddenly hit me like a bolt out of the blue. I was no longer interested in food. I felt drained, and I just wanted to go home, crawl into my own bed and sleep. But all my stuff was still back in the hotel room.

F, W and I piled into an unmarked garda car. F drove back to the hotel and parked right outside it. As we alighted from the car, a number of passing pedestrians started to yell abuse at the two lads. Obviously these 'law-abiding' citizens had identified F and W as detectives. Verbal abuse was also thrown in my direction – something to the effect of 'a new effin' pig'. I was tired and irritable, and it depressed me when I realised that this type of abuse was a common occurrence. In my view, the lads had done a great job.

As we approached the reception desk, F and W produced their warrant cards and asked to speak to the duty manager. The lads outlined the events of the night to him and identified me as having worked undercover to help resolve the case. The duty manager appeared to have some difficulty in grasping the salient points of the story and said he would have to telephone the area manager at home. While he returned to his office to make whatever calls he wanted to make, the three of us went up to my room. I threw my belongings back into my suitcase, checked that I hadn't left anything behind, and we left the room, leaving the door open. I think that was something of a symbolic gesture on our part.

I returned to reception to hand in the room key. I was somewhat stunned when the receptionist presented me with a bill. W took a pen from his pocket, scrawled across the face of the account, 'Refer to Head Office' and handed it back to her without comment.

I picked up my car from Store Street and drove home.

―――

Paddy was sacked immediately. He took a case for unfair dismissal to the Labour Court, which he lost. Clearly any other employees who may have been involved in these scams realised that the hotel management were prepared to go to extreme lengths to deal with such problems. From that point, the hotel had no further problems with internal theft.

To this day, I have never set foot in that hotel again. Somehow, it just wouldn't be the same.

02 | 'TAXI!'

It seemed to me that certain types of compensation claims were cyclical. There would be a spate of claims arising from, say, motorists driving into holes in the road or rear-ending utility vehicles because the van driver had 'slammed on his brakes', or people tripping over uneven kerbstones. Sometimes it seemed like a particular defendant, generally local authorities, Bord Gáis and/or Telecom, were 'flavour of the month'. Then it was the turn of taxi drivers. No doubt some of the accidents were genuine, but I'm not so sure about some of the others.

I had just completed no fewer than six investigations of taxi accidents. The predominant feature in each was that they had all been rear-ended by another taxi. All had been carrying passengers. So for each accident, there might be six, eight or ten compensation claims. The driver and passengers in the first taxi would sue the second taxi driver, and the passengers in the second taxi would also sue their driver.

The other feature was that only one insurance company provided cover for taxi drivers, so all these accidents were proving to be hugely costly for that company. They had made a policy decision that all claims arising from taxi accidents would be investigated.

This particular case was slightly different. The taxi had been rear-ended by another taxi, but there were no passengers in the first taxi. There were three passengers in the second taxi, so four claims had been made in respect of this one accident. I was going to concentrate on the driver of the first taxi, 'Kevin'.

My office felt crowded at our usual Friday afternoon planning meeting. Apart from Sam and myself, there was David, who had been working for us for about three years, and Michael, a retired garda. He had a huge number of contacts, which was a great asset, and, some years earlier, had spent time based in the Carriage Office, the regulatory authority for taxis. I spent a considerable amount of time 're-training' Michael when he first joined us. As a serving member of the force, his personal mantra regarding criminals had been, 'thou shall not get away'. It took a little time for him to adapt to the fact that our job was not to apprehend or arrest, but to observe and report.

At the meeting, we reviewed the cases we would undertake the following week, and I then briefed the others on the new taxi case.

Kevin lived in an old, well-established housing estate. He was unmarried and lived with his widowed mother. He claimed that as a direct result of the accident, he was not fit to drive and accordingly couldn't work as a taxi driver.

Some taxi drivers work days only; some nights only; others only at weekends. Rather than tie up manpower on static surveillance, I decided that any time one of us was in Kevin's neighbourhood, we would drive by his house to see if we could establish any pattern in the movement of his car. Days and times were to be noted.

Michael dropped into the office on Monday afternoon. He had obtained details of Kevin's car registration number, his taxi plate number and, lo and behold, he had even managed to get hold of a copy of his photograph. I didn't ask him how or where he had obtained this information.

Already we had a head start on this investigation. Without having spent any time on surveillance, we now knew the make, colour and registration number of his car and his taxi plate number. We also had a good, clear head and shoulders photograph, so identification shouldn't be a problem.

Sam and I drove by Kevin's house early the following Tuesday afternoon, on our way back to the office from another job. It was a corner house beside a small cul-de-sac. There was no driveway. The car was parked on the roadway immediately outside the house. I couldn't believe our luck!

Diagonally across the road was a two-storey building used as offices, with car parking to the front, behind some palisade fencing. We could park in that car park and use it as a base for static surveillance. We would have a clear line of sight to the house, which was far preferable to parking on a public street where an observant neighbour might spot us. And the top floor of the building was occupied by a business owned by a close friend: the gods were really smiling on us. I had known Bernard for many years. He was an accountant by profession, and at one time he and I had contemplated opening a small restaurant business together. Neither of us wanted to give up our respective day jobs, so the proposed restaurant was going to be a sideline for both of us. In the long run, we decided against the restaurant project, but we remained firm friends.

I spotted Bernard's car in the car park. I buzzed the intercom. 'Hi, Marie, it's Shirley; is Bernard free?'

He came out of his office to meet me on the first-floor landing. Hugs and kisses all round.

'Hello, sweetheart, how are you?' he asked.

'I'm great,' I said. 'Any chance of a cup of tea?'

All the windows in his offices had vertical blinds, which were closed at an angle. Mug in hand, I walked over to his window. It was perfect. I had a clear line of sight to the front of Kevin's house, and the angle of the blinds covered me. Anyone looking up at the windows wouldn't be able to see me. What's more, I could clearly see the front door, which was partially obscured by hedging when you looked across from the car park.

'What are you looking at?' Bernard said, standing directly behind me.

'That house over there,' I replied.

'What's he done?' he asked with a grin on his face. Bernard

knew what I did for a living. I trusted him so I outlined details of Kevin's claim.

'I've a couple of favours to ask you,' I said. 'You can say no, if you want to, I won't get mad.'

Sitting back at his desk, he looked at me as if to say, 'Go on, spit it out!'

'Can I use one of your car parking spaces when we are doing the obs?' I asked. I started with the easy question. I knew he would say yes to that request.

'Sure, no problem. You can use one of the meeting rooms at the other end, if you want to.'

Great, I thought: he was one step ahead of me. That would have been my second favour.

'Thank you so much . . .' I said, and stopped mid-sentence.

Looking at me with a big grin on his face, he said, 'Anything else?' This man knows me so well!

'Well, just one other thing.' I knew I had a hard neck asking him for this favour but if you don't ask . . .

I took a deep breath. 'You know that camera on the end of your building? Well, if we were to tilt it upwards ever so slightly and adjust the focus . . . It would still be covering the entrance to your car park . . . it would only be for a few days . . .' I finished lamely. I waited. As an afterthought, I added quietly, 'Sam could do all the adjustments . . .'

Bernard said yes, with the proviso that the camera had to be put back into its original position by the following Friday afternoon. I could have hugged the guy. Well, in fact I did.

'Well?' said Sam as I got back into the car.

I told him. Everything was in place; it was now down to Kevin. Either he was a genuine claimant or he wasn't.

Later that afternoon, Sam returned to Bernard's office with a ladder and equipment and adjusted the camera.

On Wednesday morning, Sam checked the video footage from
Bernard's camera. Kevin had left home the night before at
8.10p.m. He drove his car away and didn't return until 1.45a.m.
The 'score' so far was one–nil; he claimed he couldn't drive at all.
On Thursday morning, I checked the video footage. Kevin had
left home at 8.30p.m. on Wednesday and returned at 1.15a.m. on
Thursday morning. Score: two–nil. By Friday morning, it was
three–nil. He had left the night before at 8.00p.m. and returned
at 2.31a.m.

At that stage we knew that he was driving when he said he
couldn't, but there was no sign of his taxi plate on his car, so we
couldn't say if he was working or not. We decided that we would
carry out surveillance on that Friday night. We also put David
and Michael on standby to work Saturday night if it proved
necessary.

Sam collected me from home just after seven on Friday
evening. Bernard's car park was locked so we parked on the
roadway between two houses. This is an old trick in the
surveillance business. If the occupants of either of these houses
happened to notice us in the car, they would be inclined to
assume that we were visiting the house next door.

At 7.58p.m., Kevin came out of his house. It was dark so I
couldn't see clearly what he was wearing. I like to note details of
the clothes being worn by a subject on a given occasion: it helps
identification later on. He drove away and turned left, heading
towards Whitehall.

Approximately three miles later, he pulled into the car park of
a pub.

'We've passed three pubs so far. He doesn't like to drink
locally,' I said to Sam. As Sam parked our car, I legged it into the
pub behind Kevin. I wanted to see what he was wearing. He
propped himself up at the bar, and Sam and I sat in an alcove near
the door. It looked as if he was a regular in this pub. He chatted
to a couple of barmen and to one of the waitresses. Other
customers had brief conversations with him.

He was about two-thirds through his fourth pint of Guinness
when he headed for the gents' toilets. Then he came back to the

bar, swallowed the remainder of his pint in one go, and headed for the door. It was 10.10p.m.

He drove out of the pub car park, with us following at a distance. He turned right into the entrance of a small housing estate and brought the car to a halt on the left-hand side of the road. There was a high boundary wall on his left. The nearest houses were about a hundred yards further up the road.

We drove past him and parked outside one of the houses.

'What the hell is he up to?' Sam said as he watched him through our rear view mirror.

I had turned around in the passenger seat and was watching him through the back window of our car. 'The crafty bugger . . .' I said.

Kevin had opened his boot, removed his taxi plate and was in the process of fixing it to the roof of his car. He got back in his car, drove out onto the main road and then switched on his taxi plate light.

The simple process of turning on the plate light meant that he was now plying for fares: in other words, we had caught him working. He had drunk four pints, so he was also over the drink drive limit, and his insurers were our clients.

He came to a stop at the taxi rank in the centre of Raheny village. There were three other taxis ahead of him at the rank. He chatted to the other drivers for a few minutes before returning to his car and driving away towards Dublin city centre.

His next stop was the rank opposite the Gresham Hotel in O'Connell Street, where he got in line with the other taxis. We parked illegally in Cathal Brugha Street. If he got a fare and headed south, all we had to do was turn left into O'Connell Street. If he headed in a northerly direction, we might be in trouble. We would have to do a left-hand turn and then an illegal right-hand turn and hope to God that no gardaí were in the vicinity.

The line of taxis was moving quite quickly. At 10.45p.m. he was at the front of the queue. Two women climbed into the back of his taxi. He headed straight ahead and stopped behind two cars at a red light. We did the right-hand turn and fell in one car behind him. He stayed in the outside lane, which indicated that he was probably going to turn right and drive up along Parnell Square. It was all one-way traffic on those streets.

About half way up Parnell Square, there was a garda checkpoint. Because he was driving a taxi, he was waved through, but the car in front of us was stopped. By the time we got through the checkpoint, Kevin was well and truly gone. After all our efforts, we had lost him. It galled me somewhat that he had been waved through when he was over the legal limit. But that's life. There's no point in letting these things upset you, or you'd be in bad form a lot of the time.

We decided to pick up surveillance again the following Friday night.

———

Some of my friends thought I was a workaholic, but I really enjoyed my job. I wondered at times whether being single and not having kids was the cause or an effect of doing this job. At times it was a lonely life, and sometimes I was scared stiff. I felt empathy for some of the people I was investigating, but mostly it was challenging with moments of great excitement and satisfaction. I would often spot a claimant while I was out and about, off duty so to speak, and without thinking I would be back on the job.

On one occasion I was a guest at a formal dinner in a north County Dublin golf club when I spotted one of 'my' claimants. I had already completed my investigation and filed my report, but I couldn't resist this opportunity.

It had been a routine investigation. She had alleged a serious back problem, which meant her movements were seriously restricted, and she couldn't work. But I had established not only that was she working but that she had opened her own small retail business since the accident. She had no employees and worked in the shop six days a week.

So much for her serious back problems and the major restrictions in her ability to move: there she was, up on the dance floor . . . jiving! Many of the people at the function were taking photographs, so I was out to my car in a flash, camera out of the boot and back inside within a couple of minutes.

She was still out on the dance floor having a wonderful time. I was having a very nice time, too: I used up a roll of thirty-six exposures in under a minute.

––––

Sam was of a similar mindset: don't look a gift horse in the mouth, grab your opportunities whenever they present themselves. So I wasn't too surprised when he handed me a taxi receipt and a roll of film on Thursday morning.

'Well?' I said with a big grin on my face.

He told me that he and his girlfriend had been driving out of town on Wednesday night when he spotted Kevin's taxi on the Howth Road. He followed it to the taxi rank in Raheny village. There was only one other taxi in the queue. A couple of men emerged from the pub across the road and got into the first taxi. That left Kevin.

Sam's girlfriend was a learner driver with no licence, and he didn't want to risk her being stopped by the gardaí, so he couldn't do the job himself. The girlfriend agreed to take a taxi ride.

'I told her to take the taxi to the Lord Mayor pub and I would meet her outside.'

In an effort to stem her obvious enthusiasm, he told her that all she had to do was imagine, really believe, that she was going to the Lord Mayor to meet friends.

She got into Kevin's taxi. Sam waited to make sure that the taxi took off and then he headed at speed to Swords. He arrived at the Lord Mayor ahead of Kevin.

He saw the taxi being driven up Dublin Road and it came to a halt outside the pub. In the interest of discretion, he obviously couldn't use the camera flash, but in any event the front of the pub and footpath were floodlit. He took photographs of the taxi arriving at the front of the pub and Yvonne alighting from the taxi. She was smart enough not to pay when she was inside the taxi, thus delaying Kevin's departure to give Sam an opportunity to take photographs. Yvonne stood outside the pub as if waiting for someone.

Kevin switched on his taxi plate light, did a U-turn and drove back down Dublin Road.

'How did she get the receipt?' I asked.

Apparently Kevin had passed a comment to the effect that it was 'well for her' going out for a few pints on a Wednesday night. She gave him some tale about it being 'business'; her boss was flying out to London early the next morning and he had forgotten his passport, which was in the office safe!

'You want to watch that,' I said jokingly. 'She has the potential to be an inventive liar.'

Sam glared at me. He and Yvonne had been an item for only a couple of months so I guess the rose-tinted specs were still in place.

'Anyway,' he said, 'she asked him for a receipt so that she could get the fare back from petty cash.'

We got Sam's photographs of Kevin developed. While it was too dark to identify the driver, they clearly showed Kevin's taxi and we had the receipt to tie in with the journey.

The Carriage Office records had no information as to whether or not Kevin had what was known as a 'cosy' – another licensed taxi driver who used his vehicle when Kevin was not working. I rang my clients, who were Kevin's insurers. He had no named driver on the policy. It was reasonable to assume that the person we had observed was Kevin.

I prepared and submitted my report and the photographs.

Over the next couple of weeks, we got on with our other investigations, but Kevin was niggling away at the back of my mind. While innovation and determination are important factors in our work, luck played a part in some investigations, and in this one we had been very, very lucky. Everything had fallen into place easily – maybe too easily.

Not only was our reputation as good investigators at stake,

can you imagine my embarrassment if we had got the wrong man? And there was quite a lot of money involved. Insurance companies use our evidence to revise their estimates of settlements to be agreed or awards likely to be made by the court. I discussed the file with Sam and then I called the insurance company's claims manager, Brian. After exchanging the usual pleasantries, I mentioned Kevin's claim.

'Have you a medical lined up?' I asked.

'I think so, I'll check.' He gave me the details. Kevin was due to be examined by a consultant in three weeks.

'Do you mind if I have another look at him?'

'No,' he said, and then asked, 'Is there a problem, Shirl? Do you think you've got the wrong fella?'

I assured him that I was happy we had the right guy but I would just like to check.

Maybe it was insecurity on my part, but I would be a lot happier if I could confirm that the same man driving the taxi turned up for the medical examination.

I telephoned Bernard and arranged that we could use one of his meeting rooms for about thirty minutes on the day of the medical. Sam, David, Michael and I met in my office to plan our strategy. It may have seemed a bit over the top, but I didn't want to leave anything to chance.

'This fella just fell into our laps,' I said to the lads.

'On the balance of probabilities, we have the right person, but it's been just a bit too easy. I just want to check him again, to make sure', I added as I handed out copies of Kevin's photograph from the Carriage Office.

We decided that David would be in Bernard's office and he would photograph Kevin, or whoever left Kevin's home, using a telephoto lens. As soon as Kevin had driven off, David was to get to the venue of the medical, in Fitzwilliam Square, as soon as possible.

Michael's job was to be in position near the entrance to the consultant's rooms to try and confirm that the person who turned up for the appointment was the same guy in the photograph. Sam and I would take the mobile surveillance and follow Kevin.

The medical appointment was fixed for 12.30p.m.

We took two cars to Bernard's place. While Sam was parking our car, I took David into the building and introduced him to Bernard. We did a final check of the photographic equipment and I returned to our car. It was just gone 10.45a.m.

I think I must have affected Sam with my uncertainty. Several times he checked to make sure that David couldn't be seen from the roadway. I guess we were both a little on edge.

At 11.15a.m., Kevin emerged. He was heading for the Swords Road when he turned left. That was unexpected.

He drove into an old, well-established local authority housing estate. He came to a halt outside one of the houses, alighted from the car and knocked on the door. We positioned ourselves on the far side of a large green open space. We had a clear line of sight to the front of the house.

Two or three minutes later he emerged from the house, accompanied by another male. They got into the car and Kevin drove away. We followed at a distance. He turned right onto the Swords Road heading for the city centre.

Neither Sam nor I was in a talkative mood. I was fiddling with the camera equipment. If I checked it once, I checked it a dozen times: the battery in the motorised winder; the film in the camera; spare rolls of film; the selection of lens. I could tell that I was getting on Sam's nerves so I plonked the camera bag on the floor at my feet.

'What if the other guy goes in to the medical?' I said to Sam.

'Let's just wait and see,' he replied.

I took the street map of Dublin and tried to visualise what route Kevin would take to the medical.

'Hello,' said Sam.

I glanced up. We were travelling down Drumcondra Road. Kevin's left-hand indicator was blinking. He came to a stop outside some houses, just past the Cat and Cage pub. Sam drove up onto the footpath, outside a row of shops. I grabbed the camera, just in case.

Kevin alighted from the driver's side and the passenger from his side. Kevin got into the front passenger seat, and the passenger into the driver's seat. They literally exchanged places in the car, and drove away.

'Did you get that?' Sam asked, meaning photographs.

'Think so,' I replied, praying that I had. Sam was the photographer on the team, so he could do this kind of thing on autopilot. As for me, I clicked away and generally hoped for the best!

I began to feel a bit more cheerful. If our original man was Kevin, there could be only one logical explanation for the exchange of places we had just witnessed. Kevin was on his way to a medical examination arranged by the insurance company against whom he was claiming. He was maintaining that he couldn't drive because of his injuries: was he really so cautious that he wasn't going to risk being seen driving near the venue? Did it mean that he was expecting to be under surveillance once he arrived?

I got on the radio to Michael, gave him an outline of what had just happened and warned him to be careful, not to get too close. David came over the radio to confirm that he had heard my message to Michael.

We arrived at Fitzwilliam Square at 12.15p.m. Sam dropped me off further up the square and drove on.

I spotted our van; this time it had our '24-hour Emergency Plumbing Services' signs stuck on the side panels. It was parked nose in, like all the other vehicles, directly across the road from the consultant's rooms.

I hoped Michael had forgotten his personal mantra, 'Thou shall not get away', and that he wasn't too close to the venue. I didn't spot him at first, but I couldn't help but smile when I did see him. He was sitting in his shirtsleeves, minus his tie, on the front steps of a house three doors away, chatting to an old bag lady.

Michael was quite a crafty actor. He had the patience of a saint and (unlike Sam) could sit on surveillance duty for hours on end without a complaint. Watching the clock while on surveillance is self-torture, and Michael would cover the clock on his car with a duster to prevent the natural tendency to keep glancing at it. On a couple of occasions when he was sitting in cars on surveillance duty, thoughtful (and/or nosy) neighbours would bring him cups of tea and biscuits while he, a nice older gentleman with a forlorn look about him, sat waiting for . . . whatever it was he was waiting for.

He would make up some cock and bull story to suit the situation. He often told people who found him sitting in a car in the early morning that he had a hangover and was 'sleeping off a skinful' until he could drive legally. These good (and nosy) Samaritans must have got a surprise when he suddenly came to life and took off like a bat out of hell in pursuit of whoever he was tailing.

At 12.25p.m., Kevin rang the front door bell of the consultant's rooms. He was admitted and he was alone.

I walked on up Fitzwilliam Square. Glancing behind me, I saw Michael about two hundred yards back, following me.

I spotted David on the other side of the road. Sam was waiting on the corner of the square.

We had a brief chat. All four of us were happy that the guy in the photograph, the one in the pub and the one driving the taxi was one and the same person, i.e. Kevin.

We could have stayed on to see what he got up to after the medical. However, he had been cautious enough to change places with his passenger en route to the consultant's rooms, which suggested that he was suspicious or that his legal team had warned him that he could be placed under surveillance.

I didn't want to risk losing any of the advantages we had gained to date. We quit while we were ahead and adjourned to a coffee shop in Baggot Street for lunch.

Later I rang Brian and gave him an oral report, confirming that I was fully satisfied that we had the right guy. I told him I would send in my final report, and he promised to send me a copy of the consultant's report.

The first time I went down to the Four Courts at the start of each law term, I got a copy of the legal diary from Albert, the chief usher. This diary lists all the cases that are due for hearing in the current term. I used the diary as a form of advance warning and Christine, my secretary, would go through the listings, mark all the cases we are involved with and note the dates in our office diary. That way I could plan for a few days' holidays here and there and Christine could pull the relevant files from storage when we needed to prepare for the hearings.

Kevin's case was listed for hearing during the Trinity Sittings, which is a quaint way of saying during June and July.

I had received a copy of the last medical report from Brian. Kevin had told the consultant that he still wasn't able to drive and that his brother had to drive him everywhere, including to that appointment. That was the day we saw him swap places with his passenger halfway through his journey. I was really looking forward to giving evidence in this case. To say that Kevin was telling fibs was putting it mildly!

One beautiful warm, sunny afternoon in early May, Sam and I were driving up Ballymun Road on our way back to the office following a hearing in the High Court, when I spotted Kevin's car parked on the southbound side of the road adjacent to Hampstead Park.

'Whoa,' I said, 'isn't that Kevin's car?' and pointed to the other side of the road.

'Looks like it,' Sam said as he did a u-turn. He pulled up behind it. There was no taxi plate on the roof but it was the right registration number. Sam reversed our car back a distance so that we wouldn't be right behind Kevin's car. We decided to 'take a walk in the park'.

The landscaping was fairly open plan so we could see for some distance. There were some people around: kids playing; mums with buggies; couples walking. We couldn't see Kevin. We continued walking towards the far end of the park towards the back of Dublin City University. About halfway down the path, we could see some high wire fencing surrounded by some trees and tall shrubs. The path veered to the right and then left. Behind the

fence were public tennis courts. I happened to glance in through
a break in the shrubbery at the entrance to the tennis courts. I got
quite a shock. There was Kevin and another man enjoying a game
of tennis. I was so taken aback that I stopped dead in my tracks.

Sam had spotted them too. He gave me a very sharp elbow in
the ribs and pushed me forward past the entrance.

'You sit there,' he said, pointing to a park bench farther along
the path.

With that, he took off at a gallop across the grass towards the
gate we had used to come into the park. As usual, the camera
equipment was in the boot of the car. So was the video camera. It
seemed like he was gone for ages but in fact it was only a few
minutes. I sat on the bench and prayed, 'Please, God, don't let
them finish the game before he gets back.'

Finally I saw Sam loping back across the grass, laden with the
camera bags, which slowed him down. The big camera bag was
slung across his shoulder and bouncing against his hip as he ran.
He was also carrying the steel case containing all the video
equipment.

He dropped the camera bag at my feet and started to get the
video camera ready. I squatted down beside the bag and put some
film in the camera. I was all thumbs.

'Please, God, don't let them finish the game before we're
ready.' I must have said it out loud, because Sam looked at me as
if I was weird.

'Keep an eye out,' he said, and then, after hooking the video
camera strap around his neck, he scrambled on his hands and
knees into the shrubbery. I knew I'd get an earful from him later
as he was wearing his good 'court' clothes.

I looked around. The only person I could see in the distance
was a woman with her dog. The dog was having a great time,
running around in circles and then back to his owner. I could
hear the two lads on the tennis court enjoying their game and
having a bit of banter. I couldn't see Sam through the bushes. The
black mongrel came bounding across the grass, with his tail
wagging furiously. He sniffed along the bottom of some shrubs,
and then lifted his leg, then headed in my direction, followed by

his owner. The dog lifted his leg again, very close to where Sam had disappeared into the shrubbery.

'Piss off!' I heard a loud whisper from the shrubs.

'Oh God!' I thought.

I had to do something. Hoping the dog was friendly, I walked towards him. Patting my knee, I said, 'Who's a good boy? Come here,' in the friendliest voice I could manage. The dog stopped and looked at me. Then he wagged his tail. 'Come on, boy,' I said again, bent down and grabbed his collar. The woman was about a hundred yards away. I had to keep her at a distance in case Sam had to beat a hasty retreat out of the bushes. I walked over to her with the dog and we exchanged comments about the weather or some irrelevance. She put the dog back on the lead.

I was about to walk back towards the tennis courts when I heard voices. I glanced over to see Kevin and his tennis partner coming out of the gate, and kept chatting to the woman as the two lads walked towards the entrance to the park. When I turned back to the path I saw Sam sitting on the park bench.

'That bloody dog missed me by bloody inches,' he said as I approached.

'Never mind the dog, did you get any video?' I asked.

He rewound the tape, pressed the 'play' button and handed the video camera to me. It was wonderful. The footage showed Kevin running across the court, leaping in the air to return balls, serving. At one point he fell over and jumped up immediately to scramble back to the base line.

As I handed the camera back to Sam I said with a big grin, 'He's rightly buggered now.'

'Mind your language,' he replied, with an equally big grin on his face. Then his face fell as he suddenly noticed the mud stains on the knees of his trousers.

———

Any time I was down in the Law Library or in the Four Courts for a hearing, I would take another look at the legal diary, which was updated every day when the courts were sitting. I could see Kevin's name gradually make its way up the page. His case was eventually listed for the second week of July. I booked a consultation room for my team and all the equipment.

On the day, we arrived at eight thirty, even though the courts don't start hearings until after half past ten. Part of our equipment was a large television, which would be used to view the video evidence. In the interests of discretion, the fewer people who saw the TV being carried in, the better. If the case was to run, we had five witnesses to give evidence: Sam, David, Michael, Yvonne and myself. Each of us had worked on the case.

On our way round to the Law Society Office to collect the key of the consultation room we bumped into Albert, the chief usher.

'Morning, Shirley, I see I'd better order in the popcorn and ice cream,' he said, looking at the TV and video equipment.

'Morning, Albert,' I said. 'You didn't see any of this stuff, of course.'

Albert was the soul of discretion. He had worked in the Four Courts for many years. On occasions in the early years, we had to use his office to show our videos in private, as some of the consultation rooms didn't have any electrical sockets. I soon learned which rooms had the necessary sockets, so I knew which rooms to ask for when I was booking a consultation room.

We trooped downstairs to our room and while Sam and David set up the equipment, I went back up to the Law Library to find our client's counsel and solicitors.

I sat in on the pre-trial consultation, which was held in another room. There were seven of us present: senior and junior counsels; Joe, the solicitor, and his articled clerk; Brian, the claims manager, and his claims inspector, Declan; and myself. My role was to clarify any points or matters that arose after the other witnesses had left the room.

A procession of witnesses followed.

First came the three medical consultants, two of whom knew me from previous cases. Those two would know why I was there. Counsel went through their various medical reports with them. Without disclosing any of the information I had obtained, he asked them some questions that had arisen as a result of my evidence. For example, would Kevin, with his physical complaints, be able to go jogging or play any sports? Barristers like to know in advance the answers to any questions they might put to a witness in open court.

Next came an officer from the Carriage Office with his records. A subpoena (a witness summons) had been issued to cover this officer's attendance. That was straightforward; we primarily wanted this officer to confirming Kevin's taxi plate number and that there was no 'cosy' listed for that plate. Under the regulations, all drivers of any specified taxi must be noted on the relevant records in the Carriage Office, together with a copy of their Public Service Vehicle Licence (psvl). That would cover the eventuality that Kevin might say in evidence that he was still not working and that he had a 'cosy' driver.

The next witness due into the room was the driver of the second taxi, the one that had run into the back of Kevin's vehicle. That presented something of a problem.

He was standing directly outside the door of the Consultation Room. He was on my list of future investigations so it was important that he shouldn't see that I was connected with Kevin's case. There was a quick discussion as to what I should do. I could walk out of the room but I would literally have to brush shoulders with him. Someone half-jokingly suggested that I should hide under the conference table.

I had a better idea. I walked over to the big sash window and pushed it up.

'I'm off for a cigarette break', I said as I sat on the windowsill. I swivelled round to face the yard and stepped off. Well, we were on the ground floor! I could hear the raucous laughter as I walked away. I couldn't help smiling myself. I sat on the parapet wall across the yard and had a couple of cigarettes.

After about ten minutes, Joe, the solicitor, stuck his head out the window and signalled that the coast was clear. I went back into the consultation room – by way of the door this time. The slagging and the craic were mighty: I reckoned they would probably dine out on this episode for months.

After we had gone though our evidence we all adjourned to my consultation room to watch the video evidence.

As is the usual practice in such cases, the horse trading started. Kevin's legal team opened the negotiations by asking for £85,000 compensation. That meant that they would probably settle for about £60,000.

Our side offered £5,000 in full and final settlement of his claim, including costs. They came back looking for £75,000. Our side simply said 'No'.

That should have put them on notice that the insurance company had some evidence that could scupper Kevin's claim. In their wisdom, rather than come back looking for a more reasonable amount, they decided to run the case.

The case was called on at 11.10a.m. Unfortunately for me, our legal team didn't want me to be seen anywhere near the courtroom – I was too well known around the Four Courts. This meant that I wouldn't be able to hear Kevin's evidence. He was first up in the witness box. Sam, David, Michael and Yvonne went into court to hear what Kevin had to say, while I headed for the coffee shop in the basement.

Sam joined me later. He had sat through Kevin's evidence. Kevin had stated in his evidence-in-chief that he still couldn't drive and therefore remained out of work. He had been cross-examined by our senior counsel and had stuck to his guns. Our counsel had then told the judge that he would like to recall Kevin later. That statement would have set down a marker to the other side that the evidence Kevin had given was going to be challenged. Sam had left the courtroom once the medical evidence began.

At ten to one the judge announced that he was going to adjourn the hearing for lunch until two fifteen. As a matter of protocol, our senior counsel told the judge that he intended to introduce video evidence in the afternoon. At this point a legal argument broke out. Kevin's counsel objected, supposedly on the grounds of 'disclosure' (each side is supposed to disclose information to the other). He ranted about the fact that, as he was unaware of the nature of this video evidence, he was being put at a disadvantage, etc., etc. Frankly, his arguments were a load of hot air.

In his wisdom, the judge decided that the video evidence was to be shown to Kevin's senior and junior counsel and his solicitor only, on the strict understanding that whatever they saw on the video would not be discussed with Kevin or any third party. He stated that the video would be admitted as evidence in the case. He adjourned the case until two thirty.

As the video only dealt with the game of tennis, I sent David, Michael and Yvonne down to the coffee shop. There was no point in alerting the other side to the fact that we also had evidence of Kevin working.

Sam and I were in the conference room when the legal teams arrived. I knew Kevin's senior counsel quite well and had worked with him on other cases.

'Oh, dear! And what has my chap been up to?' he said in a resigned tone of voice as he walked into the room. I smiled but said nothing. They watched the video in silence. It lasted twenty-two minutes.

I think their legal team were very taken aback. Most lawyers have major problems with clients who deliberately lie in support of a claim. They all expect a little, shall we say, 'exaggeration', and are inclined to turn a blind eye to it, but outright perjury in court is totally unacceptable. Without a word, they gathered up their papers and left the room.

At twenty past two, ten minutes before the hearing was to resume, Brian came back into the consultation room and told me that they had settled the case for £7,500 including his legal costs. Kevin would be very lucky if he received £1,000 of that sum.

As we were chatting, the four barristers came back into the room.

'I've just outlined the nature of the rest of the evidence we had against that chap. I think my colleagues believe that I may be exaggerating,' said our senior counsel. 'Would you give them a run through, Shirley, and show them the photographs?' he asked.

I did just that. I omitted the bit about Bernard's CCTV camera. After all, Bernard's office was just across the road from Kevin's house and I didn't want to run the risk that they might mention this to Kevin – I had no way of knowing how Kevin might have reacted. While I was a little disappointed that the case had been settled, I was glad that I had not come face to face with Kevin, so he didn't know what I looked like.

More important, though, was the fact that the next taxi driver I had to investigate was the guy who had rear-ended him – and he had been there as a witness. I would have been starting that new job at a marked disadvantage; in effect with one hand tied behind my back.

But sometimes the best laid plans can get derailed.

———

I remember a case when Sam and I were doing surveillance on another taxi driver one evening. Our subject left his house and drove to a nearby taxi rank, which was located outside a shopping centre. We decided that I would ask him to take me to a certain hotel about six miles away; Sam would drive on ahead and photograph him arriving. We hung around until he was second from the top of the queue. Sam drove away, heading for the hotel.

When the taxi driver had reached the front of the queue, I approached his taxi. 'x Hotel, please,' I said with my hand on the rear passenger door.

The taxi driver behind butted in. 'I'll take you, love.'

I was taken aback, but obviously I couldn't insist that my subject should take me. He didn't seem to have a problem with his colleague's offer. I could only assume that taxi drivers exchanged fares when the destination was convenient for one of them. The hotel I had asked to be taken to was out of the city and I assumed my taxi man wanted to end up in the city, where he'd have an easier time getting another fare. Who knows? Anyway, I found myself taking a ride in a taxi I didn't want to be in, to a hotel I didn't want to stay in. But I had to go through the motions, as if I were a regular customer.

Sam, surprised to see me being dropped off by 'another' taxi, picked me up at the hotel. We decided to call it a night and dropped in on some friends in the area.

A couple of hours later, we happened to be passing a different taxi rank. I nudged Sam. 'There he is.' Coincidences do happen sometimes.

Sam pulled over. We had a quick decision to make. 'He'll never remember me; it was dark when I was at the earlier taxi rank, and God knows how many customers he's had since we last saw him.' I decided to take a chance. Sam pulled over.

'I'll ask him to take me to the Comet.' This was a pub that I knew had a bright floodlit area outside, which would help Sam get the photos we wanted.

I got out of our car. This time Sam waited until I was inside the taxi before driving off. I approached the driver's window and ask him to take me to the Comet pub. 'Did you enjoy your night out?' he said, looking at me in the rear view mirror.

Oh, blast, I thought, he remembers me.

'Sorry?' I said.

'At the hotel?' he continued. 'One of my mates picked you up earlier outside the shopping centre.'

'My God,' I said, 'it's a small world. Fancy meeting you again!'

I told him I'd decided I didn't like the look of the fella I met at the hotel and had managed to get a lift halfway home, and I was glad to see some taxis at that rank. I added, 'I'll pop into my local so the night's not a complete waste of time.'

He seemed satisfied with my story and we chitchatted for the rest of the journey to the pub.

My little scheme could have backfired but I did manage in the end to get the right taxi with the right driver – and Sam got his photographs.

03 | INSIDER TRADING

Scammers usually get caught out as a direct result of information that initially relates to a very minor or insignificant aspect of their scam.

Let me explain. Over my twenty years or so as a private investigator, I found that scammers frequently pre-plan all the major aspects of a particular scam but very often fail to even think about minor points. Based on my past experiences, in the early part of any investigation I tended to pick out at random one relatively minor detail of the case and set about verifying that point. If it didn't check out, a red flag would go up. If it did, I would select another aspect and repeat the process.

Take, for example, the case of 'Stanley'.

One of my clients, a solicitor, had passed my name to one of his clients, directors of a company who thought they might have a problem with a member of staff. He gave me the contact information and confirmed that he had given my details to his client. Before I had a chance to telephone them, I received a telephone call from the managing director and we arranged to meet for lunch the next day. I met with 'John' and 'Peter', two directors of the company, and over lunch in Jury's Hotel, Ballsbridge, they outlined details of events that had recently come to their notice.

The company was a major computer software supplier and about a quarter of their business related to stationery printing. They specialised in printing 'logo' stationery and cheques. We've all seen cheques like these. Apart from the individual company name, they generally have a holograph superimposed on each cheque. Companies who specialise in this type of business need prior approval and clearance from the Central Bank.

One of the company's employees, Stanley, had worked for them as an area sales manager for just over four years. He was considered an excellent employee. He had a good attendance record, steady sales and repeat business. Stanley had a very customer-orientated approach and there had been no negative feedback from any of my client's customers. So, you may ask, what was the problem with Stanley?

John told me that a casual comment by a member of staff who worked in their payroll department was overheard in the staff canteen. On the surface, it was just a simple throwaway comment. Apparently, Stanley had not claimed his expenses for six months. On the surface, this was not a major event, but in the four years he had worked for the company he was always one of the first sales reps to file his monthly expenses/commission claim, generally on the first working day after the end of each month. So this was a very major change in his behaviour.

Apart from a basic salary, Stanley received commission on his sales, motoring expenses and meal allowances. His net expenses ranged from £2,000 to £5,000 per month. Stanley, a single man, had purchased a new house one year earlier; his car was a two-litre top-of-the-range vehicle, and judging by various conversations he had had with other members of staff, he enjoyed a very good social life which could even be described as somewhat lavish. So the first question was: How is Stanley continuing to finance this lifestyle without the monthly top up of his expenses and mileage?

Peter continued, 'Some three weeks later, another out-of- the-ordinary event occurred.' The finance director had been checking a pile of invoices that were due for payment. Among the invoices was one that he found quite odd. It was from one of the company's suppliers, but the invoice was addressed to one of the company's customers and not to the company itself, as would be the normal practice. The finance director checked the invoice against their sales records and found no details of any sales made to that particular customer in the previous six months. Furthermore, based on previous usage, the customer would have run out of stock of this particular item some two months before.

The finance director made a quick telephone call to the customer, during the course of which it became clear that the customer had indeed received a further supply of the items, three months earlier, and the order had been placed with Stanley. The finance director made some discreet enquiries in-house and satisfied himself that his company had definitely not supplied these particular goods to the customer.

During the following month five credit notes were received from one of the company's major suppliers, a printing company. However, when staff in the accounts department tried to enter the credit notes, the computerised accounts system would not accept them, as they had to be allocated against specific invoices. The accounts department staff had brought the problem to the attention of the finance director as they thought there might be a glitch in the system. He rang the printing company and spoke to the woman who handled their account. It appeared to him that she was stalling; she failed to give a satisfactory explanation.

The combination of these incidents was a cause of concern to the directors, and when they checked their records they found that the sales representative concerned, in both cases was Stanley.

They now had two question marks against Stanley. The first was his failure to claim his commission and expenses on time; and the second, potentially much more serious, was that goods which had not been supplied by their company were apparently being sold, by Stanley, to at least one of their customers.

Peter and John initially requested that I should place Stanley under surveillance for one week. I told them that this course of action would be not only expensive but also very problematic. For close surveillance, in order to avoid alerting the subject and to have any chance of success, a minimum of two vehicles, each with two agents, would be required every day. Furthermore, Stanley covered the Greater Dublin and north Leinster areas. He had no set routine or route; part of his duties involved cold calling on potential new customers as well as dropping in to see existing customers. On any given day, he could be anywhere from the Wicklow to Louth borders. He had only one fixed appointment each week, and that was the sales staff meeting held in the company offices at eight o'clock every Monday morning.

I suggested that, before any surveillance was carried out, they should perform a mini-audit of their sales records for the previous six months, particularly with regard to customers they had supplied with the same type of products. I suggested they should look for unexplained gaps between order dates, particularly taking into consideration their customers' previous usage of the product. They should then analyse the same sales records to identify customers who should, based on previous usage of the product, be due to place an order in the near future. This may sound like a complicated procedure, but their computerised accounts software could easily produce such reports.

I explained how these reports could be helpful. First, they would highlight any gaps in past customer orders, thereby giving an indication of the level of possible scams being operated. Second, by identifying potential orders from existing customers for the following month, we would be able to target areas and locations for surveillance purposes. Third, this kind of background information would enable me to formulate an overall plan.

Over coffee, I gave Peter a list of the information I would need, apart from the sales analysis reports: Stanley's full name, address, date of birth and PPS number (this always comes in handy); his car registration number, and its make, model and colour; a copy of the photograph from his HR file; and last, but not least, two temporary swipe cards to give us access to the car park at the company premises. We agreed to meet for coffee at two o'clock the following Thursday.

On my way back to the office, I called in to see Sam, to brief him on the background to this new job.

Sam can be a bit negative at times. Well, perhaps I should rephrase that. Sam always sees, and mentions, the pitfalls and problems that are likely to arise in each case. I am a born optimist: there will always be problems or practical difficulties with a case, but as far as I am concerned we'll get over them, whatever they might be. So he's a 'glass half empty' type of guy, whereas I'm a 'glass half full' character, so we balance each other out, and I guess that's why our working relationship lasted so long.

So here we were standing in his kitchen, mugs of tea in hand, discussing the case. Sam, as usual, was bringing up all the likely problems. How were we, practically, going to follow this guy around for hours on consecutive days without being spotted? My response: 'No problem, we'll use two vehicles and three operatives, prepare as detailed a plan as we can and then go for it.'

I lit a cigarette: I always did that when I was thinking. Without a word, Sam, a reformed smoker, opened his kitchen door, stood to one side and glared at me. Ignoring his stare, I stepped out into the back garden and perched on his coal bunker.

I continued, as if nothing had happened, 'When we get the computer read-outs, we'll be able to make some sort of plan.' I didn't quite catch his reply.

I called into the office on my way home. Christine had some reports for signing. She had sorted through the post; there were some cheques in. My corporate clients had thirty days' credit and most of them adhered to that arrangement. Lay clients, the very few we dealt with, paid half the agreed fees up front and the balance on receipt of my report. There were another four new cases in. We were averaging between twenty and thirty cases a month, a healthy, busy practice. I told Christine she could head off and I would look after the phones. I settled down to deal with the paperwork, and it was nearly eight o'clock before I called it a day.

———

My arrangement to meet Peter for coffee at two on Thursday afternoon didn't quite go to plan.

Sam and I had been doing early morning surveillance in Walkinstown for one of our insurance company clients. We had taken up observation position at 6.40a.m. The claimant (in other words the plaintiff in an insurance claim) alleged that he could not work as a result of a road traffic accident. I had my doubts.

He drove away from his house in a white Transit van at 8.10a.m., heading for Dublin city centre. We followed.

It can be very difficult to maintain surveillance in traffic, particularly rush-hour traffic. If you let too many cars get between you and the target vehicle, there is a high risk of losing visual contact, particularly at traffic lights. As long as the target vehicle stays on the main routes, we tend to tuck in directly behind it. After all, there are hundreds of other vehicles all travelling along in the same direction, which should make us harder to spot. Another useful tip is to keep the sun visors down. Then all the driver in front can see of your face is your nose and chin. Following a vehicle gets more difficult once the driver leaves a major road: when this happens you must keep your distance.

We were successful in following this guy to a small yard just off Cork Street. We cruised past the entrance to the yard a couple of times before we saw him emerging from a building carrying some lightweight cane furniture, which he began to load onto the van, both inside and on top. We really needed to get some photographs of this activity without being obvious.

Lateral thinking, improvisation skills and a hard neck are some of the essential tools of the PI trade. Partnering the same person over a number of years also helps, as it eliminates the need for lengthy discussions when something is going down.

Grabbing his jacket and the camera, Sam said, 'Meet you at the entrance to the yard.' He walked up the footpath on the opposite side of the road from the yard, crossed the road, turned and started walking back towards the yard entrance. He was carrying a camera in his right hand. Checking for pedestrian activity, I got out of the vanette, crossed the road and started walking towards Sam. We met right in the middle of the entrance.

I turned so that my back was facing the entrance, and Sam moved around to face me. While we casually chatted, Sam hung his jacket over my left shoulder. He slid the camera lens to wide angle and rested it on my shoulder, under his jacket.

'Hold on to the jacket,' he said as he adjusted it to make sure that only the lens was showing, and started to photograph the subject loading up his van. My stomach was churning – every 'click' of the camera shutter sounded so loud I was sure that the subject would hear it. As Sam was giving me a running commentary of his actions and movements, I was keeping a lookout for pedestrian traffic approaching.

'Granny approaching from your right,' I muttered.

Sam can be very cool in tense situations. He simply adjusted the jacket so that it covered the lens. I glanced at the elderly woman as she neared us, looking for any reaction. Her shopping trolley, which she was pulling behind her hit an uneven slab in the pavement and wobbled precariously. Our eyes made contact.

'Bloody Corpo – ye'd break yer bloody neck round here for all they care,' she said.

'You okay?' I asked, smiling at her.

'Grand, love – grand morning,' she said as she trundled past.

'He's on the top of the van tying down some furniture,' Sam said, as he moved the jacket so that he could continue to take photographs. After a few more shots, Sam lifted the camera from my shoulder and slung the strap over his right shoulder. 'See ya,' he said, and walked away.

I walked on for about fifty yards, then crossed the road and headed back towards the vanette. Sam was in the process of sticking magnetic signs to the side panels. As I got closer I saw that today we were a digital company. One of the best investments we ever made was getting a range of those magnetic signs made. At the drop of a hat – well, after finding a suitable parking space – we could change from our digital company to painters and decorators to traffic surveyors or florists, depending on the job in hand and/or our location. It also helped to swap the signs if we were engaged in any lengthy surveillance.

We settled down in the vanette to await developments.

At 9.25a.m., the subject drove out of the yard and turned right. We gave him a couple of hundred yards' head start and then pulled away from the kerb. He turned left onto Davitt Road and left again at the T-junction onto the Long Mile Road, heading south. On the Naas dual carriageway we were able to stay well back behind him, narrowing the gap between the vehicles only when we were approaching major junctions, in case the traffic lights changed in his favour.

Just past the Red Cow roundabout, I noticed that the load on the top of his van was moving around quite a bit. I was commenting on this to Sam when a cane chair slid off the roof of the van and hit the road, scattering its cushions. A two-seater chair and its cushions followed.

The subject pulled over onto the hard shoulder. I thought Sam would stay way back, but he didn't. He pulled over about two hundred yards from the subject's van.

Sam lifted the video camera, which was tucked, ready to go, between the two front seats, and started recording.

The subject literally ran down the hard shoulder, darting out onto the road to scoop up the cushions, which he threw onto the hard shoulder. Traffic on the inside lane was cutting out to the outside lane to avoid the chairs lying on the road. Horns were honking; irate drivers were giving each other rude finger gestures; the subject himself gave a few rude gestures to passing motorists.

I realised that there could have been a serious accident, but I could see the comic side of the situation. I started giggling as the scene developed in front of our eyes. Always the professional, Sam continued filming.

After retrieving his goods, which he placed on the hard shoulder of the carriageway, the subject ran back to his van, jumped in and reversed it back to where he had piled up his furniture. He lifted the furniture back up onto the roof and then scrambled up to tie it down securely.

He got back in the van and continued south.

We could have terminated surveillance at that point, but one doesn't like to look a gift horse in the mouth. Here was a chap who was alleging quite serious disabilities as a result of a road traffic accident. But so far that morning, we had evidence of him driving a van, going to a business premises, loading furniture into and onto the top of his van, literally running up and down a section of the dual carriageway, clambering up on top of his van again, all without apparent difficulty!

We would have to make some enquiries in relation to the business premises, but we decided we would continue with surveillance for the time being. Suffice it to say we reached Kilkenny city without any further mishaps, where the subject double-parked in Main Street. We did likewise farther down the road from his vehicle – well, needs must! While I kept a lookout for traffic wardens and the gardaí, Sam proceeded to obtain further photographic and video evidence of the subject offloading the furniture and carrying it into a store on the street.

Now I had just one problem: I wasn't going to get back to Dublin in time for my two o'clock appointment with Peter. We could have made it back to Dublin by three, but we were starving – we had been on the road since a quarter to six that morning, had had nothing to eat since the night before, and we were exhausted. Staying focused and fully concentrated, not only on the driving and surveillance, but also on all the subject's actions and movements so that one can note anything that might be inconsistent with his claim, can be mentally very tiring.

I rang Peter and rescheduled my appointment for eleven the next morning, Friday, and Sam and I headed off to have some lunch.

———

I picked up all the paperwork and relevant information from Peter the following day. Sam and I agreed that, provided we could formulate some plan, we would start on this investigation the following Monday morning.

Having completed the usual Friday afternoon chores – staff payroll, allocation of work for the following week, going through reports with the lads – I left the office at about half past three, taking with me all the paperwork, notes and files relating to the Stanley investigation.

Good preparation always pays dividends; and so I settled down to work. I have a general routine in such circumstances: a quick shower, change into tracksuit bottoms, a T-shirt and trainers; make a big pot of coffee, ensure ample supply of cigarettes; turn on the telephone answering machine; and stock up the CD player with some favourite music. When I'm working from home, I generally work in the dining room, which is at the back of the house, so that I can ignore the doorbell.

It was five thirty when I started to collate the information from the various computer records.

I took a break at eight fifteen to have dinner. Well, that's an exaggeration – I stuck a Weight Watchers frozen meal in the microwave and opened a bottle of Côte des Villages. I took my plate and a glass of wine back into the dining room to eat as I surveyed the progress I had made in the intervening period.

I find it easier to recall information if I initially make a visual presentation of the available data.

I had pinned a large-scale map of Dublin on the wall. The large green pin showed the location of my client's premises in Sandyford. The smaller red pins showed the location of Stanley's clients in the Greater Dublin area; the blue ones indicated the location of his clients who regularly purchased the stock item that had been the cause of concern to my client; finally, the yellow pins indicated the clients who should be reordering the stock item in the immediate future, based on their previous usage. 'So far, so good,' I thought.

We could not realistically drive around with a large-scale map of Dublin, stuck with coloured pins, propped up on the back seat. I had to devise some method of transforming that information into a more 'portable' version. I poured myself another glass of wine and sat staring at the map, hoping for some inspiration.

Index cards, I thought, and highlighters. I had ten minutes to make it to the local shops before they closed. The index cards were a bit larger than I needed and I had to compromise with a shocking pink highlighter rather than a red one, but otherwise the shopping trip was successful.

Back at the table, I returned to the computer read-outs and began the tedious task of highlighting appropriately each customer's name on each list.

During the course of Saturday morning, I transferred the data onto index cards for each postal district of the greater Dublin area and included a map grid reference for each address listed. Finally, I filed each card in alphabetical order for each area or location.

Later, I admitted to Sam that my plan might be a little complicated, but one of its main advantages was that we could maintain a discreet distance from the subject and if we lost Stanley visually in any given area, we had to hand a list of his known customers. We agreed to start the surveillance, as planned, on the following Monday morning.

Sam picked me up at 6.45a.m. He had all the camera equipment in the boot. I carried the file and all my index cards. We arrived at our client's premises at 7.35a.m. We parked on the street, which was preferable to using their car park, which was empty at that hour. Cars started to arrive at 7.45 and Stanley drove into the car park at 7.55.

Sam and I had agreed that we would concentrate purely on surveillance. Tedious work, but it had to be done. We would simply note details of where Stanley went and how long he spent in each premises.

He drove out of the car park at 9.15a.m. and headed south, then cut across country and drove into Sandyford Industrial Estate at ten. The building he went into was not on the customer list provided by Peter. We noted details of the company occupying that property. There were two cars parked directly outside, and I noted the registration numbers, which might produce some leads for further investigation. Stanley came out of the building at 10.30a.m.

He called at four more addresses on the south side of the city, spending fifteen to thirty minutes at each address. All four were legitimate customers.

Sam and I were both beginning to get a bit tetchy at this stage and we were having our usual moaning session about how boring surveillance could be.

'Told you I didn't want to do this job,' Sam said.

I could see that there was a row brewing, so I said nothing.

Stanley reappeared and headed for the city centre.

'We'll check his next call and leave it at that for the day,' Sam announced. I agreed. I was hungry and I really wanted a cigarette.

At 1.15p.m. Stanley drove into a yard in Irishtown. There were four separate buildings in the yard and Stanley entered the building nearest the road. There were no customers listed for the Irishtown area, so we had to get details of the occupiers of each building.

Sam drove through the entrance and parked at the far end of the yard. While he checked the names on the plaques outside each building, I noted all the car registration numbers. Apart from Stanley's car, there were five cars in the yard. We took up an observation position farther down the road and waited.

'Maybe he's having lunch or something,' I ventured. It was now 2.15p.m. and he had been in the premises for an hour.

'We'll stay until he comes out and then call it a day,' Sam replied.

So we waited. And waited.

It was 4.10p.m. when Stanley drove out of the yard. We let him go.

'What on earth was he doing in there for four hours?' I said.

'Don't know, but it's worth following up,' Sam replied.

I spent the next two and a half days doing research. I love this type of work: making enquiries, gathering information, searching for connections, leads or a common denominator, however tenuous. I really enjoy the mental agility and lateral thinking involved.

I was concentrating on two lines of enquiry: the property/company in Sandyford Industrial Estate and the yard in Irishtown. I carried out vehicle registration checks to verify the owners of each car we had seen. I checked out all the company names for directors and secretaries; I visited the Rates Office to establish the rated occupiers of each property. I obtained information about the employees of each company.

By Thursday morning, I was checking and cross checking all the information I had gathered. I prepared flow charts that showed any links between the various companies and/or employees, and pinned them up on the walls of my office. Then I telephoned Peter and arranged for him to come to my office on Friday at eleven. It was easier to show him the connections by way of the charts rather than make detailed notes for him at that stage.

Both Peter and John arrived for the meeting. I outlined Stanley's route and the calls he had made the previous Monday. I started with the Sandyford address. The name of the company occupying the building meant nothing to them. I then told them that, according to the council's rates inspector, Stanley was the person listed as occupier. He had been paying commercial rates on the building since the previous March. Peter and John seemed quite perplexed by this information.

Then we came to the property in Irishtown. I told them that there were four companies listed for the building Stanley had entered: three were involved in the computer business and the fourth was a printing company. They immediately recognised two of the company names.

The printing company was one of the printers they used, but their office was in the north city area of Dublin. When I told them the names of the employees of the Irishtown company they immediately recognised one of the names: she was the lady who handled their account. This same lady was the registered owner of one of the cars parked in the yard at Irishtown. I suggested they make a phone call to the north city office and ask for her by name. Peter rang his finance director, since he was the person who would normally contact this woman with queries about their account. Within minutes the finance director called back. Ann was on a week's holidays.

They recognised one of the three computer companies at the Irishtown address, who was also one of their suppliers. My clients purchased bulk supplies of pre-printed forms from this small firm. When one of their clients ordered certain stationery products, my clients would send over the forms – you've guessed it – to that same printing company to be over-printed.

As for the remaining two companies, one sold, supplied and installed specific computerised accounts software, the same accounts software that Peter and his company sold. The sale of these accounts packages accounted for seventy-five per cent of Peter's business.

I saved the worst news until last. It concerned the fourth company. I gave John and Peter a copy of the full company search I had carried out. First I drew their attention to the memorandum and articles of association. All limited companies have such a document; it basically sets out details of the main business activities of the company. The wording of the main section was identical to that contained in the 'memo and arts' for Peter's company. In other words, this company was a direct business competitor.

But there was more: Stanley was named as a director and secretary of this company.

Peter and John were stunned.

'Have a look at the signature at the bottom of the returns,' I suggested. 'Does it look like Stanley's signature?' They nodded.

We discussed the possible implications.

On the surface, it looked like Stanley had set up a business in direct competition with that of his employers. There was prior evidence that he had diverted some orders to his own company, which had been formed two months after he had started to rent the office in Sandyford. It appeared that Stanley had some business relationship in his own right with two of their suppliers, but at that stage we did not know the nature or extent of that relationship. I suggested that we might try to gather more evidence, evidence of a physical nature.

John wanted to sack Stanley immediately, but Peter didn't seem quite so sure. I suggested they seek the advice of their company solicitors before they did anything at all. They eventually agreed. It was also agreed that, pending legal advice, I should see if I could obtain any further evidence.

I had an idea, but I needed to run it by Sam before taking any action. I made a quick phone call and then went into Sam's office. He was talking on the phone so I mouthed, 'Cup of tea?' He nodded.

I was standing in our little kitchenette beside his office watching the kettle boil, or rather thinking about the case and gathering my thoughts, trying to decide the best approach to make to him. I knew that, for some reason, Sam didn't like this particular job. As far as he was concerned, the job was finished; we had obtained the information our clients wanted. But I felt we needed a bit more evidence, something to show that Stanley was actively involved in these other businesses and not just a shadow director.

'So how did the lads react?' I hadn't heard Sam come into the kitchenette. I filled him in, including the bit about my recommendation that they consult their solicitors. He nodded his agreement.

I cleared my throat. 'How do you feel about doing a bin collection on Monday morning?'

He gave me one of his looks – the one that says, 'Oh God, what are you up to now?'

'You know, a bin lift,' I said. 'We had great craic doing the last one,' I added, pointing to a framed photograph standing on top of his filing cabinet. The photograph showed a grinning Sam wearing overalls and holding a large sweeping brush. He appeared to be bald on top with tufts of red hair sticking out over his ears – thanks to a Hallowe'en wig worn to hide his blond hair. Scruffy Doc Martens completed his attire.

'*You* had great craic. I was the one who had to sweep the road and empty the bins,' he muttered, but I could see that he was trying to suppress a grin.

———

Four months earlier we had been involved in the investigation of a man who claimed he couldn't work. Before his accident he had worked as a wholesale jeweller. Surveillance had been carried out on many occasions but we were getting nowhere.

He lived in a small, detached house at the top of a cul-de-sac in a neat housing estate in Rathfarnham. He drove a top-of-the-range car. His wife didn't work outside the home. I had established that he was in receipt of state disability benefit.

On two occasions we had watched him and his wife doing their weekly shop in the supermarket. On both occasions their bill came to just short of £200: on both occasions he had purchased six bottles of wine. In other words, his lifestyle was inconsistent with his visible means of support. Clearly there was an income or funding from some other source.

One of the other things we had established was that his 'bin day' was Thursday: he carried out two metal bins around eight a.m., left them on the roadway beside the kerb, and the bin men arrived between 8.45a.m. and 9.00a.m.

His row of houses overlooked a flat green open space with houses on three sides of the square. Another road leading further into the estate ran alongside his side garden, the boundary of which was a high hedge. We could monitor activities around his house by looking across the green from the main road.

With a view to obtaining further information and/or leads, we decided to assist the local authority refuse department by helping them with their bin collection.

Sam arrived at my house at a quarter to six on Thursday morning, and we hitched an open trailer to the back of our car. Sam stuck our 'Landscape Gardeners' magnetic signs to the sides of the trailer. They weren't an ideal fit, but they would pass from a distance. A couple of tarpaulins and the big sweeping brush were thrown in the trailer. Sam was wearing the overalls and the Doc Martens. He waited in the car while I collected the file, set the alarm and locked up the house.

I jumped in the car and he drove away. I was rabbiting on about the case, then he nudged me with his elbow and I glanced at him. He was wearing a baseball cap, but there were tufts of red hair springing out all around the base. I grabbed the cap off his head, thinking it was a joke hat, but the top of his head looked bald and the tufts of red hair were still there. He was wearing a wig. I laughed so hard I cried.

At first he got a bit huffy. 'Well, you wear wigs sometimes,' he said.

'Yeah, but mine are real wigs,' I said, wiping the tears from my eyes.

'I thought it went with the image.'

I stared straight ahead, trying to contain my laughter, periodically glancing at him out of the corner of my eye. In a way he was right: the wig completely changed his appearance. From a distance he would look at least fifteen years older.

'You're right, it really does help,' I said. 'I'm sorry I laughed, I was taken completely by surprise.'

We arrived in Rathfarnham at 7.45a.m. We waited on the main road looking across the green at the subject's house. At 7.55a.m., Sam left the car and, taking the sweeping brush from the trailer, he walked across the bottom of the green to the end of the cul-de-sac. He started sweeping the gutter area beside the footpath, heading up towards the subject's house. From a distance he looked the part. I slid over into the driver's seat.

At 8.02a.m., the subject came out of his house, carrying the first bin. I saw him glance in Sam's general direction but he didn't appear to think it out of the ordinary to see a road sweeper. Having put the bin on the roadway, he turned and walked back around the side of his house.

I drove around two sides of the square, past the side hedge of the subject's garden and did a u-turn when I was out of sight of the house. I drove back up to the corner of the subject's house and stopped. I turned the engine off. I had the car windows open. I couldn't see through the hedge, but I could hear movements at the side of the house and snatches of conversation from behind the hedge. I heard the lid of the second bin being banged down. Whatever was going to happen was going to happen in the next few minutes.

I made a mental check: keys in ignition; neutral gear; hand brake on. My stomach was churning with anticipation.

I eased open the driver's door and quietly climbed out of the car, leaving the door slightly open. I was wearing trainers so my footsteps made no noise. I lifted the tarps and left them on the grass margin a few feet from the back of the trailer; I didn't want Sam to trip over the bloody things.

Seconds later Sam came charging around the corner clutching one of the bins. He tipped the contents into the trailer and disappeared back round the corner. I spread the contents to flatten them down; next the sweeping bush was flung around the corner. I ran, snatched it up and went back to the trailer again. Sam appeared again, carrying the second bin, and tipped the contents into the trailer.

I threw the tarps over the load in the trailer and was struggling to get them fully open to cover the contents when Sam came back. 'Come on, come on,' he muttered.

We straightened out the tarps and I threw the sweeping brush on top. Hopefully, it would keep the tarps weighed down until we were out of the estate and could stop to tie them down.

Sam ran around to the driver's side of the car and I jumped in the passenger side. He eased the car away from the kerb and drove slowly up the road towards the estate exit. The entire exercise had taken less than two minutes.

I turned in my seat and was looking back at the subject's house. As he turned the last corner of the green, I said, 'Slow down.' He slowed to a crawl.

'He's out again,' I said.

The subject was standing by his first bin with a small white plastic bag, which obviously contained some rubbish. In his other hand he was holding the lid of the bin. He was looking down into the now empty bin. He replaced the lid and lifted the lid of the second bin and looked down. It was some seconds before he replaced that lid. He stood and looked down to his left towards the end of the cul-de-sac. He walked to the corner and stood looking down the road that ran parallel to his garden. He turned and went back to his own bins and took another look inside.

'Yep, they're still empty, buster,' I said, and burst out laughing.

He walked back around the side of his house, still carrying the little white plastic bag of rubbish. In a way I felt sorry for the man: he must have been totally perplexed by the incident.

The bin run paid off handsomely. We obtained enough details to trace a new company the man had set up to import jewellery from India and the Far East.

———

'And if I remember rightly, I came within sixty seconds of getting caught,' Sam added.

'It'll be different this time. There'll be no yucky household waste to sort, no soggy teabags, chicken carcasses or left-over food; it will just be paper,' I said cajolingly.

'It's a main road – we can't bring the trailer, the traffic will be too heavy,' he replied.

The conversation went back and forth. I noted that Sam's objections were now in the future tense: the problems we 'will' have rather than the problems we 'would' have. I was obviously gaining some ground, so I kept going.

'We'll be in and out in less than an hour,' I said. I told him I had phoned the council and they had confirmed that refuse was collected from the building on Mondays between 8.30a.m. and 9.00a.m.

'How did you get details of the times?' he asked.

I told him that I had said a friend had just moved into offices in the area and needed to know. I also told him that they had asked me to remind my friend that the rubbish must be left out on Monday mornings, and not the Friday before – that was an offence under the bye-laws.

He looked at me for a while. I could see that he was on the verge of saying yes.

'Would you like some more tea?' I asked.

'Feck off,' he said. 'Okay. We'll have one go at it and that's it.'

I blew him a kiss and went back to my office.

———

Sam picked me up from home at 7.10am on Monday morning. He had collected the van from David's house on Sunday. The signs on the side of the van read 'Emergency Plumbing – 24-hour Service', together with a fictitious telephone number.

We arrived in Irishtown at 7.58am and parked half up on the footpath. The yard was immediately ahead on our left-hand side. The solid blue doors to the yard were closed and padlocked. There were no bins or rubbish bags outside. There was plenty of activity in the immediate vicinity; black refuse sacks and other rubbish was piling up at the edge of the footpath in front of nearby business premises. We waited.

At 8.32a.m., a young woman unlocked the blue gates and pushed them open. Sam hopped out of the van and sauntered along the road. He stopped in front of the gates and glanced into the yard, continued walking for a short distance and then came back to the van.

'She's gone into the end building,' he said.

'I'll watch from over there,' I said, indicating a spot across the road.

A man in his mid-twenties arrived and entered the front building, the one we were interested in. I checked my watch; it was 8.41a.m. Sam was looking at me, so I gave him a nod.

At 8.50a.m. the same man emerged, carrying three large black plastic sacks, which appeared to be lightweight, in each hand. He turned back into the yard. I gave Sam a head signal to move forward and scarpered across the road. He stopped the van just past the gates. I opened the back door, Sam hopped out and we threw the black sacks into the back of the van. We both jumped in and Sam drove away. We had taken less than a minute to lift the bags and get going.

While he was checking the rear view mirror, I kept an eye on the side mirror, but there was no repetition of the Rathfarnham scare.

By the time we got to the East Link Toll Bridge, we had both relaxed. We decided to bring the bags to my house and I would work through the messy bit, sorting the rubbish. It wasn't until we were offloading at my house that I notice the back of the van was filthy, covered in mud. This was very unusual as David was very conscientious about keeping it clean. I made a mental note to mention it to David and then it hit me. The rest of the van was spotlessly clean. I looked again at the back; it was so dirty that it was virtually impossible to read the rear number plate.

'Would you like some breakfast?' I asked Sam.

'That would be great, I'm starving,' he replied.

I raided the fridge and knocked up a reasonable brekkie; scrambled eggs, toast and fresh coffee. We had finished eating and were having a second mug of coffee. 'Nice touch,' I said.

'I was wondering when you'd notice,' he replied with a grin.

After he picked up the van from David, he had bought a bag of compost, mixed it with enough water to make a paste and smeared it all over the back of the van, paying particular attention to the number plate.

'I suppose I'd better bring it to the car wash before I give it back to David,' he added.

We agreed that he would look after the office, deal with clients and keep things going while I worked on the rubbish bags at home. I switched on my answering machine so I could work uninterrupted.

I pulled on a pair of rubber gloves and got stuck into the first bag. I spent the next three days sifting, sorting and discarding paper. It was tedious work, but necessary. I worked on the kitchen floor. I went through each bag in turn sorting the contents into various piles of documents, one part of the kitchen floor for each of the four companies and a couple of miscellaneous piles. One of the black bags contained all their canteen waste – smelly milk cartons and dried-out tea bags – so it could be dumped immediately. What became apparent very quickly was that the rubbish was mixed. Paperwork from all four companies was found in each bag, so I could assume that on a day-to-day practical basis, the companies were connected.

When I had completed the initial sorting, I put each pile in a new black refuse sack, which I labelled with the appropriate company name.

Then I started going through the individual bags again,

reading every piece of paper. This time I was looking for any reference to Stanley. I made notes as I went along.

By Tuesday evening, I was genuinely surprised at the amount of information I had, not only linking Stanley to all four companies but also evidence of what could be described as gross misconduct in his capacity as an employee of my clients. I also noticed I was developing a case of 'washerwoman's knees' from crawling around on my tiled floor.

I made a couple of telephone calls first thing Wednesday morning to obtain some further information just to clarify my overall impression with regard to the setup in Irishtown. Then I started dictating my report.

In respect of the company of which Stanley was director and secretary, I had envelopes, incoming letters, faxes, quotations and an American Express bill, all addressed to Stanley at this company's name and address in Irishtown.

There were copies of outgoing letters accompanying quotations sent to various companies with Stanley's name and the company name at the bottom.

In addition, there was a copy of sales figures for one week (amounting to £6,500), with a handwritten note from Stanley attached. The note was addressed to a young office secretary, who, in turn, was actually on the payroll of the printing company in the same building.

I had also recovered a statement from Aer Lingus addressed to Stanley at his home address, the same address my clients had on their files.

There was also a dispatch label from a major computer manufacturer addressed to Stanley at my client's company.

There was one piece of evidence linking Stanley to the printing company, and that was a handwritten draft invoice for £30,097.98. The invoice was to be sent to my clients.

I found another piece of evidence that linked Stanley to the company that was in direct competition with my clients. It was a business card with this company's name, address and telephone number. Also printed on the business card was Stanley's name in full and the description 'Area Sales Manager'.

With regard to the last company, the one that sold the same computer software as my clients, I found some copy mailmerge letters. Dumped in the same bag as these letters was a database spreadsheet listing sixty company names, addresses and contact names. When I cross checked this list with the list of customers Peter had given me at the start of this investigation, I found twenty-four matching names. It would seem that this company was targeting my client's customers. It would be reasonable to assume that Stanley had provided details of my client's customers; he was the only known connection.

I couriered my report, which was thirty-five pages long, to Peter on Monday. He asked me to meet him and John at their solicitor's office on Thursday at 11.00a.m.

Sam and I attended the meeting. I went through my report with the solicitor, clarifying any points he raised.

The solicitor asked me to do another 'bin lift' the following Monday. I could feel Sam's eyes on me, although I didn't look in his direction. I had given him my word.

I thought for a few seconds.

Bloody clients, they're never satisfied, I thought.

'I'm sorry, no,' I said. I didn't explain any further.

Needless to say, Stanley was dismissed. I don't know if our clients took any other legal action against him; that was a matter for John and Peter to decide. It was none of our business.

04 | A LEAP OF 'FATE'

I called into 'Audrey's' as usual to pick up my Sunday news-papers. 'You're early today,' Eddie greeted me as I came in.

Eddie and Anne had recently moved into big spanking new premises across the road from their original shop, which had been a tiny eight feet by twelve feet general grocery store. They were very proud of their new premises. We chatted a while about how their business had improved since the move. I picked up my papers and left. As I let myself into my office down the street, I made a mental note to ask why they called their shop 'Audrey's' – not that it really mattered.

The best thing about working on a Sunday morning is the peace and tranquillity – no phones ringing, no interruptions, no traffic – and it was the one day in the week when parking was readily available.

While I waited for the kettle to boil, I opened all the windows. Another plus, I thought: the rest of the week we had to rely on fans to keep cool because of traffic noise and pollution. It was a beautiful sunny morning.

At 7.20a.m., with a mug of coffee beside me and cigarette in hand, I sat at my desk and opened the file to review the operational plan.

David, my apprentice, was due on duty at eight and Sam was due to start at nine. I toyed with the idea of making alarm calls to both lads, just to be sure that they were up, but decided against it. This was the third consecutive Sunday we were all working and they were grumpy enough without having me checking up on them. They had to do the worst part of the job – static surveillance.

David had drawn the short straw. He had the earlier start and he would have to cope with the difficulties of trying to carry out surveillance on a Sunday morning, in a small housing estate, without drawing attention to himself.

Sam was responsible for the technical side of the business: cameras, videos and equipment. As for me, I guess I was responsible for everything else.

The main reason I was in the office was because the base station for the radio equipment in each car was located there and I would be radio controller for the earlier part of the job – if anything at all happened, that is. As I said, this was the third Sunday we had attempted to complete this job.

David came through on the radio at 7.55a.m. He had checked the subject's house (we'll call him 'John'). As there was no car in the driveway, he would have to have a direct line of sight to the front door, which could be problematic. David had to cover a number of possibilities.

Carrying out surveillance is not as it's often depicted on TV or in films, where the PI or detective locates the target's house, finds a very convenient empty parking space nearby and has a direct line of sight to the target's premises. The fictional target, on leaving the premises, usually drives away in the same direction the PI's car is facing, which means the PI doesn't have to carry out an illegal or dangerous U-turn without being noticed. And how often have you seen on TV a target who realises that they are being followed? Real life is somewhat different.

The first thing that has to be done, prior to any surveillance being carried out, is a preliminary reconnoitre or recce. It is essential that the exact location of the target premises is known so that the PI is not, in effect, kerb crawling and drawing attention to him or herself. It is a very good idea to scout around the immediate area to familiarise yourself with the layout of the adjoining roads and access to the nearest public transport routes, shops and main roads. This preliminary work can dictate the choice of the surveillance position.

Then there is the matter of making, in most cases, an almost instantaneous decision as to identification of a target. Even with the benefit of photographs, positive identification can be problematic. For example, a male target might have a brother of a similar age, which could cause problems with positive identification – is it the target or a member of his family? Checking the electoral register for a list of the occupants of a house can assist in this regard, as can vehicle registration checks.

The best time to check 'home premises' for vehicles is very late at night or in the early hours of the morning, and preferably not on weekend nights, when there is a greater possibility that a target may be out socialising. Once the registration number of any vehicles or vehicles at the premises is known, a check of the local licensing authority's records will generally provide the names of the registered owners, which can be cross checked against the electoral register.

But what do you do if there are no vehicles at the premises, as was the situation in John's case? The static surveillance position has to afford a direct line of sight to the target premises, in case some unknown third party collects the target from his house. We all knew what John looked like, we even had photographs, but they were distance shots taken some time earlier. He could have dyed his hair, shaved his head, grown a beard – all of which would materially affect his overall appearance. Positive identification in these cases can be a process of elimination.

I re-read the file, even though I knew the details of what had occurred over the previous two weekends.

———

There had been a routine road traffic accident. A vehicle belonging to one of my clients, a semi-state utility company, had rear-ended John's car. Technically, there was no legal defence, but my clients had asked me to carry out a routine investigation simply to verify that John's complaints were continuing.

Primarily John was alleging that he had severe and ongoing back problems. He couldn't work, drive, play football or walk for any reasonable distance. I had completed my investigations and was about to submit my report when I received a telephone call from the claims manager of my client company.

I thought she was chasing her report, as the claim was listed for hearing at the start of the next sessions in the Circuit Court. But no, she had received an anonymous telephone call. Anne said that judging by the sound of the voice, the caller was a female in her twenties. The information she offered was very scant – John was to take part in a bungee jump in Dublin city centre on a Sunday morning. That was it – no date, no location, nothing more.

From an investigator's point of view, anonymous calls can be a pain. They are often nothing more than malicious, although some are well intentioned, but all such calls have to be followed up, just in case.

At that time, Internet connections were not available in Ireland, so 'Googling' was not an option. Private investigators had to rely on old-fashioned, time-consuming, mind-bogglingly dreary, foot-slogging research and lateral thinking.

My immediate problem was how I could find out about planned bungee jumps due to take place in Dublin.

If that anonymous telephone call was correct, all I had to work with was that it would take place in Dublin city centre on a Sunday morning. I was sure that some form of licence must be needed to run such an event and public liability insurance cover would also be required. I started with Dublin City Council, then called Dublin Corporation. I tried their Events Department first. They had no information. I checked with the Roads and Parks Department – no luck. The Environment Department also had no information, in fact they wanted me to tell them the date and location as soon as I became aware of it as there could be heath and safety issues to be checked. I finally checked the Law

Department, again with a negative result. I was beginning to feel under pressure. Time was running out and I was no further forward.

Most of the insurance companies operating in Ireland were clients, so I sent a request for information about any public liability cover they had put into effect for a bungee jump event due to take place in Dublin.

I also started phoning contacts in each of the ten city-centre garda stations. If road closures might be needed to facilitate this event, the local gardaí would be have to be informed. Whilst I was waiting for responses from these contacts, Lady Luck decided to smile on us.

During the course of another investigation, David had visited the Thomas Street/Meath Street area of the city centre. While he was having coffee in a café in the market area, he noticed a small poster displayed near the cash desk. It was advertising a local community festival week and listed the various activities due to take place during the week commencing the following Sunday.

The event was to open with a bungee jump, starting at midday. Having checked out the venue, David telephoned me to put me in the picture.

At our regular Friday afternoon meeting, we put together a plan of operation for the following Sunday morning.

On Sunday, I woke, as usual, at half past five. Without opening the blind, I knew the weather was foul. The sky was dark and it was pouring rain. After a quick shower and breakfast, I telephoned David and Sam. We Irish are known to be preoccupied by the weather, and many outdoor social activities are planned 'weather permitting'. I suspect few people realise that weather conditions often affect the activities of private investigators too.

I decided that we would run with the planned operation. David headed off at seven thirty to carry out a static surveillance in the vicinity of John's home.

By ten o'clock the weather had deteriorated badly. The rain was torrential and a strong wind had come up. I tried telephoning a pub in the festival area but there was no reply. I rang the local garda station in Kilmainham. I know the gardaí receive numerous and wide-ranging enquiries from members of the public but I am not sure how often they are asked for local weather reports. In any event the duty officer was very helpful in providing information.

At half past eleven David reported in and advised that there was no movement from John's house. I told him to stay in position and that I would get back to him. Sam and I travelled into Newmarket – a long, wide street just off The Coombe in Dublin. Apart from a pub, all the other properties on the street were small to medium-sized workshops or industrial units. There were terraces of small houses in the adjoining streets.

All the festival equipment was in place in front of an old red brick ESB sub-station at one end of the road, down from the pub, but there were few people about.

Sam and I decided to see what information we could pick up in the local pub. As we chatted with a barman over a cup of coffee, he told us that the bungee jump had been cancelled due to the bad weather. He thought that the festival would now close with the bungee jump on the following Sunday afternoon. I phoned David to update him.

Understandably, he was feeling a bit miffed; he had been sitting in his car for some five hours at that stage. The only thing that keeps you going in such circumstances is the anticipation that something might be about to happen. David was feeling cold, hungry, in need of some toilet facilities and totally fed up, and in an effort to cheer him up, we agreed to meet at the Yacht in Clontarf for lunch. On our arrival David handed me his written report. It was three lines. He had taken up an observation position near John's house at 7.50a.m. Literally nothing had happened, no one had entered or left the house, and he left the area at 12.55p.m. Over lunch, we thought over the plan for the following Sunday.

During the week, one of my garda contacts told me that a bungee jump was planned for the following Sunday week, on the quayside near the Point Depot. Reconsidering my options, I decided that whether or not John participated in the jump planned for the next weekend in Newmarket, we would also cover the proposed Point Depot jump. This would mean that I would be deferring the submission of my report to my client, but it would be worth a further week's delay; if we were very lucky, John would jump on both Sundays.

The second Sunday was a beautiful sunny morning. Even though I hadn't got to bed until one in the morning, I woke early. I pulled on my tracksuit and trainers and set about my exercise routine. In an effort to lose weight and get fit, I had set up a mini-gym at home. I had kept it very simple: an exercise bike, a step machine, a rowing machine and some weights. I had promised myself that I would do my routine every morning, but I find that when the weather is wet and miserable, I am inclined to forgo the exercises and hug a mug of coffee and a cigarette instead.

I had two hours to kill before I needed to be in the office. The adrenaline was going. I needed to do something to settle myself. Cutting the grass at 5.45a.m. was a non-starter – my neighbour wouldn't have been impressed – so I decided to do a late 'spring clean' of the bathroom. I am lucky enough to find housework therapeutic – sometimes.

I let myself into the office at 7.20a.m. and David came through on the radio at ten past eight. He was in position overlooking John's home. Nothing was happening. He radioed again at 11.20a.m. to say that John had emerged at around eleven, walked a very short distance to a local shop, had purchased some newspapers and was now sitting on his front doorstep reading the paper.

Sam, who had arrived a little earlier, decided to join David on the surveillance. In the interest of discretion, a change of vehicle at that stage would be a good idea and, anyway, he would be company for David.

Waiting for something to happen when you are carrying out surveillance is stressful, to say the least. Sam and David had each other for company; I paced the floor in the office. By two o'clock I couldn't stick it any longer, so I drove down to John's area and met up with the lads. There was no real need for me to be there, but I felt I had to be doing something. I was intensely frustrated.

At least we could see John in and around his home, so we knew we hadn't missed him, which is always a worry. Lapses in concentration can happen on lengthy surveillances.

The bungee jump was due to start at three. By four fifteen we gave up and went home. Even though I would be paid for the hours covered by my team and myself, there is always a sense of disappointment when nothing happens.

So here we were again, working on the same file for the third consecutive Sunday. I had decided that if nothing happened today, that was it; no more time and effort would be spent on this case. I would file my report and tell the client that if I heard of another bungee jump taking place before the court hearing date, I would automatically cover it.

Thinking about the previous two attempts, I started to feel a bit anxious, so I made radio contact with David at 8.45a.m. As I was talking to David, John emerged from his house. David watched him as he walked down the road. He turned into the local shop. David and I were debating whether or not he should follow John on foot when John came out of the shop and walked back to his home.

Damn and blast, I thought, but David rightly pointed out that John had left his house some two hours earlier than he had the previous Sunday.

Sam came through on the radio at 9.05a.m. He had been loading the camera gear into his car when he heard David's report over the radio and had decided to join David to await developments. I started to pace up and down the office as my sense of anticipation grew.

At 9.30a.m. Sam reported that he and David were now in Sam's car, watching the house. At 10.10a.m. the radio crackled again.

'Are you receiving?'

I tripped over the office bin as I ran to the desk.

'Yeah?' I said.

'He's out again,' David said.

This time, he had turned right on leaving his house – if he had been going to the shop he would have turned to his left.

Excellent! A different route, I thought.

'What's he wearing?' I yelled into the microphone.

'No need to shout,' came Sam's cool response. I know I'm inclined to get a bit excitable at times, but he's so laid back I could slap him!

'Grey tracksuit bottoms, white short-sleeved tee, left sleeve is bright red, white trainers,' Sam replied. 'He's heading towards the Dart station,' he added. 'David's following on foot.'

And after a few minutes, 'He's gone into the Dart station.'

I really wanted to be there, in the thick of it, instead of being stuck in the office. I didn't know what role or function I would fulfil, but, hell, I had waited three weeks for this, and I didn't want to miss any of the action.

'Will we assume he's going to the Point?' I asked.

'Okay,' came Sam's response. I didn't need any further encouragement.

'I'm on my way,' I said, as I threw the microphone onto the desk.

I ran down the stairs and jumped into my car. I am really glad that there were no such thing as penalty points in those days; I am equally glad that it was a Sunday morning and traffic was very light. I have no doubt that I broke all the speed limits. As they say, I hit the road in spots. I reached the Point Depot in seventeen minutes.

I abandoned my car in Castleforbes Road and literally ran around the corner onto North Wall Quay and down to the Point Depot.

There was a small crowd of onlookers but I located Sam quite quickly. He was carrying a video camera and hanging around his neck was a stills camera with a telephoto lens. I took the stills camera and draped it around my neck. Looking around, I could see no sign of David or John.

The crowd was getting bigger and more animated by the minute. Men, women and kids were milling around, and it would be difficult to spot John from a distance. I was relying on picking David out from the crowd – he's six foot two, so it shouldn't be too difficult.

David appeared from the direction of Castleforbes Road at 10.50a.m. I nudged Sam and pointed towards David. Then we spotted John, about thirty yards ahead of David, walking in the direction of the Point.

There is no point in rehearsing what to do in situations like this. You just have to go with the flow, taking advantage of any situations that may arise, in order to complete the job in hand.

Looking around at the crowd, I could see a number of people had stills cameras and small camcorders. There were a couple of larger video cameras in evidence as well, so Sam did not look out too of place with our large video camera sitting snugly on his right shoulder.

'I need to get a locating shot,' Sam muttered to me. When video evidence is submitted in court cases, it is essential that the location and date of the activity is clearly identified, ideally at the beginning of the recording session. Sam is a very experienced cameraman. This is a great advantage when we have to take videos of subjects, as he is totally familiar with lighting, shot angles and the workings of cameras.

The crane was so high that Sam had to move a considerable distance away from the onlookers so that he could get a photograph of the whole of the crane that would also indicate its height in relation to neighbouring buildings.

A beaming David joined us. He started to relate the events leading to their arrival at the Point. As I listened to David I watched John, who had by then joined the queue of people at the barrier who were waiting to jump.

'Get in the queue behind him,' I muttered to David, 'and earwig what he is saying.'

'There's no way I'm jumping,' David said as he walked towards the queue.

I sauntered over towards David as he joined the queue. 'Back out at the last minute,' I whispered in his ear.

Having taken his 'locating shot', Sam pretended to film the event by sweeping the camera over the crowd, turning in John's direction as he did so. Then he pressed the record button. Sam periodically filmed John's progression along the queue of jumpers. For the sake of something to do, I snapped away with the stills camera, taking distance shots of John.

Using the telephoto lens, I focused on a guy two places ahead of John. I wanted to get a full-face close-up of John for identification purposes, but I didn't want to point the camera directly at him. When he moved up the queue, I simply had to lift the camera, make fine adjustments to the focus and squeeze the shutter.

Gotcha, I thought, with a smile on my face.

I walked back to join Sam, who had now moved to the front of the crowd of onlookers.

As John was being fitted with the harness, I yelled over to him, 'Give us a wave!', which he did.

He shouted back, 'Wait till you see this!'

You bet, I thought.

It's no exaggeration to say that John was now posing for our video.

Grinning broadly, he entered the cage, turned and waved to us. I waved back. Someone in the crowd yelled, 'Go for it!'

'Yeah, go for it,' I prayed silently. Some of the earlier jumpers had backed out of jumping when the cage had reached the top of the crane, so I kept my fingers crossed that he would go through with it.

While the evidence we had obtained at this stage was worthwhile, if he backed out its value and impact would be reduced.

Most of the other video cameras were domestic camcorders. Ours was a large Super vhs professional model. Maybe John thought we were a television or film company and that this would be his fifteen minutes of fame.

He continued to play to our camera, grinning and waving down in our direction, as the cage slowly rose to the top of the crane.

I saw the minder check John's harness when the cage reached the top of the crane. The cage gate was opened.

Holding on to the upright with his left hand, John leaned out as far as he could, waved to the crowd below and then, turning in our direction, gave a final wave, saluted with his right hand and jumped.

He plummeted headfirst towards the River Liffey. As the elastic rope reached its maximum extension and was beginning to retract upwards, John carried out a manoeuvre that none of the previous jumpers had – somehow he managed to propel himself into an upright position as he bounced back up towards the cage. The crowd cheered and clapped. I will never know how he managed this feat – especially since he was supposed to have a bad back.

He repeated this manoeuvre twice more before gently bouncing, head first, a few times until the bungee rope was still.

'Did you get all that?' I said to Sam, who was standing beside me.

'Yup,' he replied, grinning from ear to ear as he kept the camera rolling.

I looked over at David. He looked very happy too. I glanced back at John who was being lowered onto a padded groundsheet by two hefty-looking lads from the bungee company.

Once up on his feet, John sauntered over in our direction.

'Keep it rolling,' I whispered to Sam.

'Did you enjoy that?' I said as he reached the barrier.

'It was effing great.'

'Would you do it again?'

'Can't wait.'

'What's your name, anyway?'

'John,' he said.

Thank you very much, mate, I thought.

————

Whilst the road traffic accident was genuine, John received substantially less than the amount he had originally claimed in compensation. The judge also ordered that his file was to be referred to the Director of Public Prosecutions to investigate whether there was sufficient evidence to warrant a prosecution for perjury.

John did eventually get his fifteen minutes of fame on an RTÉ Television current affairs programme. The topic of the programme was personal injury claims, how some such claims are exaggerated to a lesser or greater degree, and how some of these claims are borderline fraud.

A segment of our video was shown as an example, but they 'forgot' to mention my name!

05 | FACE TO FACE

Unless a case specifically involves working undercover, a private investigator beavers away in the background, digging around looking for information. If surveillance is necessary, we like to maintain a discreet distance, simply observing the target, or subject, going about their normal daily routine: where they go; who they see; what they do. That way we can build up a picture of their lifestyle. All of my investigations involved research and enquiries and about eighty per cent also required surveillance.

Generally one of my team, David or Michael, carried out the initial periods of surveillance. We normally met every Friday afternoon to review the cases each of us had worked on during the week. I suppose you could call these meetings 'case conferences'.

Apart from the reviews, we would kick around ideas or suggestions on any follow-up actions that needed to be taken on each file. If we had gathered enough information, the file would go in the pile for the preparation of reports for our clients.

Sometimes it was necessary to get very close to a target, even meeting them face to face using a pretext or cover story. As a rule, that role fell to me.

No Can Do

On one investigation, we were checking a guy who lived on the seventh floor of one of the tower blocks of flats in Ballymun. We knew he was married with three young children: but the problem was we didn't know what he looked like, so how the heck were we supposed to follow him? I came up with the bright idea of doing a 'survey', and, to increase the chances that the subject would agree to participate, I thought it would be a good idea to give away something useful. I decided on cans of food!

When I discovered that the lifts were out of operation, maybe I should have reconsidered my idea. Instead I tramped up seven flights of stairs carrying a heavy tray of canned foods. I did a trial run at a neighbour's flat. It worked like a dream; I gave her four tins of food. Next stop, our subject's flat. His wife opened the door. There was a scruffy little fella of about three years of age hanging on to her leg. I started my spiel. I was in luck. My subject walked down the narrow hallway to the door; I smiled at him and restarted my 'story' about 'a taste test' survey on a range of products from a well-known Irish company. I handed her two cans and bent down to pick up another two. Your man exploded: yelling abuse, cursing and swearing at me. He grabbed the cans from his wife and lobbed them over the balcony down into the yard seven floors below. 'Get the fuck outta here!' he roared.

I stood there gawping.

His wife, who seemed a nice, quietly spoken woman, put her hand on my arm. 'Sorry, love, they sacked him three weeks ago.'

Talk about bad luck. On the positive side, though, I had achieved my objective. I would certainly recognise this subject in a crowd.

Elizabeth

'Elizabeth' was one of our bog standard, routine insurance company cases. She had been involved in a road traffic accident and claimed she couldn't return to work because of ongoing disabilities.

My pre-surveillance routine enquiries had disclosed that she was in receipt of disability benefit from the state. Both David and

Michael had carried out periodic surveillance and hadn't spotted anything untoward. She had been seen on a number of occasions; the most demanding task she had performed was shopping.

At one of our Friday meetings, we went over the information we had obtained through enquiries and surveillance.

'Looks like she's okay,' said Michael.

David nodded in agreement.

Before putting her folder in the 'for reports' pile, I glanced through the lads' various written reports.

'Hang on a minute,' I said.

I flicked through the surveillance reports again.

'Mondays, Tuesdays and Wednesdays, she potters about; Thursday afternoons and Friday mornings she has a number of women calling to her house, right?'

They both nodded.

'So what's she doing on Thursday afternoons and Friday mornings?'

'Maybe they're just friends or family calling,' said David.

I decided to put her file back in the active investigations pile.

The following Thursday morning, I headed out to her neighbourhood in south Dublin. I found Elizabeth's house without any difficulty. I had three vantage points from which to monitor the property, so I could move my position periodically. I also had the benefit of photographs taken by David, which would help me with identification. I settled down to wait, to watch and to note activities.

A woman went into the house at 10.45a.m.; she came back out again at 11.30a.m. I judged her to be in her mid-sixties. Another woman went in at noon and re-emerged at 1.10p.m., and a third woman, who looked in her early seventies, went in at 2.30p.m. She didn't come out until just before four o'clock.

I had taken photographs of the first two women when they emerged from Elizabeth's house. When the third lady came out, I lifted the camera to take a couple of photographs; as I looked at her through the lens, I felt there was something different about her. Then I put my finger on it – yes, I was sure of it. When she went into the house, she had whiteish grey hair. Now her hair had a distinct pink tinge.

The old lady headed off towards the main road. I quickly drove around the block, so that now I was driving towards her. I wound down the passenger window and leaning across, with a big smile on my face, I said,

'Can you help me? I think I'm lost. I'm looking for Elizabeth, the hairdresser's house?'

'Of course,' came her reply. She pointed out Elizabeth's house. 'I've just come from Elizabeth's myself.'

She seemed quite chatty, so I got out of the car and we talked for about ten minutes. She mentioned that Elizabeth did her hair every Thursday afternoon. I also got the impression that Elizabeth had been hairdressing from home for about two years.

I resumed surveillance. I waited until five o'clock, just in case another customer had gone into the house in my absence. No one came out.

I knocked on Elizabeth's door at half past ten the following morning. A small, smiling, dark-haired woman opened the door. She was wearing clear plastic gloves. A navy towel was slung across her shoulder. I recognised her from David's photographs.

'Hi, are you Elizabeth?' I asked in my most ingratiating voice.

'Aha,' she said smiling at me.

'I don't know if you can help me: I'm staying with my cousin round the corner. We have a wedding this afternoon and I can't get an appointment at any of the local salons. Any chance of a quick wash and blow dry?'

'Sure – if you don't mind waiting a few minutes, I can do it.'

'That would be great. Thanks.'

I followed her upstairs and into the back bedroom.

'Have a seat,' she said.

She went back to her other customer, a woman in her forties. She had clearly coloured the woman's hair. As she did a strand test, I had a good look around.

'I'll just rinse this colour, I'll only be a few minutes with the blow-dry,' she said to me.

The two women went into the bathroom next door.

I knew that I had less than five minutes; that's all it would take to rinse out the colour and then shampoo and condition her customer's hair.

The bedroom was about fourteen feet by nine. There was a proper salon table with mirror fixed to the wall opposite the door, and a standard salon chair in front of the table and mirror. A shelving unit to the left of the table contained the usual hair products – shampoos, conditioners, and treatment products – on the upper shelving. The double doors at the bottom of the unit were open; clean navy towels were neatly stacked on the bottom shelves. A plastic laundry basket stood on the floor beside the unit; I could see some used towels in the basket.

I was sitting in an armchair under the window and to my left was a two-seater sofa with piles of magazines on one of the cushions. To all intents and purposes, it was a mini salon. All that was missing were washbasins; Elizabeth clearly used the bathroom next door for washing her customers' hair.

I had my mini Olympus camera in my bag. It is an extremely useful piece of kit – no bigger than a packet of cigarettes, it has all the features of a full-sized camera. I slipped off my shoes, quietly raised myself out of the armchair and started taking photographs. Occasionally the floorboards creaked. I would cough aloud to cover the sound.

By the time Elizabeth and her customer returned to the room, I was back on the armchair and pretending to be engrossed in a magazine.

As she was blow-drying the other woman's hair, I asked, 'Elizabeth, could I use your bathroom, please?'

'Go ahead, it's just next door.'

I closed the bathroom door and sat on the toilet lid. I fished the camera out of my pocket, took a few photographs, flushed the toilet, washed my hands and went back into the 'salon'.

As Elizabeth saw her other customer to the front door, I surreptitiously slipped the camera back into my handbag.

'Right,' she said, running her fingers through my hair. 'You've got a few split ends, will I trim them?'

The usual hairdresser's conversation started.

'Are you doing anything for the weekend?' (My cousin around the corner and the 'wedding' had obviously slipped her mind.)

We covered all the usual topics: holidays, films, the latest political scandals. She finished my hair in thirty-five minutes.

I walked around the corner to where my car was parked. I sat, lit a cigarette and reflected on Elizabeth. She was a nice, friendly woman and a bloody good hairdresser to boot. In a way I felt sorry for her. She had come over as a pleasant character and, from what she told me, her husband was an extremely hardworking man. She had two children aged seven and five. Hell, she probably needed the money.

But if her case came to court and she didn't admit to working from home, even on a part-time basis, she was going to get sandbagged by the insurance company's legal team at the hearing.

Sentimentality can't come into the picture when work is concerned. I decided I should cover the possibility that her legal team might suggest that it was a 'one off' situation or that Elizabeth just did hairdressing occasionally for friends. The reality was that she was running a business from home and had kitted out her back bedroom as a mini-salon, complete with professional fixtures, fittings and equipment.

I had lunch with my sister Barbara on Sunday and asked for her help. Various members of my immediate family had helped out on other investigations in the past. On one occasion, Barbara had accompanied Mum and Dad, who were then in their early seventies, on a trip to the West of Ireland on an information-gathering jaunt. The case had involved an elderly farmer who lived in a rather isolated area. Mum and Dad provided Barbara with a suitable cover story. They did very well, so well in fact that the farmer in question invited them all to tea one afternoon.

On Thursday, I picked Barbara up at 9.30a.m. En route, I briefed her on the salient points of the job to be done. Barbara phoned Elizabeth's house from her mobile.

'Hi, Elizabeth? My name is Barbara.'

She told Elizabeth that she had 'done her friend's hair' the previous week and that she was delighted with it (completely true). She asked Elizabeth if she could fit her in for a shampoo and blow-dry that morning. Elizabeth told Barbara to call at 11.30a.m. She didn't even ask who her 'friend' was.

Both Michael and David were on surveillance duty. They were to note the car registration numbers of any callers to the house, and one or other of them was to follow any pedestrian callers to their destination after they left Elizabeth's house. I wanted to identify some of her other customers, and since it was fair to assume that most, if not all, of them were locals I hoped some would be going home after getting their hair done. I dropped Barbara at the corner of the road five minutes before her appointment.

This was before hand-held mobile phones were in common use, and we had recently installed Motorola radios in the three company vehicles with a base unit back in the office. This meant we could communicate between cars and with the office. It was a valuable method of communicating, particularly if we had more than one vehicle on a surveillance job.

I tried Michael first; David replied. 'Hi, Shirl, Michael's just gone after the first customer.'

I told him that Barbara had gone into the house.

Barbara reappeared at 12.25p.m.

'What do you think?' she said, stroking her hair as she settled in the passenger seat.

'Feck the hair – tell me exactly what you saw.'

'Well it's obvious that she doesn't remember you exactly . . . I think she has loads of customers.' She described the details of the back bedroom, the bathroom, and the 'hairdresser's chat'. 'Her next customer arrived just before I left.'

'Okay, make your notes,' I said, handing her a notebook and pen. 'Your hair is lovely, by the way.'

Michael and David arrived in the office at two o'clock on Friday afternoon. They had successfully followed and identified three of Elizabeth's other customers.

Elizabeth's claim was not settled. It was down for hearing in the High Court. Sam, David, Michael, Barbara and I arrived at the Four Courts at 8.45a.m. and went straight to a consultation room on the ground floor.

The two legal teams met to see if they had any common ground to agree. The insurance company solicitor came back to the room to keep me posted on developments. 'She's still maintaining that she's not working.'

Barbara and I had to remain in the consultation room until the case was called. Michael and David could go into the courtroom if they wished, but Sam had to stay outside too, even though he hadn't been directly involved in this case. Like myself, he was too well known as a private investigator.

The first witness to give evidence in these cases is the plaintiff, the subject of our enquiries. After completing their evidence in chief, which is given on oath, they are then cross-examined by the defence senior counsel, who tries to pick holes in the plaintiff's evidence.

Barbara and I discreetly slipped into the back row of the public seats when Elizabeth was in the witness box and the insurance company's counsel had just started his cross-examination. The sandbagging was about to begin.

Counsel questioned Elizabeth about her accident, her injuries, her pre-accident work history and her current medical complaints.

'And tell me, Mrs X, have you worked since your accident?'

'Oh no, I am not able to work.'

I dropped my head; Elizabeth was still under oath and she had just committed perjury.

What was just as bad for her, I knew that our side had subpoenaed someone from Social Welfare. That witness was sitting beside the insurance company's claims manager. Elizabeth was still receiving disability benefit, so the department would be going after her too.

'Have you tried to go back to work?'

'No, no, I can't work,' replied Elizabeth.

She sounded so plausible, so nice.

'Not even part-time?' our counsel said. He was speaking quietly, and his tone seemed sympathetic.

'No.'

I caught Barbara's eye and shook my head. I had hoped she would 'fess up, but she didn't. I stared at our counsel's back and waited. He turned around. He gestured to me to stand up.

'Do you recognise that lady?' he said to Elizabeth, pointing at me.

Her counsel and solicitor turned around and looked at me. Both knew me well. They turned back to face the judge. Both heads went down. The judge also knew me: I had given evidence to him on a number of occasions in the past.

I looked at Elizabeth, making eye contact. Her face never changed. Bloody hell, she should get an academy award, I thought.

She was sitting in the witness box with a smile on her face. She actually gave me a little wave!

'Oh yes, she's a friend of mine . . . eh . . .' She hesitated; she was trying to remember my name. 'Sheila,' she added.

'No, she's not a friend of yours, Mrs X, she's a private investigator.'

He turned back to her. I sat down.

'Did you dress her hair?'

Bloody hell, what century did he live in? 'Dress her hair'?

'Well, yes, but I only did it as a favour, she was stuck.'

'Did you charge her for your "favour"?' he asked in a sarcastic tone.

Elizabeth said nothing.

'Did you do favours for anyone else?'

'No.'

Stop digging a bigger hole for yourself, I thought

I nudged Barbara in the ribs and muttered, 'You're next.' Counsel turned and gestured to Barbara. She stood up.

'Tell me, is this another friend of yours?' He pointed at Barbara.

Elizabeth said nothing. She looked at her counsel and solicitor. They still had their heads bowed. They weren't going to be any help to her.

Our counsel's voice changed.

'Do you know Mrs Annie C?' he demanded.

No reply.

'Or Miss Yvonne L?'

Silence.

'What about Mrs Linda O'C?'

No response.

'They are all customers of yours, aren't they?'

She made no reply.

'Do you want me to have to bring these old ladies into court to confirm that you are their hairdresser? Well?'

Elizabeth started to cry.

At this point the judge intervened.

'I think this is opportune moment to adjourn for lunch.'

It was only twelve fifteen: normally we wouldn't adjourn for lunch much before one o'clock.

The judge continued, addressing Elizabeth's counsel. 'Mr K, could I suggest you have a word with your client in the lunch recess and advise her of the possible consequences of the evidence I have heard so far?'

He stood up. We all stood.

The tipstaff shouted, 'Court will resume at two fifteen,' and led the judge out of the courtroom.

We headed for the coffee shop in the basement.

'At least the place will be empty this early, we'll get a table no problem,' I said as we trooped down the stairs.

The lads and Barbara were in very cheerful form.

'Great win, guv,' said Michael, slapping me on the back.

I felt sad for Elizabeth. Why had she kept digging that hole? Sam sat beside me at the table. We'd worked together for so long, he could read me like a book. He squeezed my arm. 'It was her own fault, Shirl, she was too stupid to know that she had been caught out; and just too greedy.'

At five to two, our solicitor stuck his head around the door of the coffee shop. With a nod of his head, he indicated to me to follow him to the lobby outside.

I went out to join him.

'It's just settled, Shirley', he said. 'Great job; well done.' He started to tell me the settlement terms.

'If you don't mind, Joe, I don't really want to know; what about Social Welfare?'

'Oh, they're going after her, all right. She'll probably have to repay all her benefits.'

His parting shot as he headed for the stairs was, 'That will put a bloody big hole in her settlement.' He grinned at me and continued up the stairs.

I was reminded yet again that the one party who never seems to lose out in court is the legal profession. A 'necessary evil', someone once called them.

I went back to the lads at the table.

'We can all go home, it's settled.'

We trooped out of the side door into Chancery Place.

'Anyone for a pint?' said Barbara, pointing to the pub across the road.

We adjourned to the pub for a quick drink.

06 | EXTRA SERVICES

Before the introduction of the Personal Injuries Assessment Board, now called the Injuries Board, claims for personal injuries arising from road traffic accidents were dealt with directly by insurance companies. Investigating claims arising from these accidents was usually pretty routine. A number of insurance companies simply made a random selection of claims to be investigated that warranted only superficial enquiries, just to check the validity of the claim. If nothing suspicious arose, these claims would be settled.

However, there were a substantial number of other claims on which, for a variety of reasons, a 'red flag' went up. This might be as a result of confidential information received; discrepancies, inconsistencies or contradictions between the pleadings (the papers filed in court) and the medical reports prepared for the insurance company; or it could be that the amount of compensation claimed was so large that the claim was subject to detailed scrutiny.

This particular case was a 'red flag' claim!

The matter arose from a genuine accident. Around midnight on a wet Friday evening in September, a lorry with defective lights and hauling an unlit trailer was in the process of turning into the entrance of a yard in Ballyfermot. To make matters worse, the lorry and trailer were dirty and there were no safety markings along the sides and back of the trailer.

A car driven by a woman in her early thirties came around a bend in the road and ploughed straight into the trailer. The driver was seriously injured and the front seat passenger, her fiancé, died in the accident.

The lorry driver was held to be at fault and prosecuted by the gardaí. Therefore, liability was not an issue and the young woman filed a claim in the High Court for compensation in respect of her injuries.

So why did the red flag get hoisted? Initially, top consultants acting on behalf of the insurance company noted major discrepancies between her complaints with regard to her ongoing physical and mental disabilities and their own medical examinations. There were also variations in her stated pre-accident history.

The insurance company handed over their file to me with instructions to fully investigate her pre-accident history and her current activities.

I started by reading all the court papers and all the available medical reports and noting any obvious discrepancies.

The accident had happened fourteen months earlier, and I decided that the best place to start was right back at the beginning. I had a copy of the garda abstract report, an official document that summarises details of the accident. Very often the investigating garda has other information, which, though not strictly relevant to the report, can be of assistance in investigating the claim. So I started by talking to the two gardaí who had investigated the accident, and in the course of that conversation I obtained some information that I felt warranted detailed investigation.

'Marian', as I shall call her, had said during the course of the legal proceedings, that she couldn't remember anything for a period of one week before and six weeks after the accident. Yet, in her statement to the gardaí, which was taken during that period, she had said that she had left home at 10.45p.m. and had driven to a named pub in Ballyfermot to collect her fiancé: clearly she could remember that much. That begged the question of why, in the context of her claim, she appeared to want to conceal her activities immediately before the accident.

Then there was the matter of where was she actually living? One address was given in the court paperwork, but I had noticed a different address on one of the copy receipts provided by her solicitors. And there was a third address, in a south Dublin suburb.

The other piece of information I obtained at that meeting concerned her identity. Following the accident, the car was towed to the local garda station. With a view to trying to identify the two occupants of the car, Marian's handbag was checked. There was a very substantial amount of cash, £1,383 (over €1,700), in the bag. This was in the mid-eighties, at the height of a recession. In addition, there were two building society passbooks in the bag. Both accounts were with the EBS, and both had very substantial balances. The first account had been opened in the Rathmines branch in 1984 and the second, opened in 1985, was with the Westmoreland Street branch. Both accounts were in the name of Murphy, and two different addresses were provided.

So who was Murphy? And, if she was our lady, how had she amassed such substantial assets, particularly since, in her court papers, she said that she was a part-time secretary earning £150 per week?

I decided the first thing to follow up was the matter of the various addresses. When I checked with Dublin Corporation, I found that Marian was the registered owner of the car she had been driving, and the address was the one in south Dublin. The insurers specified were clients of mine. They told me that cover had been effected through a broker in north Dublin, but that the broker had withdrawn the insurance cover. Their records contained a note that the broker had referred the matter to the Fraud Squad, but they had no further details. This information warranted a visit to the broker's office in Dublin 9.

It was a small firm, just the owner and a secretary. They had no difficulty – for a number of reasons – in recalling Marian, and pulled her file from their system.

First, she had walked in off the street. While that was normal practice for people who lived or worked in the area, it struck them as unusual that someone who lived in south Dublin (this was the address she provided) would walk into their office in north Dublin.

She had told them that she had just bought her car and needed insurance in order to register herself as the owner and get road tax. She had filled in the proposal form and produced a provisional driver's licence, but had claimed that she had held a full UK licence since 1974. She was asked to produce evidence of her driving experience in Ireland, so she returned next day with a letter from a garage/workshop with an address in south-west Dublin. I didn't know then that this area would feature in this investigation. The letter stated that she had worked for the company since April 1985 and that she was named on their 'garage policy'. The letter specified yet another address for Marian, this one in Rathcoole, which is west of Tallaght on the N7. The brokers gave her a temporary cover note.

When they received the paperwork from the insurance company they sent it on to Marian at the address in south Dublin, the address she had specified on her proposal form. Their letter was returned by An Post marked 'no such address'. They then sent the correspondence to the Rathcoole address. Once again, it was returned by An Post, marked 'no such address'. This rang alarm bells, so they passed over the file to the Fraud Squad. All this had occurred just two months before the fatal road traffic accident.

I was getting bogged down with addresses; by now we had six different addresses for Marian. I needed to verify her current address for surveillance purposes – our clients wanted to know her daily routine. I also needed her previous addresses if I was to build up a picture of her background and pre-accident activities.

My partner Sam and I detoured over to the south Dublin address on our way back from a job in Greystones. We sat in the car, counting and recounting the houses. We didn't really think that An Post had made a mistake, but I wanted to see the layout of the road myself.

'There're definitely only sixteen houses,' Sam said. (On her insurance proposal form, Marian had given a house number higher than sixteen.)

Sam was right, there were only sixteen houses, numbered consecutively from one to sixteen. The development, which was fairly new, continued into another road, and there were no spaces between the two roads for any infill of houses that might have been numbered seventeen and above.

We decided to cut cross-country and check out the Rathcoole address. The address we had there seemed to be a townland as opposed to a specific road.

When in doubt about an address in a rural or semi-rural location, particularly if there is no local garda station, or if it is closed, you head for the local post office. If you get lucky, and the local staff are friendly enough, you can usually pick up extra information.

It was always my part of any job to approach people for information. Sam reckoned that I was a better actor than he; I believed that generally people felt more at ease, perhaps less suspicious, if they were approached by a woman rather than a man. But I accepted that 'acting' was a part of my job. It was critical in some investigations that you could role-play and adapt to local surroundings and situations.

In Rathcoole, the post office is located on Main Street. I scribbled the address we were interested in on a piece of paper and went in. There was an elderly man and a young woman working behind the counter. I chose to approach the man; generally I get on better with men and, in this case, because he was older than the woman, there was a fairly good chance that he was a local.

'Hi, I'm sorry to trouble you, but I hope you can help me,' I said, with a big smile on my face.

Returning my smile, he said, 'I'll do my best, dear. What can I do for you?'

Proffering my bit of paper, I said, 'I'm looking for this address.'

He recognised the address and gave me directions.

He appeared to be receptive, so, chancing my arm, I said, 'I'm dropping in on a friend as a surprise – she's just moved in there.'

He looked at me with a quizzical expression. 'You must have the wrong address, me dear,' he said. 'There's nothing up there but fields.'

'No houses at all?' I asked.

He shook his head.

'I don't suppose you would know her yet, having just moved in and all, but her name is Marian . . .', and I gave her surname.

He shook his head again.

'All that land is owned by xxx family,' he said, and then proceeded to give me a rundown on that family.

I thanked him profusely and left.

Back in the car, I was giving Sam a summary of the information, when it hit me like a bolt out of the blue. 'Bloody hell, the family who own that land has the same surname as the chap who died in the accident,' I said.

Maybe it was coincidence, but I mentally filed away a note that we should take another look at that family. After all, they had also filed a claim for compensation against the lorry driver.

I called in to see the insurance company's claims manager. He agreed that Marian appeared to be going to extraordinary lengths to cover up something, but what it could be we didn't know. I suggested that he organise another medical examination for Marian as soon as possible. Our objective would be to positively identify her and place her under surveillance when she came out of the medical, with a view to establishing her current address. He readily agreed.

We had one further hurdle to get over. Most consultants refuse to assist investigators in any practical way, such as by allowing access to their waiting rooms. They are all aware that insurance companies engage the services of private investigators, but they can't be seen to be involved in any way. For my own reasons, I suggested the insurance company use the Blackrock Private Clinic on Rock Road in Blackrock. Frank, the claims manager, telephoned the next day. The medical was fixed for the following Thursday at half past two. He gave me details of the suite number and consultant's name.

We took two cars. Sam and I travelled together and David, our assistant PI, travelled in the company van.

We arrived at one fifteen and headed to the small coffee shop on the ground floor. David hadn't 'done' a medical at the Blackrock before, so I explained the set-up. Each consultant occupies a separate suite of rooms, which is fronted by a small reception area. All the suites are identical: a glass entrance door; sofa-type seating against the left- and right-hand walls; and, directly opposite the entrance door, a glass sliding partition, usually closed, behind which the consultant's secretary sat. The patient would go to the hatch, give their name to the secretary and wait to be called.

'So we hang around and see who goes in at two thirty,' David said.

'You do, but I don't,' I said. 'You stay with Sam.'

Just before a quarter to two, I took the lift to the second floor and walked past the suite. As I expected, the roller blind on the front door was pulled down. Lunch hour was from one to two and the first afternoon appointments were usually at two o'clock. Bang on time, the secretary raised the blind.

Meanwhile, Sam had taken David back out to the main doors into the clinic. There was a main reception desk to the left as you entered the clinic. People attending for medical examinations, particularly if they have not been to the clinic before, often go to the main reception and say that they have an appointment with so and so at such and such a time. Sam and David hung around that reception area, just in case Marian announced herself to the receptionist. This might help us identify her, just in case my plan didn't work out.

I leaned against the wall between the door to the stairwell and the lift. I had a clear line of sight to the suite I was interested in, which was to my right.

Just before two o'clock, an elderly couple emerged from the lift. They looked around as if they weren't sure where they should go. 'Hi,' I said in my friendliest voice, 'you look lost.' Bingo! They were looking for my suite.

'I'm going there myself,' I said as I guided them along the passageway and pushed open the door, holding it open for the couple to enter. The husband approached the reception desk.

'We can sit here,' I said to the woman and guided her to the sofa. Having given his name to the secretary, the husband joined us, and we chatted while we waited – at least I listened and they talked all about the husband's medical complaints. I had wanted to give the secretary the impression that I was with the couple, rather than just hanging round, and it worked. After a while the man was called into the examination room.

At two fifteen, a blonde woman entered. She looked in the right age group for Marian. I overheard her give her name to the receptionist. It was Marian. She sat on the sofa opposite and started to read a magazine. She didn't even glance in our direction. While she read and the elderly lady chatted, I made a mental note of what Marian was wearing. Tight-fitting light blue denim jeans tucked into white leather knee-high boots; a crisp white shirt with the cuffs turned out over the edge of the sleeves of a light blue denim jacket; matching light blue silk scarf knotted French style; and a good-quality black leather shoulder bag. Overall she was well put together: in my view a bit tacky looking, but chic.

Wish I could dress like that on a hundred and fifty quid a week, I thought. The bag alone would have cost over £100.

Just before two thirty, the receptionist said, 'Marian, you can go through now.'

As soon as she walked through the doors to the consulting room area, I said to my companion, 'My friend is late, I think I'll go out for a cigarette.' Downstairs I met up with Sam and David. They had identified Marian at the main reception desk. We had thirty minutes, at most, to get ourselves organised.

Sam had already retrieved the camera bag from the car. He and David went back to the van and drove around the back of the clinic building to the service area. I headed for the car.

Nice one, I thought as I saw the van reappear: today we had selected 'landscape gardeners' from our magnetic signs.

David parked beside a bed of shrubs directly opposite the

main door to the clinic. He appeared to be on his own but I knew that Sam was tucked away in the back of the van ready to take photographs. Dave turned his back to the driver's window and appeared to be reading some paperwork. If Marian was in any way suspicious, all she would see when she came out the door was a landscapers' van with the driver's back towards her.

It was my job to alert Sam and David over the radio as soon as I saw her emerge. All I said was, 'She's out,' and checked my watch. It was 3.07p.m.

'Okay,' came David's acknowledgement.

Now we had to be flexible enough to cover a number of eventualities. We didn't know her mode of transport. If she was on foot or travelling by public transport David would follow her; if she travelled by car, we would use both our vehicles to follow her to her destination. Outside the clinic door there is a footpath to the left and right. The right-hand path is closer to the main gates out onto Rock Road, and there is also a small car park to the right; the left-hand path leads into the main car parking area. Marian stood outside the main door and glanced to her left and right. She took the left-hand path.

I pushed the talk button on the radio. 'Looks like she's heading for the main car park.' As she walked past the back of our van and turned to her left, David slid out of the van and followed her on foot, stopping for a moment to open the back door of the van. He now had to identify the vehicle she was travelling in.

Sam hopped out of the back, whipped off the two signs, threw them in the back of the van and headed for our car.

I could see David running back towards the van.

'That's why he does that bit of the job – he's only a young fella,' I said to Sam.

David's voice came over the radio. 'Dark red or wine-coloured, looks like an old Escort; driver male with white hair.'

We fell in behind the Escort as it approached the main gates. It turned left, heading towards the city centre. David was two cars behind us. We stuck to the tail until the Escort turned left along the Grand Canal. Traffic was light.

'David, can you take over?' Sam said as he slowed down.

David moved in ahead of us. 'Indicating left,' he said as we approached the Suir Road junction.

The little convoy turned left at the traffic lights; David went through on the amber light and we went through on red. I had a quick glance around: there was no sign of any garda cars.

'All clear,' I said to Sam.

I think Sam would have gone through the red light anyway – needs must.

'Indicating right, no junction,' said David.

Sam slowed right down so that he could see the road ahead, past the van.

'Keep going, David,' I said into the radio.

David overtook the Escort on the inside lane. Sam pulled over and parked on the left-hand side of the road.

The Escort came to a halt on the footpath outside a row of red-brick houses. Marian and the driver alighted from the car and walked up the garden path. We saw Marian use a key to open the front door. They both went in. Ten minutes later, the driver left the house.

It's very satisfying when things go to plan on a job. We had achieved our objectives of the day: to positively identify Marian, to photograph her and to follow her back to her base, her home. I reckoned I had the easiest part, getting myself into the consultant's rooms without raising suspicion. The lads, on the other hand, had the stressful part, mobile surveillance.

I picked up the radio handset. 'Anyone for a pint on the way home?' I asked.

There was unanimous agreement.

David, Sam and I sat in my office to review the file. We agreed to split the workload. Sam and David would take over the surveillance aspect and I would look after the enquiries.

First we dissected the medical reports and listed all Marian's numerous alleged physical and psychological disabilities. Sam and David would pay particular attention to items on this list when carrying out surveillance. I left them to sort out the practical arrangements relating to days and times for surveillance.

I made my notes on the various lines of enquiry I was going to follow up. I now had Marian's name, date of birth, current address and a list of other addresses she had given at various times in the past. I started by calling my contact in Social Welfare.

While he was checking his records, I decided to go to the pub in Ballyfermot that Marian had named in her statement to the gardaí. I brought with me copies of some of the photographs taken when she had attended the medical in the Blackrock Clinic. A good time to talk to a bar manager is about thirty minutes after the pub has opened, when they have set up for the day's business and before there are too many customers. I went in just after eleven o'clock. I ordered coffee and asked the barman if the manager was around. He muttered the usual response, 'Not sure if he's in.'

I put a ten-pound note on the counter. 'Keep the change,' I said. 'Oh, by the way, you could tell him I'm not trying to sell him anything, just need a few minutes of his time.' I smiled ingratiatingly and headed for a table at the far end of the bar.

The manager appeared within minutes. 'Can I help you?' he asked.

I did the usual spiel: 'I'm an insurance investigator. . .' I mentioned that I was interested in a fatal road traffic accident that had happened on such and such a date. He instantly recalled having heard about the accident. I think he may have thought that I was interested in the amount of alcohol that Marian and her fiancé had consumed. He went on to tell me that 'the couple involved in the accident' organised and ran wet T-shirt competitions once a month on a Friday. That's how he remembered the accident! Neither he nor the owner of the pub had any problems with this competition taking place on the premises. As he put it, the punters would be hanging out of the rafters: the turnover on those Friday nights was huge and the organisers also made a hefty sum.

I was stunned by this information. We went back and forth over the details, and he started to explain what was involved in the competition.

'I get the picture,' I said. I didn't need graphic details.

'Can you remember the organisers' names?' I asked.

He stopped and thought and then shouted across the bar to the barman. 'Mick, can you remember that blondie one's name who used to run the т-shirt competitions last year?'

Without hesitation the barman replied, 'I think it was Marian or Marie, something like that.'

'Do you remember what she looked like?' I asked.

'Well, she had blonde hair to here,' he said (indicating his shoulders) and paused.

Mick wandered over to our table.

'Do you remember what she looked like?' I asked Mick. He started to describe Marian. I interrupted: 'Would you recognise her from a photograph?'

'Possibly . . .'

With that, I produced three photographs from my bag. The first was a distance shot. I handed it to Mick.

'That looks like her okay,' he said.

I then handed him two more photographs, a close-up full facial and the second a facial profile.

'That's definitely her,' Mick said as he handed me back the photographs.

The manager was adamant that Marian had never participated in these competitions, she merely organised them. During the course of conversation, he offered his thoughts on Marian's activities for the rest of each month. Based on that conversation, I added another line of enquiry to my list – did she have a criminal record?

I had an arrangement with the fraud investigation section of the Department of Social Welfare, which basically involved exchanging information. In return for their assistance, if I found evidence of a claimant working when they were in receipt of disability benefit or dole, I would pass back details to the fraud section. We saw ourselves as part of the same team, working to reduce fraud.

Marian's records had been checked. She had had a child when she was twenty-one years old and since 1973 she had been receiving unmarried mother's allowance, now, in the mid-eighties, set at £60.10p per week. Her specified address was in Walkinstown, the same address that had appeared on one of the medical receipts in the court papers. It was her old family home, so that eliminated any need for me to make any further enquiries about that address. The child's grandmother, Marian's mother, was the recipient of the monthly children's allowance payment.

The unmarried mother's allowance was means-tested, so any income or salary Marian earned would be taken into consideration. Marian had told the department that she had no income; that she had had no income since 1973. Yet in the papers filed in the High Court, she was claiming loss of earnings of £150 per week.

She was also claiming that her disabilities arising from the accident were such that she would never be able to work again. On that basis, her loss of future earnings was potentially huge, given that she was only in her early thirties.

My contact had also checked the files for Marian's history of tax and social insurance contributions. She had no record of any such contributions. This in effect meant that if she had worked, she was working in the black economy or for cash in hand.

She had provided some details of previous employers in the context of her claim. I would have to go through those details with a fine-tooth comb – and very diplomatically, as some of the employers named were highly reputable and high-profile companies. I doubted if they would be involved in the black economy, but one never knows.

Working on a complicated investigation like this is a bit like taking a long train journey, with passengers getting on and off all the time. At regular intervals we have to take on board new information that might come from our enquiries, from the claimant's solicitors or from further medical examinations. Some lines of enquiry lead to a dead end or to the elimination of a particular element of the investigation, so they are dumped. You have to be totally familiar with every aspect, every nuance of the information you have, so that you are in a position to pick up on any oddities that might become apparent.

On reading a new psychologist's report I found a new

inconsistency. In an earlier report, Marian had said that she owned her house, but in this one she clearly stated that she was renting. I could see no logical explanation for this discrepancy: whether she owned the house or was renting it had no material relevance to her claim. However, bearing in mind the enquiries we had made to date and the fact that nothing we had checked out so far had confirmed any of her statements, I decided to take a look at this question. I searched the Land Registry records, both under her name and under the address, and found nothing. Then I spent a couple of hours poking around the records in the Registry of Deeds in Henrietta Street. I found details of the property and the ownership register. The owners were identified as a doctor and his wife who lived on the same road as the garage/car workshop mentioned earlier.

The doctor lived only six doors away from the alleged employer at that garage. Coincidence? Maybe, but I decided to visit the doctor anyway. Perhaps he would be prepared to give me some information: was Marian a tenant, perhaps, or had she bought the property from him?

I called to the house. The doctor's wife opened the door. I opened with my usual, 'I'm an insurance investigator . . .' After I assured her that I was not seeking medical information, she invited me in for a cup of tea with her and her husband, who was now retired. I gave them an outline of the accident details and, trying to keep as close to the truth as I reasonably could, I indicated that I was interested in the property in the context of the financial aspect of the claim.

The doctor told me that the property had been sold to a young couple but he couldn't remember their names offhand, nor did he know anything about them. He had never personally met the purchasers. I asked him if I could approach his solicitors for this information. He agreed and left the room to get the solicitors' details. He returned a couple of minutes later with a file relating to the sale of the property.

'Ah yes, here we are,' he said. He had been flicking through the correspondence from his solicitors. The purchasers were named in a letter sent by his solicitors shortly after the beginning of the property transaction. Marian and the man who had died in the road traffic accident were names as joint purchasers. It had been a cash sale: no mortgage had been involved.

Back in the office I reviewed the file and the information I had obtained to date. Sam and David were dealing with Marian's current activities: I was concentrating on her life before the accident. It was clear that I was going to have to look at the financial aspects of the investigation.

According to Social Welfare records, Marian's only income was £60.10p per week, her unmarried mother's allowance. But she had over £1,300 in cash on the night of the accident; she had two building society passbooks with substantial credit balances; and now it appeared that she had bought her current home for cash. I was going to have to get on the money trail and start digging.

Even though Marian's Revenue/Social Welfare records disclosed no employment history, I would have to go through the motion of checking out two of the three employers she had declared in her court claim.

Her first employment on leaving school, she stated, was as a clerical officer in a government department. I knew from her Social Welfare records that this was factually untrue.

From 1973 to 1980, she specified two employers. I checked out both companies. Both had been very reputable companies and both were no longer trading: in fact, one had ceased trading before the date she said she started working for them. Somehow, I didn't think either company would be party to paying employees under the counter.

So I was back to digging around again, and I started with her car insurance proposal form. I had a copy of the letter from the garage/car workshop where she had claimed to work, and I also had a work contact telephone number that she had given on the form itself. I called the number. It was a very well-known food company. I asked for her by name, but they didn't know her. However, I did establish that Marian's sister worked for this company.

I decided to visit the garage rather than phone them. It was a very small workshop located at the rear of a separately owned/operated petrol station forecourt. The garage was a two-man operation, just the proprietor and one young mechanic. The owner claimed that he had never heard of Marian.

At this stage I was getting totally fed up – every lead was turning into a dead end. I had used the 'insurance investigator' approach but I hadn't mentioned the road traffic accident up to that point.

I admit I did get a wee bit shirty. I pulled the letter from my file and said, 'You are Mr X?'

'Yes,' he replied, somewhat hesitantly.

'So how come you wrote this letter stating that she was a member of your staff and on your garage insurance policy?' I sounded as irritable as I felt.

He hummed and hawed a bit so I added, 'That's conspiracy to defraud an insurance company!' I didn't know if it was or wasn't fraud, but it sounded good at the time.

It worked, because eventually he admitted that he had written the letter as a favour for a friend, but he was still adamant that he didn't actually know Marian personally.

Now I knew that she hadn't worked for this guy, but I was still drawing a blank on what the hell she had been doing to earn money prior to the accident. I wasn't too far from the garda station where the accident investigation officers were based, so I decided to call round to see if they could help any further. One of the investigating officers was due on duty at two o'clock so I hung around until then. Over a mug of tea, I told him of my efforts to get information and all the blanks I had drawn.

He sat there and grinned at me.

'Oh, I thought you knew,' he said. 'We think she is a prostitute.'

I sat there and just looked at him. I didn't know whether to hug him or throttle him.

'That could account for all the money,' I said. 'Any convictions?' I added.

'No,' he replied. 'But the lads down at the Gibbon [Fitzgibbon Street Station] could probably fill you in.' At last I was getting somewhere. We had another mug of tea to celebrate.

I had a contact from an earlier job who had recently been transferred to Fitzgibbon Street.

I phoned the Gibbon and found out when he was next scheduled for duty, then rang him and arranged a time to call in and see him. After a chat about the old job I asked for his help. Mugs of tea and coffee seem to a ritualistic part of my life. To be invited to have a cup or mug of something seems to indicate, at the very least, that people are willing to listen; it is generally a good omen for me. Over a mug of tea, I gave W an outline of the Marian case, the enquiries I had undertaken and the dead ends I had reached. I explained that the last lead I had obtained suggested that Marian could possibly be involved in the sex industry. I asked if he could help me.

W had no personal or first-hand information, so he went to check with his colleagues and the resident collator. The collator is the officer who, in addition to recording convictions, compiles information from various sources.

When he returned, he told me that Marian was 'known' to them. She had no recorded convictions, but she was suspected of being involved in the operation of a number of brothels on their patch. These businesses operated out of the basement flats at various addresses. She was also suspected of using a number of aliases, including the surname Murphy. This tied in with the two building society passbooks found in the car on the night of the accident. W gave me four addresses, all of which were in the immediate vicinity of Fitzgibbon Street Station.

In all the years I had worked as a PI, I had never been involved in any investigation that had even the remotest connection with the sex industry in Dublin. I simply didn't know what I was dealing with or likely to face in this phase of the investigation. W outlined how these businesses generally operate; what signs I should look for; and what circumstances I should avoid. All very scary stuff, but I felt it was a challenge. The problem I was facing was simply, if all this stuff was true, how on earth I would obtain evidence of Marian's alleged activities in this field, particularly as she had no convictions.

After leaving the Gibbon, I drove past the four addresses I had been given. W had told me that when these massage parlours/brothels were open for business, whether day or night, an outside basement light would be turned on. The basement lights were on at three of the four addresses.

The basement of the fourth address gave me a bit of shock. Instead of a basement light indicating they were open for business, I found a large sign headed, 'A Group of Christians Meet Here', with details of the days and times of Bible group meetings and contact telephone numbers. That threw me. Bloody hell – was the Bible group a front for the massage parlour?

I headed back to the garda station and spoke to W again. The Bible group was genuine. Apparently one of the women who had worked for Marian had quit her 'job' and opened up a similar business on her own at that address. Within three months, the premises had been petrol bombed and the young woman put out of business. W was very matter of fact about it all, as if this sort of event was the norm.

Holy shit, I thought. 'I'm not sure I'm being paid enough to deal with this stuff.

But I can be very stubborn. I love a challenge but I'm also realistic. In the context of the claim in the High Court, how could I obtain the evidence I needed?

The following Monday morning, Sam, David and I had a case conference. Sam and David updated me on the results of their surveillance. They had obtained enough visual evidence to refute Marian's claims about her physical and psychological disabilities.

I told them the results of my enquiries and asked if they were prepared to visit any of the known brothels with a view to obtaining information about or confirmation of Marian's involvement in them. Both declined, immediately.

I telephoned four of my closest male friends. Without going into too many specifics, I asked each of them if they were willing to visit any of the brothels. They, too, declined. I rang Frank, the claims manager, updated him and asked if he or any of his male claims inspectors were willing to visit any of the brothels. They also declined.

This was one occasion when being a female PI didn't help or advance an investigation. I really couldn't present myself at any of the brothels. Or maybe I could have, but like all my colleagues, I wasn't willing to.

Now I had to look at what our options were.

I'm quite good at lateral thinking, so I tried to think of any ancillary information that would positively link Marian to the brothels. Property taxes, rates and water rates came to mind. So, since all the properties were within the jurisdiction of Dublin Corporation, off I went to Dublin Corporation Rates Department.

The rates office was based in Dublin Castle. I had dealt with the council's rates officer on previous investigations, so we knew each other. Over yet another cup of tea, he checked his records. They showed that a sheriff's warrant had been issued against Marian in relation to one of the four properties identified by W as a brothel. The warrant remained unexecuted, as there were insufficient goods upon which to levy. This tied Marian into at least one of the brothels. The rates officer also identified the owner of the building, who operated an antiques business on the ground floor. The tenant of the basement was probably liable for the rates bill for the basement, though this would depend on any leasing agreement or contract, but I decided I would take a direct approach. At that stage, I really needed some more third-party confirmation of Marian's activities. I decided to tackle the antique dealer.

Call it intuition, but I expected a level of resistance from this guy. I was right.

I am interested in antiques and collectables, and I had attended some courses over the years, so I knew a little bit about the subject. The dealer's showroom displayed a good and varied range of antiques. When I went in the owner was talking to an elderly couple who were examining a tantalus. He was assuring them that the decanters in the tantalus were original. Why did I feel that I didn't believe him? Maybe I was still feeling a bit pissed off about this entire investigation. I had spent so many hours investigating this claim, and it had come down to this: this little guy who might or might not give me the information I needed. The elderly couple left and the dealer walked over towards me with a smile on his face. The smile never reached his eyes.

Rightly or wrongly, I decided to take a formal approach. I didn't think a friendly or even somewhat subservient attitude would get me the information I wanted. At this stage, it would not really make any difference if Marian heard about our enquiries; we had obtained enough evidence on surveillance to discredit her claims about her alleged physical disabilities. In addition, none of the information provided by her in support of her claim for loss of earning could be substantiated.

'Mr Joe D?' I asked.

'Yes, how can I help you?' he replied. The smile was still in place.

'I am assessing a claim for loss of earnings for a young lady, Marian X. I think she worked for you for some time,' I said.

Silence.

I looked around. 'It's not a very big premises, Mr D: surely you would know if she worked for you?'

I had deliberately made eye contact with him. I could nearly see the wheels turning in his head. His smile faded somewhat. After a moment he said, 'Ah, yes, Marian. Yes, she worked for me part time for a while.'

'And, what was her job? What did she do?' I asked.

'She helped me here in the showrooms,' he replied.

I frowned, as if puzzled. I plonked myself down on the arm of a nearby antique Carver chair and rooted through my file.

I am sure he would have loved to tell me to shift my butt off the arm of his chair. But he didn't.

I glanced through some of the court papers and, resuming eye contact with him, I asked, 'And what exactly did she do in the showroom?'

I knew I was chancing my arm adopting this attitude. He could have told me to sod off or asked me to leave. My intuition told me that he just wanted to get rid of me as fast as possible. I don't think he had ever anticipated a visit from the insurance company's representative.

'Sales,' he said. 'She was a very good saleswoman.'

I bet she was, I thought.

'Says here that she was your secretary.'

He replied, 'Well, yes, she used to help me with my paperwork.'

I felt we could be waltzing around this subject for hours, so I decided to be quite blunt with him.

'How come you didn't pay tax or insurance for her?' I asked.

Silence.

'Look, Joe, either you talk to me or you talk to Revenue and Social Welfare – your choice.'

Silence.

'I have no problem either way,' I added.

At that point, I reckoned he was considering his options: would he throw me out or would he cave in? He eventually caved in. I took a full and detailed statement from him. He confirmed that Marian was the tenant of his basement and also verified the nature of the business that was being carried on there.

As far as I was concerned this investigation was over.

I prepared my final report and submitted it to my client, the insurance company.

Marian's case was listed for hearing in the autumn of 1990. The night before the hearing, our senior counsel bumped into the senior counsel who was representing Marian. Our man told his colleague that he was really looking forward to the case the following day. He also mentioned 'in passing' that Marian was precluded from claiming loss of earnings as her pre-accident earnings arose from illegal/immoral activities. He didn't expand or explain this statement.

The following morning, the you know what hit the fan. Our legal team was approached by Marian's counsel and her claim for compensation was settled out of court – minus any claim for loss of earnings.

My client, the insurance company, was delighted with the result. As for me, I had hoped that all the evidence we had obtained would be put before the court. I would have been interested to see what reaction a judge would have had to our evidence and, based on that evidence, what decision he would have arrived at.

Disappointingly, in this case, it was not to be.

07 | HARD ACT TO FOLLOW

We always had to bear in mind that any case we were working on might end up with a court hearing, and that I might have to go into the witness box, open to cross-examination by our subject's legal team. We always had to make sure our evidence was unassailable, and in order to maintain our own personal integrity and professional standards, we had to be absolutely rigid about working within the law. If we had any doubts whatsoever about a course of action we were considering, I would get advice from my own solicitor and/or my garda contacts.

There were times, of course, when a decision had to be made instantaneously, right in the middle of events that were unfolding around us. Thankfully, those decisions always related to infringements of road traffic regulations.

In those days the Irish population generally had a more laid-back approach to minor traffic offences: things like double parking to run into a shop for a newspaper, and so on. Needless to say that was before the introduction of the Garda Traffic Corps or penalty points.

Sometimes we had to make conscious decisions to 'bend' the road traffic laws – run a red light or make an illegal u-turn – but we always made sure that it was safe to make the manoeuvre. We justified our actions, in our own minds, usually by saying we had been following a subject for x amount of time and, heck, we didn't want to lose them on the basis of a minor traffic infringement. These were calculated risks and, as it happened, they always paid off.

Only once did we get into any difficulty with the gardaí. Which is a nice way of saying we were caught red-handed.

We were involved in an investigation of a woman who lived in County Offaly. She was twenty-eight years of age, single, and lived on her own in a small housing estate about five minutes' walk from the centre of the town in which she lived. Both David and Michael had carried out routine surveillance on a number of occasions and had made enquiries locally, with zero results. According to neighbours, they knew nothing about her; she didn't mix locally; she had no car; they were merely on nodding terms. We did get one snippet of information. An old lady who lived opposite ventured the opinion that she was working 'somewhere'. She would see her leaving her house around six o'clock each weekday morning and she wouldn't return home until after seven each evening.

I contacted one of my sources, who told me that, while her basic details were showing up in Revenue and Social Welfare records, access to her records was blocked. There could be only one reason for this: she had to be working for some government department, somewhere. After reviewing her file, Sam and I decided that we would take over the surveillance aspect of the case.

Sam picked me up from my house at a quarter to four one morning and we drove to Offaly. To avoid alerting our subject, or worrying any neighbours who might be up and about, Sam switched off our headlights as we turned into the small estate. Using the lads' reports, we had no problems locating her house. The light was on in the downstairs hall. We tucked ourselves into a small cul-de-sac from which we had a direct line of sight to her house. We waited for developments.

At 5.57a.m., the light in the hall went out. It was still dark outside, so it was difficult to see who had emerged. We could just make out the outline of a person of medium height, stocky build and wearing dark clothing. We couldn't even tell if it was male or female.

I switched off the interior car light; I didn't want the inside of the car to light up when I opened the door.

'Have you enough cash on you?' Sam asked as I eased my way out of the car. I nodded. We didn't know what her means of transport was going to be, whether she would get a lift, taxi, bus or train. Our plan was simple. If she travelled by public transport, I would follow her, so I had made certain that my wallet was in my bag before I left home.

The person headed towards the main street. I followed. I was dressed in black, including black trainers. Excluding accidents of any sort, the person wouldn't hear my footsteps. As we approached the junction with the main street, I narrowed the gap between us. Her gait suggested that it was indeed a 'woman'. It was important that I get a good look at her. I would have to make an instant decision – was it our subject? And if so, I wanted to get a good close look at her and her clothes. I had to be able to pick her out, possibly from a crowd of people, when we reached her destination.

We turned left into the main street. About fifty yards ahead a shop was open, its lights flooding out onto the street. I could see for sure that it was a woman I had followed.

There were about ten people standing outside the shop.

She went into the shop and I followed. As she queued to pay for her newspaper, I took a good look at her. She was of the correct age group for my subject, and I was confident that I would be able to identify her later. It would be particularly easy to spot the unusual multicoloured fabric drawstring bag she was carrying, which had knitting needles and a ball of black mohair wool sticking out of the top of it.

I left the shop and walked back towards the corner where Sam was parked with the car lights off. I slipped into the car. 'Looks like her all right'.

We sat and waited. She came out of the shop and stood with the group. She never spoke to or looked at anyone in the group.

'She's not exactly the chatty type, is she?' Sam commented.

A white fifty-two-seater single-decker coach came up the main street. It pulled in at the newsagents ahead, and the group boarded. I noted the registration number of the coach. It pulled out and drove in the direction of Kilbeggan. We followed. It picked up some more passengers in Kilbeggan, Tyrellspass and Rochfordbridge. Each time the coach stopped, we stopped some distance behind to see if our lady alighted. She didn't. It continued through Kinnegad and Enfield on towards Dublin. Traffic got steadily heavier as we approached Dublin.

The first passengers alighted in Maynooth, then some more got off at Heuston Station. Our lady was still on board.

It was from this point that we were likely to experience difficulties, thanks to the flipping bus corridors. By now it was approaching 8.15a.m., the height of the Dublin morning rush hour, and we had been on the go since 3.45a.m. Traffic was bumper to bumper, except of course for the bus lanes. If we stayed in the correct lane there was no doubt we would lose her.

Sam and I looked at each other as if to say 'Will we or won't we?'

'Go for it,' I said, pointing to the bus lane.

We tucked in right behind the coach. We crossed the River Liffey, turned right and headed down the quays towards the city centre. There was a line of buses ahead and behind us. Sam and I stared ahead, not wanting to make any eye contact with other motorists stuck in the traffic as we sailed past.

'Blast it!' I nudged Sam. We had just driven past a motorcycle garda who was parked tucked in on the footpath just across from the Halfpenny Bridge. I checked the wing mirror. Sure enough, he had driven off the path and was following us.

'I'll talk to him, you stay with the bus.'

The line of buses in front came to a halt, so we weren't going anywhere. I jumped out of the car and approached the garda as he was pulling his motorbike up onto its stand.

'I'm sorry, Guard,' I said as I pulled out my identification.

I have no doubt that traffic officers have been told all sorts of

tall tales by offending motorists, but I decided to tell him the
truth. I wasn't quite babbling but I got the message over as
quickly as I could.

'We're insurance investigators – we've been following that bus
all the way from Offaly since six o'clock this morning – we're
going to lose her now – please don't pull us over.'

He looked at my ID and then at me. I didn't realise that I was
clutching his forearm.

Sam was standing beside us but watching the passengers
alight from the white coach.

'There she is,' he said.

I watched her back as she headed for the junction with
O'Connell Street.

I looked at the garda. 'Please,' I said.

'Okay, pull it up onto the path.'

'Go after her, Sam', I said.

I assumed the officer was asking me to pull up onto the path
to unblock the bus lane while he wrote me a ticket. I turned to
walk back to the car. 'Prop the bonnet open as if you've broken
down,' he said.

I grinned at him. I manoeuvred the car onto the path and
pulled the lever to open the bonnet. The garda was standing in
front of the car. I could hardly believe my eyes: he was opening
the bonnet for me.

'Go on, then. I can't promise you how long I can stay here. Get
back as soon as you can.'

I felt like giving him a hug.

I turned and ran down towards O'Connell Bridge and
stopped at the crossing to see if I could spot Sam. I couldn't really
miss him. He was on the traffic island at the centre of the
crossing, jumping up and down and waving his arms trying to
attract my attention. God only knows what the pedestrians
around him thought. I trotted across to the centre of the road,
zigzagging my way through traffic and ignoring the drivers' dirty
looks and the verbal abuse yelled at me by one guy.

'She's over there.' Sam pointed to the opposite side of the
road. She was walking up towards Lower Abbey Street.

We followed her.

I knew there were a number of government departments operating out of buildings in the immediate vicinity. Five minutes later our subject entered one of those buildings. Sam ran on ahead of me back to the car. There was no sign of the garda when I got back.

———

On one occasion it was simply impossible for us to follow the exact route taken by one of our subjects. We had driven to a town in County Wicklow. We intended to carry out a bit of surveillance on a gentleman in his early sixties and to make some local enquiries. We found his bungalow without too much difficulty and took up observation shortly after eight in the morning. There was a Ford Fiesta parked in the driveway. We didn't have to wait long before we spotted our subject. At 8.20a.m. he opened the double gates to the driveway and went back into the house, reappearing a couple of minutes later with a small holdall, which he placed in the boot of his car. He then returned to the house. At 8.35a.m. he reappeared, accompanied by a woman of a similar age. They climbed into the Fiesta and he drove away. We followed. He turned left onto the R753, heading for Rathdrum, and driving at a steady forty miles per hour.

'Wish he'd speed up a bit,' Sam said.

I agreed. In practical terms, it is more difficult to discreetly follow a slow driver driving a small motor, particularly when you are in a two-litre car. It made us feel somewhat conspicuous but there wasn't much we do about it except stay way back and only move in closer as we approached major roads or small towns.

The man drove through Rathdrum and towards Wicklow town.

To ease the boredom on surveillances, Sam and I sometimes played a guessing game: in this case the guess was 'maybe they're going shopping in Wicklow'. They didn't. In Rathnew, they turned left onto the road for Greystones and eventually ended up in Dublin. The journey was uneventful.

They parked in the ILAC car park, and we followed them on foot. We spent a relaxing day watching them shopping in a number of the stores around Dublin city centre. Not exactly mind-blowingly exciting, but our client's instructions were to monitor our subject's activities. That is exactly what we did.

Eventually, they headed back to the ILAC car park, laden with their purchases. Off we went again.

'We're not following them all the bloody way back to Wicklow.'

Sam agreed. 'We'll stay with them until they reach the road back to Wicklow.'

They took a slightly different route out of the city. We thought they would head for the N11 but instead they drove through Rathmines, Terenure and into Templeogue.

'He certainly knows his way around town,' I said to Sam.

We started the guessing game again.

'Look's like he's heading for the N81.'

'That's too far inland for his home.'

We looked at each other. The penny dropped with both of us at the same time.

'The Square!' we said in unison.

The Square is a large shopping centre in Tallaght on the outskirts of the city.

'Ah, heck.' Despondency descended. Neither of us particularly liked shopping or shopping expeditions. I could never understand how some people made a pilgrimage into town every weekend to shop. Even when I shopped for Christmas presents, I made out a list of gifts, hit the shops just after nine on a Monday morning in November, did the business and was heading back out of town by ten thirty at the latest.

The Square Shopping Centre loomed up ahead on our right. Sure enough, on flashed his right indicator and he manoeuvred into the outside lane.

'Okay, we drop him as soon as they leave the shopping centre.'

Sam nodded his agreement.

We tucked in directly behind him. We had to stay really close to his car so that we wouldn't lose visual contact with him as he went around the roundabout ahead. There were just too many car parks at the centre. We approached the roundabout. He got to the top of the queue; we were right behind.

There was a gap in the flow of traffic coming around the roundabout to our right, plenty of space for him to move forward – and enough room for us to move out directly behind him. I will never know how or why he suddenly made a sharp right-hand turn. Now he was driving, albeit slowly, in the direction of the oncoming traffic.

We both burst out laughing.

'I'm bloody well not . . .'

'Of course not,' I replied.

We waited and watched. Cars approaching our friend slammed on their brakes. Horns blared. He stopped. I clearly saw the wife giving him a smack on the back of the head, and it looked as though she was also giving him an earful. He didn't panic or appear to get flustered. As cool as a cucumber, he reversed slowly, inch by inch, back towards our junction. As he tried to straighten out so that he could drive around the roundabout in the right direction, he came within inches of reversing into the front of our car.

Instinctively, Sam leaned on the horn to alert him. He stopped and got out of the car, and walked slowly towards us, stopping to check that he had not made contact with the front of our car. He seemed totally oblivious to the cacophony of car horns and abuse from other drivers, and to the fact that traffic in the entire area had come to a halt.

'Sorry about that, Mister, but I didn't hit your car.'

'That's okay,' Sam replied.

He nodded in my direction. 'Sorry, Missus.'

I smiled but said nothing.

He moseyed back to his own car as if he had all the time in the world. He mounted the edge of the roundabout as he straightened up and drove towards the entrance to the shopping centre.

There was little point in our following him any farther: he had seen both Sam and me at close quarters.

'Let's call it a day.'

We did.

———

In contrast to our friend from Wicklow, meandering around at thirty to forty miles an hour, we were around the same time involved in an investigation of a female hospital doctor who was alleging psychological disabilities that prevented her from working. She claimed that her problems were so acute that she was terrified to travel even as a passenger in any vehicle, let alone drive herself. She claimed she was housebound.

'This should be a doddle – either she can travel or she can't,' I said to Sam when we received our instructions.

The case turned out to be not such a 'doddle' after all.

The address we had for her was in a north Dublin suburb. When we checked this address, we discovered that she had moved. We traced her to a nearby town, only to find her gone again. We eventually traced her to a small town in County Kildare.

She lived in a new, partially completed, housing estate on the outskirts of the town. Her house was located near the top of a small 'keyhole' cul-de-sac. There was no car in the driveway.

During the first couple of occasions surveillance was carried out, she was observed walking from her house into the town centre to do some light shopping. She was also observed jogging along the banks of the local canal. At the weekly case review, having discussed their reports with Michael and David, who were our operatives, my first inclination was to file our report. But there was something niggling away in the back of my mind.

She claimed not to be working and I knew through one of my contacts that she wasn't in receipt of any state benefits. Even if she had income protection insurance, I couldn't figure out how she had sufficient capital to buy this house. I phoned local auctioneers and enquired about property rents in that estate. I was told that that the average rent was £800 per month, which would be rather high for someone with no visible means of support. It was the beginning of July and I asked David to carry out a period of evening surveillance the following Monday evening, starting from about five o'clock.

David phoned me on Tuesday. From his tone of voice I knew he had come up with something. Our lady doctor had got home at 8.25 the previous night. She had arrived driving a silver Opel Ascona and had driven past her house to the bottom of the cul-de-sac, where she parked her car. She had then walked back up the road and entered her home. David had subsequently checked the car registration number and found that she was the registered owner.

'The doc is playing silly buggers,' I told Sam when I gave him the information. We agreed that her case warranted closer examination.

On the mornings when she had been seen jogging, she had left her house at around eight fifteen and had returned at approximately nine o'clock.

The following morning Sam and I were in observation position shortly after seven thirty. She emerged from the house, wearing shorts, T-shirt and trainers; at 8.05a.m. and trotted off. We followed in the car, at a distance. She arrived at the T-junction. The main part of the town was to the left; if you turned right you would eventually end up on the N4; to the east of that road lay the main road to Dublin; in the opposite direction was the main road to Athlone.

She crossed the road and scrambled down an embankment onto the path that ran alongside the canal, increased her speed and jogged off into the distance. I stayed on the bridge, watching her progress until she disappeared from view. Sam drove back into the estate and checked out her car.

She reappeared in the distance at the end of the canal bank at 8.40a.m. I took photographs, using a telephoto lens, before moving to the far corner of the bridge so that I wouldn't be in her direct line of sight as she got closer. When she scrambled back up the embankment onto the footpath, she jogged towards the nearest shop, reappearing almost immediately with a carton of milk and a newspaper. She didn't slow down until she reached the entrance to her estate.

'Nothing wrong with her flippin' legs – she's been jogging for about forty minutes,' I said to Sam as I slid back into the car. I checked my watch: it was 8.50a.m.

We didn't see her again until 11.10a.m., when she left the house and walked down to road to her car, which was still parked at the end of the cul-de-sac. Sam took photographs of her climbing into the car, reversing and driving out of the estate. We followed at a distance.

She turned left onto the N4, travelling towards Dublin. As soon as she hit the dual carriageway, her speed increased. Sixty miles an hour ... seventy ... eighty-five. Now she was cruising at between eighty and eighty-five.

Not bad for someone who can't drive, I thought.

She manoeuvred smartly and cleanly, often without indicating. I was trying to take photographs, while Sam concentrated on the driving.

'Flippin' heck, I'd hate to see her driving if she wasn't afraid to get into a car.'

She was in the outside lane as we approached the slip road for the M50. Suddenly, she indicated and immediately cut across the inside lane and onto the start of the slip road. The driver she cut up banged on his horn. At the earliest opportunity we moved to the inside lane and approach the slip road. She was out of sight. Luckily for us, she had to stop in a line of cars waiting to get onto the northbound carriageway of the M50. She shot out onto the motorway and took off again. We followed.

I gave up on trying to take photographs, bearing in mind that at the speed we were doing to keep up with her, they would probably only be a blur. I kept my eye on our speedometer, noting the speeds we were travelling at; she reached ninety-three miles per hour.

Within minutes, we were approaching the Blanchardstown turnoff. She indicated left, we followed suit. She turned into the main street of the village and then indicated right.

'She's going to the hospital, there's nothing else down there,' I said.

We followed her at a distance and as she turned into one of the parking spaces at the front of the hospital, Sam hopped out of our car and, using the telephoto lens, took some close-up photographs of her locking her car and walking in through the main doors of the hospital.

We parked in the main parking area. I didn't realise the effect the high-speed chase had had on me until I tried to get out of the car. My hands were sweating; I didn't think my legs could support me. I leaned against the side of the car to support myself.

'Bloody hell, I need a strong cup of tea.'

I plonked down on the grass and lit a cigarette.

When I calmed down a bit I realised that we needed to maximise the opportunity that had been presented to us.

'I'll go in and make some enquiries.'

I approached the reception desk. I didn't know what role or function our subject had in the hospital, so I was deliberately vague. 'Doctor X, please,' I said pleasantly to the woman behind the desk.

'Through the double doors, take a left and it's the third clinic on your left.'

'Thank you.'

There were about twenty people sitting in the waiting area of the clinic. I sat down at the back of the room and waited.

'Thomas Kelly?' a male voice called out. I looked up. A male doctor was standing at the entrance to a small corridor with a hospital chart in his hands. A man stood up and approached him. I scribbled in my notebook as if I was interested in what was going on around me.

'Shauna Campbell?' I looked up. There she was, my doctor lady, wearing a white coat and holding a hospital chart. A woman in her late twenties approached her. She smiled and shook hands with the woman. There wasn't a hair on her head out of place; she looked totally relaxed, oozing confidence. Me, on the other hand, I couldn't wait to get home to change my clothes – my T-shirt was still stuck to my back after the rollercoaster ride she had just led us on.

She disappeared down the corridor. I walked back out to the car. Sam suggested we adjourn to a coffee shop in the village and I readily agreed. We discussed the case over our mugs of coffee. I lit another cigarette.

'That's your third since we came in,' he said, scowling at me.

I glared back. 'The way I feel I could eat the whole damn packet without even lighting them.'

He backed off.

'I think we're going to have to do it again, Shirl.'

'No way. Why?'

'The photographs aren't going to show enough; they'll show her, her car, but not the bloody speed she was going at; we're going to have to film her.'

On reflection I realised Sam was right, and we spent the next thirty minutes discussing how we could get to film her. We couldn't fix the camera to the dash of the car because we needed to be able to video her through the front windscreen of our car and then pan back to record our own speedometer showing the speed at which we were travelling. I dreaded the thought of going through that experience again.

'If you're caught, you could lose your licence and then where would we be?'

'We'll have to take that chance.'

I thought for a while. 'I know, I'll phone Celtic Helicopters and see how much they'd charge.' I was only half joking.

'Don't be daft, they would never pay for a helicopter ride, and anyway I'd prefer to drive,' Sam replied.

The only way I was likely to get Sam up in a helicopter was to knock him out cold first. He's not too keen on heights – and that's putting it mildly.

'I'll drive and you can film. It'll keep your mind off the speed thing.'

So it was settled: that's what we would do.

The following morning, we took off again.

As I got into the car, I looked around. 'Where's the crash helmets?' I was trying to make light of the subject but had Sam produced his two motorbike helmets I would have used one, no matter how stupid I would have looked.

On our way over to the doctor's house, Sam went through what he wanted me to do. When he started to repeat it for the third time, I glared at him. 'I know, you told me twice already,' I snapped. I realised I was getting tetchy. 'Sorry, I'm a bit jumpy.'

Forgetting our agreement that I wouldn't smoke in the car, I lit up and started to wind down the window.

'It's okay this time!' he said.

I gave him my best smile.

The doc went for her jog and returned home, as usual, reappearing at 11.07a.m.

'Ready?'

I nodded. It was exactly the same pattern as the previous day. As soon as she reached the N4, her foot hit the floor. I got so engrossed in working the video camera, I didn't have time to think about the speed at which we were travelling. I zoomed in and out, a distant shot of her car, easing nice and gently to a close-up shot of her number plate, zooming back again and turning the camera slowly to bring our speedometer into focus. I continued this sequence after she turned onto the M50. I did make a sort of gasping sound when I saw through the video lens that our speedometer was reading ninety-five miles an hour.

'You okay?' I heard from beside me. I nodded and the camera nodded with me.

We reached Blanchardstown Hospital in one piece. I still had my eye stuck to the viewfinder.

'Get closer, get closer,' I urged Sam. 'I want to get a good shot of her getting out of the car and going in.'

'This close enough?' Through the lens, she looked at if she was standing right in front of me.

I eased the lens back and recorded an overview of her walking in through the hospital doors. I then focused in on the hospital name above the door.

Sam nudged me. 'That's enough.'

I switched off the camera. I handed it over to him with a big grin. 'I think it's good'.

As a rule, when I was working on investigations that could involve a high compensation award, I liked to keep an eye out for any further developments that might arise during the period after I submitted my report and the court hearing. This was such a case.

Sam and I were on our way to a job in Kinnegad one morning and, at around seven o'clock, we made a small detour to check the doctor's house. The car she had used before was parked in its usual position at the bottom of the cul-de-sac.

There was one potentially interesting development, though – an estate agent's For Sale board in the front garden. I made a note of the agent's details, and on our way back from Kinnegad we stopped off at the estate agents' offices in the village. Details of the doc's house were included in the display of properties in the front window. I went in and, posing as a prospective purchaser, began chatting to one of the staff. As I wanted to come over as a genuine prospective purchaser, I expressed an interest in three of the properties advertised, one of which was, of course, the doc's house. Two of the three properties were some distance from the village so my first preference was naturally the doc's house, which was closest to the village. I hoped that chatting with the estate agent might net me some extra relevant information, but I was somewhat taken aback when, there and then, she offered to show me the house.

Go with the flow, Shirl, I thought, and agreed immediately. She drove to the estate and Sam and myself followed.

I wasn't particularly interested in looking over the subject's house; but I felt that this might be an opportunity too good to miss. Maybe I could get some information about why the doc was selling her house and where she was planning to move to. This information, even though it would be from a third party, could help if my clients wanted me to update my report before the hearing.

I adopted the role of a prospective purchaser and acted accordingly. At the house, I went through the motions of viewing the property and asking the agent appropriate questions, including 'Why are they selling? It's a new estate.' She told me that the vendor was a doctor who was expecting her first baby and she was moving to a four-bedroomed house in a (named) village some twelve miles away. She had already paid her deposit on this new house, which was in a new housing development in the village, and was anxious to sell as quickly as possible. She also mentioned that the vendor wanted to bring up her child in a more rural environment. Interestingly, the estate agent told me that the doctor had recently been appointed to a (named) hospital, which wasn't Blanchardstown.

By the end of the house inspection I knew, at least according to the estate agent, where the doc intended moving; that she had been appointed to another hospital; and that she was pregnant.

I submitted another report to my clients.

On the Monday of the week the case was listed for hearing we were in the solicitors' office for a showing of 'my movie'. It was good. We got on film all that we needed.

'It's great, we'll show it in court,' Joe said. 'We're not going to settle, we'll leave it to the judge to decide the amount of her award.'

Sam was silent for a moment and then he said, 'Hang on a minute, we're going to show evidence of her driving, and we're also showing her breaking every speed limit in the book.'

Joe and I nodded.

He continued, 'but we're also showing video evidence that I broke every speed limit in the book too!'

Joe looked at him as if to say, 'So?'

'I could get done for breaking the speed limit.' Sam was sounding just a bit petulant.

'Don't worry, it won't happen; sure if it does I'll defend you', Joe said with a grin.

08 | ALL THAT GLISTENS ...

Counterfeiting products and passing them off as originals is a multimillion-euro business. From 'Gucci' handbags, 'Rolex' watches, films, videos, DVDs and CDs, to logo sports kits and leisurewear, you can find fake goods everywhere – on street stalls and markets, and being sold by casual traders all over Europe.

The average man or woman in the street doesn't see this as a crime. No one has been hit over the head and robbed, no one's been mugged, it's not stolen property, so what's the problem? It's a bit like slightly exaggerating an insurance claim. Many people know someone who had a bit of a prang in their car, nothing serious, no other car involved. They go to a main dealer to get the estimate for the repairs and claim under their comprehensive cover, and then they get the repair job done by a back street garage and pocket the difference. Or someone's been involved in an accident, nothing too serious, but they exaggerate their injuries until after the compensation claim has been settled.

'So who are we hurting?' they ask. 'Sure, isn't it only the big insurance companies, who have been charging huge premiums over the years?' Or one of the big record companies, or a major sportswear manufacturer, and they make millions in profits each year, don't they?

Mr and Mrs Joe Public may not have a problem with people who sell counterfeit goods, but what they often overlook is this: just as retail stores build in a margin on their prices to cover the cost of shoplifting, which most people do agree is a crime, some manufacturers add on to their wholesale prices a margin to cover counterfeiting of their products. And that means higher prices for everyone.

In Ireland, in the early and mid-1990s, the sale of counterfeit copies of football shirts, including the national football team kit, was huge business. The same was true of the major UK football team strips. The Irish team's home and away strips were frequently changed, and within days of a new kit being released into the major stores, counterfeit copies would hit the streets and could be bought on stalls and in markets around the country, but particularly in Dublin.

I was instructed by a major sportswear company to carry out an investigation to establish the approximate quantity of this counterfeit merchandise that was for sale on the streets and, if possible, to identify the source of these goods, the location of the warehouse or storage facility where the goods were being kept, and the identity of the people who were distributing the stuff.

It seemed to me that this job had more potential for a good result, and more job satisfaction, than one of our earlier investigations, when we had to deal with counterfeit safety matches! Yes, those little wooden sticks we use to light cigarettes, coal fires and the like. We were successful in tracing the origin of those matches to Eastern Europe, and helped stop their importation, but that investigation did little to fire my enthusiasm.

Prior to my involvement in this current case, my clients had already obtained a High Court injunction against a named person – I'll call him Damien – restraining him from the importation, distribution, handling or sale of any of my clients' merchandise. This injunction also covered any other person served with a copy of the injunction. Any counterfeit copies Damien had in his possession were handed over to my clients.

About eight weeks later, following another change to the Irish team jersey, the counterfeit copies were back on the street stalls and in the markets around Dublin.

It was then that I received my instructions. Apart from the court papers, the only relevant information my clients could give me was Damien's name and last known address. I noticed that in one of the affidavits sworn by Damien he stated that he had bought fifty of the jerseys 'from a man, unknown to him, in Ashford Market'. My clients had never accepted that statement, as literally thousands – not just fifty – of the copies had been on sale on market stalls.

I loved carrying out investigations of this type. They involved loads of research, enquiries and some legwork. I really enjoyed the mental gymnastics, the logical and lateral thinking that eventually led to the overall picture.

The first thing Sam and I had to learn was how to identify the counterfeit merchandise. Our clients laid out a full range of football jerseys, a mixture of original merchandise, counterfeit copies and replicas. The replicas we could pick out, no problem. From a distance they looked similar to the originals, but on handling the jerseys you could clearly see that the fabric and sponsors' logos were different, and the team crest was positioned on the opposite side of the chest. My clients weren't interested in replicas, because they weren't being passed off as originals.

It was extremely difficult to pick out the counterfeit copies. They all appeared to be the same as the bona fide jerseys. They had a similar weight and feel; the team crest was on the correct side; the sponsors' logos were correctly designed and in the right position.

We were then shown the differences between the counterfeits and the originals, including some secret or confidential details or markings that would only be on the originals. I never realised that clothing manufacturers used such methods, but, then again, we had never been involved in a case like this before.

Damien was the only known suspect, so Sam and I decided to start the investigation by checking him out.

Sam had taken a day off work to take his mother to her old

family home in County Wexford. On their way back to Dublin that night, he detoured by Damien's house in south County Dublin. He wanted to find the exact location of the house so that we wouldn't have to cruise around looking for the house on the first morning of surveillance. He also noted the registration numbers of the two cars, a Mercedes and a Volkswagen Golf, and one small van that were parked in the driveway. I subsequently checked to see who were the registered owners of the vehicles. The van and the Mercedes were registered to Damien, and the Golf to his wife, Susan.

Bearing in mind the monetary losses being sustained by our clients, we needed to get started on this investigation as soon as possible. We began surveillance two days later.

We had to make an early start to avoid traffic jams, so Sam picked me up from my home at six o'clock on Monday morning. We arrived at Damien's home at 7.20a.m. The Mercedes and the van were parked in the driveway, but the Golf was gone. We decided to take a chance and assume that the wife had left in the Golf, so we stayed put!

An adult male, presumably Damien, came out of the house at 8.45a.m. He got into the van, reversed it out onto the roadway and parked. When he got out of the van, Sam took the opportunity to photograph him. We would have to identify this man later to ensure that he was indeed Damien. He went back indoors, came out again at 9.05a.m., climbed into the Mercedes, reversed onto the road and drove off. We followed.

When he reached the main road, he headed in the general direction of Dublin City. The traffic was appalling; bumper-to-bumper stuff. If we were going to succeed in tailing him to his destination, we would have to tuck in directly behind him and stick to his bumper. I pulled down both sun visors. If Damien checked his rear view mirror, all he would be able to see was our noses and chins, not enough to recognise us if we had to get close to him later.

All went well until we reached the Red Cow roundabout, which was completely gridlocked, but at least we were still stuck to Damien's back bumper. Suddenly, he pulled out to his left and into a small gap in the traffic flow. The gap wasn't big enough for us to follow him. Sam swore and smacked the steering wheel, as I tried to keep an eye on the Mercedes. 'Lost him,' I said.

Based on our past experiences of situations like this, we tended to continue straight ahead, particularly if that road led towards a town or city. It was amazing how many times this policy had proved fruitful. Sam manoeuvred – well, actually, almost forced – his way out into a small gap; I mouthed a big 'Thank you' to the approaching driver, and we continued towards Dublin. I scanned the traffic in front.

'There he is!' I shouted, pointing to a filter lane up ahead. His right indicator was blinking. Sam allowed one car in behind Damien and then tucked in behind that car. Damien did an illegal u-turn; we did likewise. He was now heading back towards the Red Cow.

'He must have business somewhere along here, otherwise he would have taken the M50 from the roundabout.'

As usual, Sam was trying to do two jobs at once. I nudged him with my elbow.

'You watch the road, I'll watch him.'

On the Naas Road, Damien indicated left and turned into a yard. A big sign at the gate read 'Storage Containers to Rent'. Sam and I looked at each other and grinned.

Sam pulled over onto the hard shoulder, and I hopped out of the car and walked into the yard. There were large metal containers, the type you would see down around the docks or on the back of haulage trucks, pushed up against the perimeter walls of the yard. There was a double row of containers running down the middle of the yard, and tucked away in a corner was a Portakabin.

I saw Damien's car parked outside a container at the right-hand wall. Obviously I couldn't stand in the middle of the yard watching Damien, so I went into the Portakabin.

'Hiya. Have you any containers available?' I asked.

The attendant was an elderly man. He looked just like the kind of 'gotchie' or night watchman who used to be around years ago: flat cap, cigarette dangling from the corner of his mouth, a big mug of tea in his hands. All that was missing was the brazier with the burning coals. I chatted away to 'Pops', while keeping one eye on Damien through the window of the Portakabin. Damien was loading boxes into the boot of his car and onto the back seat.

I decided not to ask Pops any questions about Damien just yet – it was simply too early in the investigation – and if I did he might just say something to Damien. At an opportune moment in our conversation, I said goodbye and headed back to the car.

'He's got a storage container all right,' I said as I slipped back into the car. 'And he's loading stuff into the car.'

We decided to continue with the tail on Damien. If we were lucky, we would follow him to his destination, but we couldn't stay too close to him. We had made some good progress so far, and we didn't want to blow it by alerting him to our presence. While we waited, I took two spare jackets from the boot of Sam's car and we changed into them. Sam put on a baseball cap; I tied up my hair and donned a pair of spectacles. Checking the mirror, we agreed: superficially at least, we had changed our appearance. Unless Damien was on the lookout for a tail, we shouldn't get rumbled.

We were lucky, very lucky, this time. Damien drove out of the yard at 10.20a.m. Traffic conditions had eased a bit. He turned left just before the Red Cow and left again. He drove past some industrial estates. All we had to do was keep him in our line of sight; we didn't have to stay close to him. He eventually turned right onto the Long Mile Road. He was heading towards town. We had to tuck in behind him again to avoid losing him.

Sam is excellent at mobile surveillance. He had been doing it for about fifteen years at that stage and he knew all the tricks of the trade. He successfully followed Damien to a street just off South Great George's Street in the city centre. Damien parked his car halfway up on the footpath outside a three-storey building. He unlocked the door and wedged it open. Sam photographed him offloading some of the boxes. When the car was empty, Damien drove away.

Tempted as we were, we didn't follow him. Part of our job was to know when to back off, when not to push our luck too far. This time we decided to call it a day.

As soon as Damien disappeared from view, Sam walked up to the front of the building. I saw him make some notes.

'There are two company names on the plaque on the wall,' he said as he settled back into the driver's seat. 'Could be anything, based on the names,' and he handed me his notebook.

I recognised both names immediately. They were ladies' fashion wholesalers, whose merchandise was retailed under their own labels. Their clothes were imports, at the cheaper end of the fashion price range.

'Both rag trade,' I said to Sam.

'I wonder why Damien needs that storage container when he's occupying a three-storey building in town?'

'Maybe he wants to keep stock in a separate location, maybe he hasn't enough storage space at the moment and it's only a temporary arrangement,' Sam replied.

I looked at him. 'Maybe he's afraid that he going to be raided – don't forget about the injunction.'

'We'll get Michael or David to watch the place and see what transpires.'

As Sam was about to pull out to join the one-way traffic flow we spotted Damien walking back up the street towards the building and going in. We stayed in the car for another thirty minutes, just in case he came out again. He didn't.

The next day I had to try to verify the activities or businesses carried on at the two locations Damien had visited. I spent Tuesday morning in the Companies Registration Office in Dublin Castle researching the two company names we had noted. Nowadays, all you have to do when you're looking for information on a company is go online and type in the company name. All the general information pops up on the screen, and you simply tick the boxes for the documents you want, insert your credit card details and, less then five minutes later, you receive an email with copies of all the documents you have ordered attached. What would take about five minutes now could take up to half a day back then, when all the records were maintained in bound hard copy folders.

I queued for the microfiche to obtain the company registration numbers; I then queued to hand in my requisition docket; I waited for about forty-five minutes for the relevant hard copy files to be located in the basement; and I waited some more for the assistant to reach my two folders, which were somewhere in the last pile that had come up from the basement.

I scanned the documents. By cross-referencing the companies and searching by way of directors' names, I was able to connect four companies with Damien. His name did not appear as a director of any of the companies, but his address did come up. The local authority rates office was able to provide me with details of the company that paid rates for the yard on the Naas Road.

When I got back to the office, I telephoned both David and Michael to ask them to change their allocated jobs for the rest of the week. All I wanted them to do was note and photograph all callers to the city centre property, to get their vehicle registration numbers, and to note details of any items – bags, boxes, etc. – that callers brought into or removed from the building. Michael would cover the next day, Wednesday, and David would be on duty on Thursday.

On Thursday and Friday, Sam and I went shopping. We checked every street stall we could find around Dublin city centre. In one street alone, we found counterfeit jerseys on twelve of the twenty-one trading stalls. We prepared a rough drawing of the location of each of the twelve stalls. Each stallholder should have held a Casual Trader's Licence issued by Dublin Corporation, and I hoped the corporation would be able to help me identify the individual stallholders.

Sam and I took turns to make our purchases. While one of us bought a jersey, the other took photographs of the transaction, including the stallholder and the merchandise. By the end of the shopping expedition, we were literally knee-deep in counterfeit merchandise; and we had only purchased one item from each stall we found that had counterfeit jerseys for sale.

David and Michael's surveillance of Damien's business premises had been fairly successful. They had a list of six vehicle registration numbers, and they had identified the registered owner of each vehicle.

We had five markets to check out on Sunday morning: Fairyhouse; the North Road heading towards Ashbourne; Finglas; the Phoenix Park; and Tallaght. We found and purchased counterfeit merchandise at four of the five markets. The North Road market was the only one that didn't have stalls offering the stuff. Finglas had only a few items. Stalls in Fairyhouse, Phoenix Park and Tallaght markets were laden with the jerseys. We also found five of the six vans that had been spotted at Damien's premises earlier that week. Each of these vans was parked directly behind one of the stalls. What's more, Sam and I recognised a number of the street stallholders from whom we had purchased counterfeit merchandise on Thursday and Friday.

At that stage, working backwards, we could definitely connect these stallholders to the vans that had been at Damien's premises. Accordingly, it was reasonable to assume that Damien was the common denominator, or – to put it plainly – the supplier. By Sunday evening, the pile of counterfeit goods we had bought was waist high. It was obvious that there were thousands of counterfeit garments on the street.

Instead of asking for information over the telephone, when there was a risk of being turned down flat, I decided on making a personal approach to Dublin Corporation. Depending on the approach, most people do find it difficult to look someone in the eye and refuse to help. I did occasionally find people who refused to help, and, funnily enough, it was always women who had been a bit difficult. Over the twenty years I had worked as a private investigator, only once had I been completely blown out of the water by a man, and he was a garda working in a suburban Dublin station.

And now I had another one to deal with.

I stood looking over the counter at a small guy, in the Casual Trading Licensing Office at Dublin Corporation. He was being difficult about handling my enquiry. His initial response was that the information I was looking for was not available to 'just anyone'. I had no delusions of grandeur, neither did I think of myself as a 'somebody', but I did have a bit of a problem with his attitude and his tone of voice. He was a kid of about twenty-two years of age and was wearing the uniform that appeared to be de rigueur for people working in the public services: denim jeans and a jumper. I quietly explained for the second time, trying to keep the exasperation out of my voice.

'We have a High Court injunction to stop these traders from selling these counterfeit goods.'

He stood looking at me defiantly.

'I would like to see your supervisor please.'

He disappeared from view. I thought back to the only other 'run-in' I had had with a man during the course of carrying out enquiries.

——

He was the investigating officer in a fatal road traffic accident and I had made an appointment to meet him at six o'clock one evening. When I arrived, the station sergeant told me he was out in the patrol car. He got him on the radio and told him that his six o'clock appointment had arrived. I should have guessed that he might have an attitude problem when he kept me waiting for over forty-five minutes. He had been on patrol duty, merely driving around, so it should have taken him no more than five to ten minutes to get back to the station.

In the interview room, I introduced myself and gave him my business card (which didn't specify my occupation). Right from the beginning, I could literally feel the hostility in the air. I had no idea why this guy was so silently aggressive. I had behaved in my usual pleasant way. Wonder what his problem is, I thought.

He leaned back in the chair, crossed his arms and stared at me through half-closed eyes. His head was shaved, but you could see the shadow as his hair grew back. His smile, without doubt, was a sneer. If he took off his uniform and had some studs in his nose, he would look the same as many of the yobs frequently seen roaming the streets. With or without the studs, I'd cross to the other side of the road if I saw him approaching me.

So I was very circumspect when I ran through the garda abstract report with him. This is an official accident report form, which is prepared by An Garda Síochána and passed to the insurance company involved in the claim.

When I looked at him for confirmation of various points in the report, he didn't say a word; he just nodded. As I was reaching the end of the report, he interrupted. 'So what is it that you want to know?'

There was one thing on which I wanted clarification. The driver of the car that had hit and killed a pedestrian had maintained in his statement that he too had been injured in the accident. Medical reports suggested that his injuries had been very slight, mostly shock.

The driver had claimed that he had lain on the grass margin at the side of the road for fifty-five minutes waiting for an ambulance to arrive. That seemed to me an excessive length of time, so I had already checked with the Dublin Fire Brigade Ambulance authorities; they had told me that an ambulance had been dispatched within four minutes of the 999 call being received. That time tied in with the time recorded at the local garda station, which was literally around the corner from the scene of the accident.

Second, the accident had happened at 11.55p.m. in the middle of January. I had also checked with Met Éireann, who had provided me with actual readings of the air and ground temperatures at midnight on the night in question. I was no doctor, but I wondered about hypothermia. There was no mention in the medical reports of the driver suffering from or complaining about hypothermia when he was examined in the A&E Department at Beaumont Hospital.

So it seemed to me that there was approximately fifty minutes unaccounted for on the night of the accident, and that's what I really wanted to talk to the investigating garda about.

Because of his attitude, I felt it would be prudent to lead

gently into the question I wanted to ask him. I broached the subject of the time frame. I asked him if he thought the driver might have been confused or had given wrong information when making his statement to this garda officer after the accident. I really don't know if he thought I was being critical of him or questioning his competence. (Although I didn't mention it, the reality was that he had apparently failed to pick up on or question the unaccounted-for time.) I was genuinely shocked by his reaction.

He was sitting less than four feet from me, on the other side of a desk. He half rose out of the chair, placed his two hands flat on the desk and leaned forward. His face was about two feet or less from mine.

'I know you!' he roared. 'I'm going up to his [the driver's] house and I'm going to tell him you were asking questions about him!'

He was so close some spittle landed on my cheek. I wiped it away with the back of my hand. I gathered my papers together, grabbed my file and walked towards the door. I could feel the anger rising from the pit of my stomach. I turned and looked at him. He was still standing by the desk, still sneering.

Trying to keep my voice level, 'That's your prerogative,' I said. 'I don't know what your problem is, mate, but you are a disgrace to your uniform.'

I slammed the door on my way out.

I subsequently made a few enquiries about this officer. The garda authorities knew him as someone with an attitude problem. He had been transferred from the station around the corner from the accident location to another station in the Garda Metropolitan area and was supposed to be restricted to back office duties. Clearly someone had slipped up by letting him loose on the unsuspecting public.

It turned out that he did know me personally, although I had no recollection of ever meeting him. The year before, I had been lady captain of my golf club. I was a member of a joint sub-committee that was drawing up proposals for equal status rights for women in golf clubs. He was one of the main movers in a group of male members who were vehemently opposed to granting full membership of the club to women. I was one of the speakers at a special general meeting of the club members, at which the proposal for full membership for women was passed. I guess he though he was getting his own back!

———

The supervisor appeared within minutes, with the little guy at his side. I explained the position to him and produced a copy of the injunction. He read it carefully, line by line. 'No problem at all,' he said with a smile, and, glancing at his junior, 'Alan, look after this enquiry, please.'

I smiled at Alan, hoping to repair any hard feelings he may have had. He looked at me sulkily. It took over an hour for him to drip-feed the information to me, but we got there in the end. I now had the names and addresses of the licensed stallholders who had sold us the counterfeit stuff. I did manage to refrain from making any sarcastic remarks to Alan as I left.

Sam and Christine had bagged up the jerseys while I prepared my interim report, so when Sam and I arrived at our clients' office at eleven o'clock on Wednesday morning, we had, apart from the report and photographs, thirteen large black refuse sacks containing counterfeit merchandise.

Having liaised by phone with the garda superintendent for the area, my clients and their solicitor decided that they would not only serve a copy of the injunction on the individual stallholders, they would also attempt to recover all counterfeit garments found on the stalls.

We met up in Store Street Garda Station on Friday morning as arranged. Apart from Sam and myself, Paul and Tom, directors of our client company, attended, accompanied by their solicitor, Hugh. They had brought with them four male employees of the company.

Because of manpower constraints, the superintendent could only provide two uniformed gardaí to accompany my clients while they served copies of the injunction on the people working at each stall. They would be there to prevent a breach of the peace in case any of the stallholders got stroppy when the injunction was served.

Hugh, the solicitor, suggested that they would like to start the process at two in the afternoon. The superintendent was unhappy with that proposal. He made it clear that he had other matters to take into consideration, such as potential public order problems; after all, the street my clients wanted to target was one of the busiest shopping streets in the centre of Dublin. He could not guarantee that he would have any officer available in the middle of the afternoon, let alone two.

What the superintendent didn't know was that, in an effort to ensure maximum publicity, the media been tipped off about our clients' intentions, who were hoping that the publicity might go some way towards convincing the stallholders that, financially, it was simply not worth the risk. The stallholders would have paid for their stock and it could be taken from them. They would lose not only the money they had spent, but also the profit element on the sale of each garment.

The superintendent insisted, 'It has to be done by 11.30a.m.'

Excluding Sam and myself and the two gardaí, seven people had to cover twelve of the twenty-one stalls. The stalls were located at each side of what was in effect, a cul-de-sac about a hundred and fifty yards long. At the bottom of the small road were double doors leading into a shopping centre.

Sam and I headed off to the street in question. It had been agreed that the operation would start at 11.30a.m. and we now had about ninety minutes to go. We were going to try to close down any escape routes for the traders. Apart from the shopping centre, there were two department stores on either side of the cul-de-sac. Both stores stocked our clients' merchandise and there were at least two retail units in the shopping centre that also sold their products. I decided to try getting support from the security staff in the shopping centre, which would be the main exit route from the street.

In my job, having a hard neck is one of the essential tools of the trade. I found the administration section and basically talked myself into a five-minute meeting with the shopping centre manager. I gave him a broad outline of the problems (without mentioning the forthcoming raid) and, in particular, I emphasised how happy some of his tenants would be if we could stop the sale of counterfeit merchandise which was happening literally outside the doors of his shopping centre. I caught his interest.

'What can I do?' he asked.

'Maybe we should talk to your security manager.'

I kept looking at my watch. Seventy-five minutes to go.

'Time is of the essence,' I said.

The security manager arrived within minutes.

'Michael, I want you to listen to this – Shirley, go ahead.'

I repeated what I had told the manager. This time I told them about the raid.

'Your guys don't have to do anything, they don't have to get involved.' They were looking at each other. 'They just have to stand at the door to give the impression that they are blocking the entrance,' I added hastily.

'It's okay with me, Michael.'

Michael stood up. 'Okay, I'll get them organised.'

He stopped at the door on his way out of the office.

'Have you talked to our neighbours yet?' He was referring to the two department stores.

I stopped just short of fluttering my eyelashes at him, 'I hoped you might do that for me.' I smiled coyly; at least I hoped it came over as being coy.

'Okay.'

I galloped down the stairs and met up with Sam.

'All arranged, and they're going to talk to the neighbours,' I said with a smile.

I rang Paul on his mobile and told him the arrangements I had made. He was delighted. From his tone of voice, he seemed to be quite excited, even hyper. Maybe he had watched too many cops and robbers series on television, or maybe he was really into a new television series called *Knock Knock*, which was all about raids by the UK customs authorities. I hoped he wasn't going to go overboard and end up in some sort of embarrassing incident.

Sam and I made out way over to another department store across the road from the entrance to the cul-de-sac. We checked the first floor, the ladies' fashions department; there were far too many customers and staff around for us to do what we wanted.

'Let's try the furniture department,' Sam said.

He was right, of course. There would only be two or three members of staff to cover the entire floor. We wandered around the department, all the while heading towards the front of the building.

'Can I help you?' came a voice from behind us.

I turned and smiled. 'Just looking, thanks.'

The assistant walked away towards an elderly couple who had just stepped off the escalator at the far end of the shop floor.

We found a niche, a smallish alcove. There were free-standing wardrobes around the perimeter and backed up to the front windows. Whilst I kept a lookout for shop assistants, Sam eased one of the wardrobes away from the window.

'The lower part of the windows are blacked out,' he said quietly.

He pulled out the wardrobe further and disappeared. He reappeared almost immediately.

'If we stand on the windowsill we have a clear view.' The windowsill was about two feet off the floor.

This time, Sam phoned Tom. We hoped he was in a calmer state of mind than Paul. The idea was that we would watch from the windows to see if the traders removed or hid any of the stock from view when the operation began. Tom was to phone me on my mobile just before they turned into the cul-de-sac, and keep the line open so that I could pass over any relevant information.

'I should have asked that security fella for the loan of a couple of radios.' It was too late now. I was irritated that I had not thought of that possibility earlier. I fiddled with my phone.

It was 11.10a.m. Twenty minutes to go. I could feel the tension starting to build in my stomach. Tension makes me a bit tetchy.

'I can't find 'vibrate' on this yoke.'

Sam looked at me as if to say, 'Cool it.'

'Well, I don't want the blasted thing ringing from behind a wardrobe.'

I handed him my mobile. He clicked a few buttons and handed it back to me.

To ease my tension a bit I said, 'Just visualise us standing behind that and the unsuspecting shop assistant is trying to flog a wardrobe to a customer and my phone rings from nowhere!'

Sam is so practical about things. 'What do we do if we get caught?'

That possibility had crossed my mind, but I hadn't mentioned it to Sam. 'Oh, I'll think of something.' I wasn't going to plan for a worst-case scenario: we had other things to worry about at that moment.

I peeped around the corner of the alcove. The young shop assistant was still attending to the elderly couple. A second assistant had appeared: he was sitting at a desk about halfway down the shop floor.

I ducked back in. 'All clear!'

Sam eased two wardrobes out about two foot from the window. I kept my fingers crossed that the staff wouldn't notice that these two were not flush with the adjoining wardrobes. He climbed in first and I followed him.

We had a perfect view of the street below and the cul-de-sac opposite. I nudged Sam and pointed. There were two security men standing at the door of each of the department stores. Five security men were standing with their arms crossed at the entrance to the shopping centre. The security manager was standing outside the door.

I nudged again and pointed to my right. We could see our gang, with the two uniformed officers, approaching. I felt the phone in my pocket vibrate.

'Hi,' I whispered. 'Look up to your left – can you see us?'

'No,' Tom replied.

'Good.' If he couldn't see us, neither could the street traders. I put my phone in my left hand so Sam could speak into it if he spotted anything. The two gardaí stood in the middle of the road.

The guys split up and we watched as they set about serving the injunctions on the traders. They seemed to be negotiating with some of the stallholders. From the body language it seemed that some of the traders were refusing to hand over their stock of counterfeit jerseys.

'Second last stall on the left, he's dumped a load of stuff *under* the stall,' I whispered.

'Got it,' came the reply.

Sam nudged me and pointed to the right-hand side of the cul-de-sac. The woman on the fourth stall was running towards the entrance of the shopping centre. Her arms were so full of jerseys she couldn't hold on to them all. Some dropped to the roadway as she ran. She stopped dead in her tracks when she saw the security men, still standing with their arms crossed, at the shopping centre doors. She quickly looked around and spotted some filled black refuse sacks piled in the top right-hand corner of the cul-de-sac. Like a flash she was over at the sacks. She pulled away a couple of bags, dumped her stock on the remaining bags and threw the two black sacks on top.

'More stuff hidden in black sacks at top right,' I whispered into the phone.

'Okay,' Tom replied. For some reason he was whispering too.

We were so busy trying to keep an eye on the activities below that we missed the approach of more gardaí. A sergeant and two more uniformed officers appeared in the middle of the cul-de-sac. 'The Super must have relented a little,' said Sam, with a smile on his face.

The operation was over in minutes. We eased our way back along the sill; we were still facing the windows, as there wasn't enough room to turn around. I lowered myself to the ground in the gap between two wardrobes.

I turned round and came face to face with the elderly couple. They were just at the entrance to the alcove. She was clutching her husband's arm and had a look of surprise on her face. He was standing there with his mouth open. At least there was no sign of the sales assistants. Oh, blast! I did the first thing that came into my mind. I knocked a couple of times on the back of the wardrobe, and then on its side.

'Good solid wood all over,' I said as I flung open the door of the wardrobe. I hoped the door might cover Sam as he dropped down from the sill. I stuck my head inside the wardrobe and knocked on the wood a couple more times. 'Excellent quality,' I said to the couple as I straightened up.

I thought they were going to drop dead from shock when Sam appeared from behind the wardrobe door. They stepped back, well out of our way. To keep up the pretence, we argued over the choice of wardrobe as we walked past them and out of the alcove. We didn't look back. We made it out onto the street without being challenged by any of the staff.

We met up with Paul, Tom and their team back at Store Street Station. They hadn't got all of the stuff the traders were selling but on a quick count they had recovered over six hundred counterfeit jerseys. And we still hadn't dealt with Damien, the suspected supplier to the street traders. It was probable that Damien would hear about the events on Friday but he wouldn't necessarily make any connection to himself. Most companies would have tackled the supplier before the sellers, but my clients had decided to do the reverse.

Sam and I arrived in the High Court at nine thirty on Monday morning. Joe was going to try to obtain an ex-parte order for Damien's committal for his breach of the injunction granted earlier. 'Ex-parte' is when one party makes an application to the court without giving any notice to the other side. It was highly unlikely that a judge would grant an order for Damien's arrest on an ex-parte basis, but Joe felt it was worth a try. He had prepared affidavits setting out the information Sam and I had obtained. When we had sworn the affidavits, we all trooped into court.

As anticipated, the judge declined the request for a bench warrant for Damien's arrest. He adjourned the case until 10.30a.m. on Wednesday so that Damien could be served with a copy of our clients' application and attend court personally. Our counsel did succeed in getting an order requiring Damien to surrender all merchandise bearing our clients' name or logo. The court order was drawn up in a hurry and served on Damien's solicitor by midday.

Obviously, when his solicitor was served with the court order, he would notify Damien. Neither Damien nor his solicitor was aware that we knew his business address in the centre of the city and the location of his storage container in the yard on the Naas Road, so if he was holding any counterfeit merchandise, he was likely to try and shift it before Wednesday.

Paul and a couple of his employees headed over to South Great George's Street to await developments. Tom, Sam and I headed out to the Naas Road yard.

'Hi, Pops, brought you a little pressie,' I said as I walked into the Portakabin. I dropped a carton of Major cigarettes on his table. I wanted to get on the right side of him so that he would be receptive when I started asking questions. I didn't want him phoning Damien either.

'Any chance of a cup of tea?'

We chatted about this and that over mugs of tea. It amazes me sometimes that if I don't introduce myself, a lot of people don't ask me who I am. They just assume . . . well, whatever they assume!

'Remember that big Merc that was here the last time I was in? Does he drop in very often?'

He was informative. He pointed out the two containers rented by Damien. He also told me that Damien generally called in twice weekly, Monday and Friday mornings first thing. This was Monday, but Damien hadn't called in that morning. My mobile rang. It was 2.15p.m.

'The Merc and the van have just passed us,' Sam said.

'Don't come in yet, we need to see what he does,' I replied.

I could see Pops looking from me to the vehicles and back again.

The van pulled up outside the container at the right-hand

wall. A young man in his early twenties jumped out. The Merc stopped outside another container and Damien emerged. He unlocked the container on the right-hand side and returned to the one beside his car, which he also unlocked. The two men started loading bags and boxes into the van.

I rang Sam. 'Come on in!'

Sam pulled up directly behind the van. Tom hopped out and handed Damien a copy of the court order. Damien's face was a picture. I could hear raised voices and his denials and pleas of ignorance, and while the others were keeping him occupied, I decided to take the opportunity to check the other open container. I legged it over to the container and looked inside. There were racks of shelves all around the walls, stuffed with boxes, and sealed plastic sacks were piled in the middle of the floor.

I tore open a couple of sacks and rooted inside. I also opened the tops of three boxes. Each contained counterfeit jerseys. Stuck on the side of one of the boxes was a consignment note. I didn't take the time to read it, just stuffed it into my jacket pocket. I picked up a handful of the jerseys and went outside. Damien was still in full voice and full flight, denying all knowledge of everything and anything.

'Excuse me,' I said, stepping back out of his reach, just in case he lashed out. 'What are these?' I asked, dropping the jerseys on the bonnet of Sam's car.

Some of the language he used I had never heard before. Tom started negotiating with him. He had been caught red-handed, he would go to jail if he didn't surrender the merchandise, he was in breach of a High Court order, and so on. Eventually, Damien caved in. He agreed to hand over the merchandise. Tom phoned Paul to put him in the picture. Transportation of the goods had to be arranged, and Paul said he'd organise it immediately.

Damien and his young friend drove out of the yard. Paul's parting shot to him was, 'See you Wednesday in court!'

The three of us trooped back into Pop's Portakabin.

'Any of yis want a cuppa tea?' he asked.

We settled down to wait for the vans.

Pops looked at me and grinned. 'Never liked him anyway, wouldn't give ye the time of day.'

We were later told that 6,400 counterfeit jerseys had been recovered. I forgot all about the consignment note until I returned to the office. Our job, the investigation, was complete so I just stuck it in the file.

Our job may have been over, but the problem did not go away. Three months later, I spotted more counterfeit copies of my clients' merchandise.

09 | KEEP ON TRUCKIN'

Prologue: Tuesday, 21 November

I illegally parked my car on the footpath outside my office and grabbed the files off the front passenger seat. I was making a flying visit to the office to give Christine some work and then I was taking the rest of the morning off. It was 10.20a.m. I had about five minutes to spare before I needed to be on the road again.

The local courthouse was right next door to the office and it sat on Tuesdays. There were loads of yobs, solicitors, barristers and gardaí hanging around the front of the building. I trotted over to three gardaí who were chatting outside.

'Alan, I'll only be a minute, just dropping these files in.'

'Okay, Shirl.'

The other two gardaí acknowledged me with a nod of their heads.

I was back at the car within five minutes. I had arranged to play golf with two friends and we were due on the first tee at 10.40a.m. If there were no traffic delays, it would take me less than ten minutes to reach my club.

I kept within the speed limit until I reached the N1 and then put my foot down. Traffic was very light. I checked my rear view mirror and flicked on the indicator to change lanes. I wanted to turn onto the Donabate Road. There was no traffic on the outside lane so I made my manoeuvre. As I approached the junction, I checked my mirror again. For some reason, I happened to notice a car pulling out from behind a lorry.

The Hearse Road had a speed limit of sixty mph. I kept well within the limit, as there are some acute bends. Just as I passed Newbridge House, a 'pup' in a Volkswagen Polo passed me doing at least eighty. He had come from nowhere; I hadn't seen him behind me. I checked my mirror periodically so I wouldn't get the same fright again. There was only one car I could see, quite a way back, so there was no risk of any surprises from that car.

I pulled into the shop-cum-post office at the start of the village. A car passed.

Mary, Kate and I regularly play together. Apart from the golf, it was a social thing: friends meeting together for a bit of craic. Each of us brought 'goodies' which we shared during our round of golf.

As I was climbing back into the car I heard the beep of a car horn. I turned and saw Mary drive past, Kate with her. I waved and stood looking after her car.

How the hell does she get the two of them (both at least five foot eight), two sets of clubs and two golf trolleys into a Cinquecento? I wondered.

I rounded a bend in the village and had to manoeuvre sharply to avoid a car parked half up on the footpath, opposite a solid white line in the middle of the road.

Bloody idiots, I thought. I glared at the driver and front seat passenger as I drove past.

Now if that was a woman driver, she'd be called stupid, I thought.

Kate was leading the way from the locker room to the first tee; Mary was behind her and I was bringing up the rear. As we reached the side of the tee-box, we saw a car being driven slowly over the bridge at the back of the first tee. It turned left into the car park. We all glanced at it, expecting to see some of our fellow members.

'Fat chance,' said Mary laughing: Tuesday was Ladies' Day in the club; there was a full timesheet so there was no chance of visitors getting out to play, men or women, and we could see the two people in the car were men.

I stared after the car. I was nearly a hundred per cent certain that it was the same car that had pulled out from behind the lorry on the N1 and that had been parked on the bend in the road in the village.

Mary nudged me. 'You're up, Shirl.'

I took a couple of practice swings, addressed the ball and lashed at it with my driver.

'Shit!' The ball was heading for the ditch that ran the length of the first fairway. With a bit of luck it wouldn't go out of bounds, onto the railway track that was behind the ditch.

'That's not like you,' said Kate.

'I'll play a provisional ball,' I muttered as I stared over into the car park. Nobody was walking about; whoever the two men were, they were still sitting in their car somewhere in the car park.

I changed to a three wood, put down another ball and sent it straight down the middle of the fairway.

'That's your usual shot!' said Mary.

I was a bit on edge for the first few holes, keeping an eye out to see if I could see anyone lurking in the bushes. I didn't.

Probably just a coincidence, I thought finally and got on with my game.

Wednesday, 29 November

I had been in court most of the day and had spent some two hours in the witness box, which can be mentally draining. I called into the office on my way home to collect some files, as I wanted to draft some reports. I left at four thirty and headed home.

It was a miserable evening, cold and wet, a typical Irish winter's night. I lit the fire in the sitting room, just to bring a bit of cheer into the house. I find it quite relaxing to do paperwork sitting by the fire, glass of wine at hand. I closed the window blinds and settled down to work at about seven. Just as I reached over to get a cigarette, I saw my front security light go on. I glanced at my watch. It was ten past nine. The doorbell rang.

I am quite security conscious and I wasn't expecting any visitors. I could have gone straight from the sitting room to the hall, but instead I went through to the kitchen and glanced at my security monitor. Two men were standing outside my porch. They had obviously rung the bell and stepped back onto the path. I didn't know them. I have a monitored alarm system and one of the panic buttons is discreetly positioned within reach when I'm standing inside the front door, so I was happy enough to answer the door.

'Ms Sleator, I'm Detective Inspector X and this is Detective Sergeant Z. Could we have a word, please?'

I kept my right hand in the vicinity of the panic button.

'Can I see your identification, please?' I stuck out my left hand to take the IDs. Both looked okay. 'Come in,' I said.

I gestured the two officers into the sitting room. 'Have a seat.'

The DI looked at his notebook. 'You're the registered owner of a blue Vauxhall Carlton?' And he gave the registration number.

'That's right.' I sat back and waited. I wasn't going to deny it; they had walked past the car in my driveway.

'What do you do for a living?' said the sergeant in an abrupt tone of voice. Maybe it was tiredness, but his tone of voice was already rubbing me up the wrong way. I kept my tone of voice as pleasant as possible, though: some of my best contacts were Members of An Garda Síochána, and I didn't want to annoy him unnecessarily.

'Why do you want to know?'

'Look, Ms Sleator, we are just trying to clarify some points . . .'

I smiled and interrupted him, 'You sound just like me when I'm trying to get information.'

He looked at the DI as if seeking directions.

'Where are you based?' I asked.

'Harcourt Terrace,' said the DI. 'We cover the north city and north county.' He named the station they usually worked from.

'Do you mind if I make a call?' I intended to make the call whether they objected or not, and I wasn't bothered that they would overhear the conversation. I checked the contacts listing on my mobile and pushed the call button.

'Hi, Martin.'

'Hello, Shirley, how's the golf?'

'Great. Lost another shot last Sunday.'

Martin was a garda superintendent. We were members of the same golf club and Martin was one of my regular partners in mixed competitions.

'Martin, do you know a DI X and a DS Z?'

'Sure,' replied Martin.

'What do they look like?'

I watched the two detectives for any reactions. The DI was leaning back on the sofa with a smile on his face. The DS was leaning forward and glaring at me.

'Sorry?' Martin's tone of voice was bewildered, as if he didn't understand my question.

'I've two guys sitting here on my sofa. They say they're DI X and DS Z – their warrant cards seem okay, but I'm just checking.'

Martin gave me clear descriptions, which matched the two men.

'Do you want me to talk to them?'

'No, it's okay, thanks.'

'Ring me if you have any problems.'

'I will, don't worry – see you Sunday at twelve.'

I had rung Martin for a couple of reasons. I didn't want the two detectives, particularly the sergeant, to think that they could bully me: and now they knew that I had phoned someone in their line of work who knew them well enough to describe them. I also wanted to let someone know that I had two men in my house whom I didn't know.

I didn't want to phone Sam; he would have jumped in his car and driven over, and I would have been on the receiving end of a long lecture, once again, on taking risks and personal security.

'Okay, what do you want to know?' I asked.

The DS was still glaring at me. 'Who'd you ring, anyway?'

I stared back at him. 'My mother wouldn't ask me that.'

Well, she couldn't, bless her; she had died some years previously. Arrogant pup, I thought.

I could see that the DI was watching this exchange with a grin on his face. He leaned forward.

'Shirley, you're a private investigator, right?'

I nodded.

'Can you remember the last time you were in Ashford and what you were doing down there?'

I thought for a while. So far as I could recall, the last time I had been in Ashford, County Wicklow, was about eighteen months previously when I was checking out stalls at the Monday Street market. He seemed a bit perplexed, as if my answer didn't tie in with whatever information they had.

'Can you give me any more information? It might trigger something,' I said.

He told me that someone had been stopped in Ashford in September and when his car was searched, a list of car registration numbers, including my Carlton, was found in the glove compartment.

'That doesn't make sense.'

Before I had a chance to continue the sergeant interrupted. 'Look, it is right,' he said. Holding up one finger: 'Fact, he was stopped in September.' The second finger went up: 'Fact, he had your registration number in the glove compartment.'

He was really getting up my nose at this stage. I leaned forward. Putting up one finger I said: 'Fact, with an attitude like yours, you should be put away in some back office processing paperwork. You're not fit to deal with the public.'

I looked at the DI. 'As I was going to say: it simply can't be correct because I bought the Carlton in May this year and I certainly haven't been in Ashford since then.' Glaring at the sergeant, I continued, 'Your facts may be correct but your assumptions are wrong. He can't have noted my reg number in Ashford. It must have been picked up somewhere else.'

I stood up. I told the DI that I would think about it and if anything came to mind, I would phone him. He handed me a card.

'Wow! They give you business cards now?' I joked.

'And mobile phones too!' he said.

He tapped the card in my hand. I turned it over. His mobile phone number was written on the back. We shook hands at the front door. I looked at the sergeant. I stuck my hand out. 'Hey, Sergeant, maybe we should start again. Peace?'

'Boy, are you bolshie or what?' he said as we shook hands.

'Only sometimes,' I replied with a grin.

I double locked the front door. Back in the kitchen, I poured myself a Scotch and went back to sit by the fire.

I was worried on two counts. They hadn't identified the man they had stopped, and I had no idea why someone was interested enough to carry my registration number. Second, my car was registered to my business address. The detectives had obviously checked with the collator in my local station, whom I knew well, and that's how they obtained my home address. But information does leak from garda stations. My address could have been given to someone else as well. One other thing was niggling away in the back of my mind. I rarely used my own car for work purposes, so was this incident work-related or personal?

I checked the security lighting at the back of the house and set the alarm. The situation bothered me most of the night. I didn't sleep too well.

Thursday, 30 November

I was still mulling over the conversation from the previous night as I had my shower when it hit me.

'Never mind Ashford, could it be connected to that Meath job?' I asked myself. It was the only one I could think of for which I had used my personal car.

I was in the office in less than an hour. I pulled the Meath file. It could fit, I thought.

Sometimes I am inclined to forget that most other people don't work to my schedule. It was 7.25a.m. when I rang the inspector's mobile.

'Yeah?' He sounded as if I had woken him up.

'It's Shirley Sleator. I think I may have something for you. I'm not sure.'

'When can I meet you?' He sounded awake now.

'I'm in the office all day.'

We agreed to meet at ten thirty.

Sam arrived in the office at ten past eight, and I filled him in. As expected, I got the lengthy lecture about personal security and how I shouldn't have let strangers into the house. He seemed more concerned by that than the fact that some unknown person, of interest to the gardaí, was carrying my registration number around in his car.

I then told him what I had noticed on the Tuesday when I was playing golf. 'It's probably just a coincidence.'

'It may not be,' he replied.

'Starsky and Hutch', as I nicknamed them (Starsky being the sergeant) arrived bang on time at ten thirty, and Christine brought us coffee. Without being asked, she knew to hold all calls until we were finished.

Sam and I were both feeling a bit uneasy. Neither of us had been in this sort of situation before. I introduced Sam to the detectives.

'You've told us nothing about the person. Have we any cause for concern?' Sam asked.

The inspector blew out his cheeks. 'Don't think so – we'd let you know if there was a problem.'

Sam's voice was dripping with sarcasm. 'That's reassuring to know. Who is he?'

'I'm afraid I can't tell you that.'

I could see Sam was getting tetchier by the minute.

Touching him on the arm, 'It's okay,' I said.

I began. 'This guy had an industrial accident in Scotland. We were asked to investigate him by an insurance com. . .' I paused. Sergeant 'Starsky' was writing away in his notebook. 'Excuse me, what are you doing?'

'Making notes,' he snapped.

I looked at Sam and shrugged as if to say, 'Yes? No? Do I continue?'

The DI could see that I wasn't happy with the note-taking business. 'This is informal, just a chat,' he said to the sergeant.

I stared at the sergeant and then glanced at the DI. I now felt reasonably sure that the events at the golf club the previous week were not a coincidence. I knew I was chancing my arm, but I said, 'Before we continue, why am I under surveillance?'

They looked at each other.

'Why do you think you are under surveillance?'

'Do you always answer a question by asking another?' I replied.

They hadn't denied that it was they who were following me.

I turned to the DS. 'I saw you on three separate occasions.' I was deliberately vague about dates, times and locations. I *had* seen the same car three times, but within the space of a half an hour on the same day. I had never seen a grown man blush quite like that before. It started just below his collar and reached right up to his hairline.

'Put your book away,' the DI said.

'Well?'

The DI looked at me hard.

'All we had at first was your car registration number. We checked the address. It was obviously an office. We knew nothing about you, so we decided to have a look.'

'You didn't think of asking the local gardaí if they knew me?'

He looked embarrassed. 'We did that this week before we approached you at home.'

Sam interrupted, 'That doesn't explain why her registration number was of interest to you in the first place.'

'Okay,' he said resignedly.

'The man who was arrested in September is suspected of paramilitary involvement. We were interested in why he had your reg number.'

'This is the man in Ashford?' I asked.

He nodded.

I didn't need any further encouragement. Our job was risky enough at times, and I might need garda assistance in the future. I pulled out the file from the bottom drawer of my desk.

'I want to make it clear that I am not implying that this man has anything to do with your fella in Ashford. It's the only incident I can think of involving the Carlton. How much detail do you want?'

'As much as you can give me, Shirley: everything, no matter how insignificant it may seem to you.'

I gave them the general background relating to the industrial accident, the instructions I had received from the insurance company in April, and a broad outline of the various attempts we had made with regard to surveillance, all with a negative result – zilch. We had never caught even a glimpse of our claimant. I glanced at the DS. I thought I saw the start of a smirk appearing. I glared at him as if to say, 'Don't start pushing your luck, sunshine.'

I told them that in July I had received information from reliable sources that our man was working as a long-distance lorry driver, and was frequently away from home for as much as two weeks at a time. My sources agreed to keep an eye on his home periodically and if they saw the lorry they would phone me immediately.

I opened the folder and flicked through the paperwork until I found the relevant section of my file notes.

––––

Just after 11p.m. on Thursday, 25 August, I received a telephone call from one of my sources, who told me that the cab of my claimant's lorry was parked on the roadway outside his house. He gave me the registration number. He also told me that there was no haulage company name on the cab. I found that the truck was registered to a person in Kingscourt, County Cavan. I then phoned Sam to discuss what arrangements we could make for immediate surveillance.

We agreed that since the claimant had arrived home sometime between four and eleven o'clock that evening, he was unlikely to go anywhere before morning. We also agreed that we would organise surveillance from 6a.m. until midnight and split the eighteen hours between four of us. Sam was to take the first shift, starting at six.

I telephoned David and Michael, cancelling the jobs they had lined up for the next day. Michael was to cover from ten thirty to three, I would take over for the next four and a half hours, and David would cover from seven thirty.

The claimant – I'll call him Cliff – lived in a small private housing estate, built on a hill, on the outskirts of a small town in County Meath. Cliff's house was about halfway along the road. There was a small parade of shops at the bottom of the hill, which included a coffee shop, a hairdresser, a grocery store and a bookmaker. There was only one way in and out of the estate, a road that ran parallel to the side of the small shopping mall. Cliff's house could be monitored from the car parking area in front of the shops.

Sam was already in position when I made a courtesy call to the local garda station. I like to let the local gardaí know when we are working in their area; it saves unnecessary call-outs from the station. I provided the local sergeant with a list of our car numbers.

We had only one sighting of Cliff during the eighteen hours of surveillance, when he was pottering around his front garden. We had been waiting four months for something, anything, to happen on this job. All four of us hung around the town for most of the day and evening. We agreed that, if necessary, we would work right through the weekend.

We needed to connect Cliff to that truck. It wasn't registered in his name, so we didn't even have any circumstantial evidence.

I took the first shift on Saturday morning. By nine thirty, Sam, David and Michael had turned up. We were taking it in turns to watch Cliff's house. I knew I would not be able to justify billing our client for all the staff hours we were using, but the lads were keen, very keen, to get a result.

David was sitting on the small wall fronting the car park watching the house while Sam, Michael and I were having breakfast in the coffee shop. It was just after 10.15a.m. when David came in. I looked at him expectantly.

'Anything?'

'Just his missus, she's walking down the road in this direction.'

We didn't even have to change our position. Our table was just inside the front window. We watched her approach. David went back outside to monitor her.

'She's just gone into the hairdresser.' He returned to the wall. For the lack of something better to do, I went outside to have a cigarette. Sitting on the wall beside David, I moaned about the lack of activity.

I approached the hairdresser's salon and looked through the window while pretending to read the price list. I could see that there was only one other customer apart from Cliff's wife. Her hair had been washed and she was sitting at one of the tables, presumably waiting for a blow-dry. I pushed open the door and went in.

'Sorry, I don't have any appointment – any chance of a quick wash and blow-dry?' There were four hairdressers standing around, so the chances were good.

'Sure, would you like to take a seat at the basin?' the smiling receptionist said.

We made some small talk, and I was eventually seated at a table two down from Cliff's wife, who was having her hair cut. I pretended to be deeply engrossed in a magazine so that I wouldn't have to talk to my stylist. I could overhear most of the conversation two tables down.

My ears pricked up when I heard mention of 'a wedding today'. I listened more carefully.

Mrs Cliff left the salon ahead of me. The three lads were outside and they could monitor her activities while the stylist finished my hair.

The lads were sitting on the wall when I emerged.

'Coffee, anyone?' I nodded in the direction of the coffee shop. We sat at what was now our usual table. I waited until Sam came back to the table with coffee and scones before filling them in.

'They're going to a wedding this afternoon,' I said with a grin on my face. 'I'm not sure if the wedding is at two or they're leaving at two.'

The lads started talking all at the same time.

'There's more,' I said, tapping the table to get their attention. 'Something about his suit in the cleaners. What did she do when she left?'

'She went straight home, I watched her,' Michael said.

At last, something was going to happen, even though their attendance at a wedding wasn't going to be of much use in our investigation. We covered the various possibilities of how they might get to the wedding. The consensus was that they would travel by taxi or be collected. Unlikely as it may seem, we did make contingency plans, just in case they travelled in the lorry, or he drove the lorry into the village to collect his suit from the dry cleaners. Our primary objective, come hell or high water, was to get photographs of Cliff in the lorry: and we would have ample opportunity if he drove to the village.

The likelihood of him driving into the village was estimated at about ten to one.

A small vanette pulled up outside Cliff's house. The man who alighted was carrying a suit on a hanger covered in clear plastic. 'Ah, shit,' came the chorus of voices from around the table.

We waited. By now were sitting on the small wall. As time went on, you could actually feel the tension rising.

'Eh up!' said David. I looked at my watch. It was exactly 2.02p.m.

Cliff and his wife walked down the path and crossed the road to the lorry. 'I don't believe it,' I said. 'They're going to a wedding in a flippin' truck!' We watched as Cliff unlocked the passenger door and helped his wife as she clambered up onto the step of the truck.

'You ready, lads?' I climbed into my car. Michael went to his car and Sam and David walked to the corner of the access road to the small shopping mall.

If we were members of the gardaí, it would have been simple. We would have the authority to stop the truck and get the evidence we needed that way. We weren't. We had no choice but to resort to what was in effect a bit of a hare-brained idea. Risky as it may seem, my job was to slow the truck down at the junction, slow enough for Sam and David to get some photographs. With any luck Cliff would be concentrating on me and my car, and wouldn't spot what Sam and David were doing. Michael was to follow the truck to its destination.

I was banking on Cliff being a safe driver – most truck drivers are – but I had to get my timing spot on if I wasn't to damage my car or injure myself. We had agreed that I could abort the effort if I wasn't comfortable. I eased my car forward. Watching the lorry approach, I judged that he was going slowly enough.

'Please God, protect me. Concentrate.'

I moved forward. I was about three-quarters of the way round the junction. I silently spoke to my feet: contact point – hold – lift. The engine stalled. I braced myself for an impact. The car hopped forward and stopped.

Cliff must have jammed on the brakes. The truck stopped about fifteen feet away.

'Thank you, God, and thank you, Cliff.'

He leaned on the horn. I ignored him. I got the car going again and took off down towards the main road.

The bloody traffic lights at the end of the road were red. Cliff was coming up behind quite fast and he was still leaning on the horn. He was obviously mad at me.

Mistake – I had probably made matters worse.

I should have acknowledged him and played the dumb woman driver, I thought.

I turned left, going through the red light.

Oh, shit. He ran the red light too.

The garda station was up ahead on my right. Instinctively, I headed for it. I'd be safe at a garda station!

I drove around the back of the station. There were two patrol cars parked. At the time, the gardaí used dark blue Ford Sierras, which were a similar shape and colour to my car. I dumped the car beside one of the garda cars, jumped out and ran to the far side of the building. I waited. If he drove in, I was going to leg it down the side of the building to the front and run inside the station using the front door.

I heard nothing. I peeped around the corner. No sign of the truck. I crept towards the front of the building and peered around again. No sign of the truck.

I practically ran in the front door of the station.

'Hi, Sergeant.' He was sitting at a desk on the other side of the counter.

'Hi, Shirley, you look flustered!'

'Just called in to let you know I think we're finished here – thanks for your help.' Probably finished in more ways than one!

'Did you get what you wanted?'

'Hope so.' I really did hope so: there was no way I would go back to that particular part of Meath for a very long time if I had my way.

I went back out to the car and as I got in my mobile was ringing. I scrabbled around the floor of the car and eventually found it under the passenger seat. 'Missed call' was displayed on the screen. I didn't bother checking who the call was from – I rang Sam.

'Where the hell are you?' he yelled. 'Are you okay?'

'I'm fine.' Bloody liar – I was still thoroughly rattled.

'I'm at the back of the garda station. Are you guys okay? What about Michael and David?'

Sam told me that Michael and David were with him.

'We need to compare notes – do the three of you want to come over for dinner?'

Sam and David were unattached, and Michael's long-suffering wife, like most partners of people who are involved in the private investigation business, was used to an 'I'll expect you when I see you' type of relationship.

Cooking is one of my favourite pastimes. Not only do I find it therapeutic, but some of my best ideas had come to me while I was preparing a meal. I kept a notebook and pen on the unit nearest the worktop. I had three hungry men to feed so, tonight, quantity was as important as quality. I made a beef stew with red wine, garlic and olives. It went down a treat.

After we had eaten Michael fished his notebook from his pocket and started his report.

Michael had been ready to follow the truck, particularly if it looked as if the other two had not managed to take some photographs. Sam and David had been standing on the footpath opposite the junction, looking as if they were chatting. When I stalled the car, the two lads ran into the middle of the road. Sam concentrated on the driver's side of the cab and David photographed the front. Both had switched on the motorised winders on their cameras and each had used up a roll of thirty-six exposures in a matter of seconds. They legged it into the car park and dived in through the back door of our van. When Michael saw the truck take off after me, he followed. He saw the truck turn left on the main road. The traffic light was green when Michael reached the junction. He saw the truck had stopped on the left-hand side of the road. He drove past, and pulled into the empty driveway of a house farther up the road. He couldn't see my car anywhere.

'What would you have done if someone came out of the house?' said David. I don't think this was simple curiosity; I think he was looking for pointers from someone who had had over twenty-five years' experience in the gardaí.

'Sure, wasn't I just calling on my old colleague Paddy and I must have mistaken the house,' he said, grinning from ear to ear.

Michael continued, 'I knew the boys had got some photographs so I let him go. I thought I should stay around the area in case there was any trouble.'

Michael always called the guys 'boys'; he wasn't being patronising, it was simply the age differences.

'Poor old Cliff and his missus, they must have been scared out of their wits.'

Michael gestured to get our attention. 'Well, he wasn't. A normal person would have been gobsmacked; a normal person would have sat there scratching his head, saying, "What the hell?" or whatever. He didn't. He took off after you!'

Maybe he was right. I would have to remember his point of view if I had any future dealings with Cliff.

'It's down to the photographs now – depends on what we got and how clear they are. We won't know until Monday,' said Sam, always the pragmatist.

It was well after eleven when the lads left.

Sam and I went through the photographs on Monday afternoon. Twenty-two were clean, crisp shots; another eleven were usable.

On Wednesday, Sam delivered our report and the photographs to our clients.

———

I glanced from the sergeant to the inspector. 'That's about it, I guess. He has to be connected in some way with your man in Ashford. It's the only job I've used my own car for since I bought it.'

'You've forgotten one thing, Shirley.' The inspector paused. 'You haven't told us his full name or actual address.'

Trading information is second nature to me. 'Maybe if I knew the name of your man, it might ring some other bells?'

He told me the name. It meant nothing to me. I gave him Cliff's full name and address.

Epilogue
I don't know if the information I gave to the detectives had helped them in their enquiries. They didn't tell me.

What I do know is that Cliff was still around the following May. His case was listed for hearing in a Circuit Court in Scotland. My clients wanted me to attend the hearing to give evidence, if the case wasn't settled.

Sam drove me to the airport. We had some coffee and croissants and then joined the check-in queue for the flight. We chatted over my arrangements; a settlement consultation was fixed for midday and the case was listed for hearing at ten o'clock the following morning. I was booked into a hotel about halfway between the airport and the city centre.

The queue was moving slowly. I nudged Sam. 'Shit, that looks like Cliff up there.' I pointed ahead of me. He was about ten places in front of me in the queue. Sam went to the far side of the bank of check-in desks to get a look at the man's face. He sauntered past the queue on his way back to my position.

'It's him, okay; he's wearing a slipper on his right foot and he's got a walking stick!'

Cliff had sustained an injury to his right leg and foot in his accident.

'So he's still playing the old soldier.'

We watched Cliff as he approached the departures barrier. He leaned on the stick quite heavily and limped as he walked. At the barrier, Sam gave me a hug.

'Just keep out of his way, you'll be okay. Ring me when you land.'

I couldn't help it, it's second nature to me, but I watched Cliff as he moved around the departure lounge. There was absolutely nothing wrong with his gait. He even left his stick resting on his holdall and walked normally when he went to the bar to buy a pint. Obviously, he was being cautious while he was in the main departures hall. I kept my head down and eventually boarded the plane behind him. He made his way to the back; I sat at the window seat in the second row. An hour after take-off, we were taxiing along the runway towards the terminal building in Scotland.

I phoned Sam to let him know that everything was okay and to fill him in on the difference in Cliff's movements after he had gone airside, and took a taxi straight to the courthouse, where I met one of the insurance company's claims inspectors who worked at the Scottish office. We went into a consultation room and I filled him in on what I had observed at Dublin Airport and the difference in Cliff's gait once he went airside. The advocate joined us and ran through my evidence before going to meet with his opposite number.

Obviously they engage in horse-trading in Scottish courts as well as Irish courts. The offers and rejections went back and forth, and at a quarter to three Cliff's case was settled.

My return flight to Dublin was booked for ten fifteen the following night. I could have stayed on and spent the remainder of the afternoon and the next day sightseeing around the city, but

I felt uncomfortable. Bearing in mind the information – limited as it was – I had received from the two detectives back in Dublin, I didn't want to be in the same town as Cliff, particularly away from home and without the comfort of backup and support from the lads. I took a taxi back to the airport and managed to change my booking to the next flight to Dublin, which was leaving just after ten that evening. I phoned Sam to tell him about the change of plan.

I kept an eye out for Cliff, and even though he didn't materialise I didn't relax until we landed at Dublin. I couldn't help but smile when I walked through the doors into the arrivals hall. My three 'boys' were waiting for me on the other side of the barrier.

I was glad to be home.

10 | TILL DEATH US DO PART

They're known in the business as 'matrimonials'. God, how I hated those cases.

Why?

First of all, they usually involved night work and I'm a morning person, usually up shortly after five; and if I don't get my usual eight hours, I can be just a bit difficult to handle the following day. Additionally, a late job interfered with my early morning jobs the next day. The day jobs were my bread and butter.

They also usually involved what we called 'lay clients', Mr or Mrs Joe Public, who have spent too much time watching PI movies or television series or reading about imaginary PIs, and have no idea of what the work really entails. Dealing directly with Mr or Mrs Joe Public can be extremely difficult. The difference between matrimonials and, say, insurance scams is that, by the very nature of the beast, the erring spouse will go to great lengths to cover their tracks, whereas the 'scammer' usually goes about their normal routine and activities, apparently oblivious to the fact that insurance companies regularly use private investigators to check the validity of compensation claims.

Third, from a selfish point of view I found them about as interesting as watching paint dry. Remember, this was in the days before divorce, and even legal separations were not the norm. So what was the point? If someone was in a miserable relationship and had lost trust in their partner, why compound their misery by giving them the gory details of infidelity?

Last, and by no means least, trying to get paid for the work could be like pulling teeth. In the late 1970s/early 1980s, the average Mr Joe Public was probably earning about £200 a week; Mrs Public might be relying on whatever savings she had managed to squirrel away out of the housekeeping money. At the usual rates, I could be charging them the equivalent of one month of their net wages for one week of night surveillance. That aspect did not sit happily with me.

I considered myself lucky; the bulk of my bread and butter work came from insurance companies, semi-state utilities, corporations, etc. I did not have to rely on 'private work', and over the twenty years I worked as a private investigator, I could count on the fingers of one hand the number of 'matrimonials' I worked on.

———

Although it was only mid-morning, it was so dark that I switched on my desk lamp. The rain was bucketing down and I was really glad that I was working in the office and not stuck on a surveillance job. It was March 1980 and I had been in business as a private investigator for just over a year.

I was due to give evidence in court the following day, in a case of insurance fraud, and was sitting at my desk reviewing the files when Christine came into my office.

'There's a Mr T in reception. He hasn't got an appointment, can you see him?' she asked.

I scowled in her direction.

'He seems very nice,' she said.

Taking the hint that she thought I should see him, 'Okay,' I said, and turned over the file so that the name of the case wouldn't be visible. 'Show him in.'

He stood just inside the door of my office as if unsure about what to do next. He was small, about five foot five, of slight build and with dark hair. He was neatly dressed in navy slacks, blue shirt and navy tie. He looked to be in his mid-fifties.

'Would you like some tea or coffee?' I asked, and indicated that the chair on the other side of my desk.

'No thanks.' His voice was quite timid.

'What can I do for you?' I asked, when he had sat down.

He told me his life story; at least it felt like his life story. He had married when he was forty-four years old; his wife was four years older; they had no children; he worked as a driver of a van for the local authority in his area; his wife did not work outside the home; he was home from work by four thirty each afternoon, Monday to Friday; they occasionally went out for a meal or to the pictures. It sounded as if he had rehearsed his story over and over again.

I interrupted him.

'Sounds like a nice solid lifestyle – but you have a problem?' I asked.

Silence.

'I can't try to help you if you don't tell me the problem,' I continued.

'I think she's having an affair.'

Oh no, a matrimonial, I thought.

I could have, and maybe should have, said at that point that I don't do matrimonials, but he looked so miserable I took pity on him.

'Hang on a minute,' I said.

'You've told me that you spend every evening, every weekend, every spare minute you have together; the only time you're apart is when you go to work – right?'

He nodded.

'So when is she having the affair?' I asked.

'During the day, in the mornings.'

'In your home?' I asked incredulously.

'Oh, no.' He paused. 'She meets him somewhere else.'

Because his work took him all round the area, he often

dropped back home, usually in the late morning, for a break. Apparently, over the previous two months, his wife had been absent on a number of occasions when he stopped off at home.

'Have you asked her where she goes?' I asked.

'I didn't like to.'

We went over his account of their lifestyle again. He didn't add anything or leave anything out.

I tried to talk him out of instructing a private investigator. It didn't work. So I then told him about our fees, the mileage rate and expenses. I had hoped the cost would turn him off the idea. He wouldn't budge.

We agreed an initial fee of £400. The usual deposit is fifty per cent up front, but I just couldn't ask him for that amount of money, which I thought was probably more than one week's wages for him. I asked him for £100, but he only had £50 on him. Oh God – this is a mistake, I thought, but got him to sign our pro forma contract anyway.

He hadn't thought of bringing in any photographs of his wife and agreed he would drop some in the following day.

The next day I got back from court just after three o'clock. We had had a good win, so I was in very good form.

'Mr T dropped in the photographs and another fifty quid,' Christine said as soon as I walked into her office. 'He brought some of his wedding photographs too,' she added. I could feel my good humour fading.

'Any recent facials?' I asked hopefully.

'Ah, yes – but I had to send him home to get them,' she replied.

I looked at the photographs Christine had handed to me.

'Bloody hell, she's like my mother.' She was short, only about five foot three, overweight, with short dark tightly permed hair and pushing sixty. 'Not your average affair material – but you never know,' I said.

I hadn't seen Sam to tell him about this latest case. I knew what his reaction would be. He felt the same way about matrimonials as I did. I went into the kitchenette, which was next to Sam's office, and made two mugs of coffee. Armed with the coffee and the last of the chocolate chip cookies, his favourite, I went into his office.

First I told him about our win in court. The claimant had been looking for £50,000 compensation but had settled for £15,000 and our clients, the insurance company in the case, were very happy.

Then I told him about Mr T. His reaction was as I had expected, but it was a done deal. We discussed the best way of proceeding with this investigation.

Bearing in mind Mr T's limited finances, I suggested that if we could tie in this job with other jobs in the same general area, not only could we split the mileage charges between the jobs but we could reduce his hourly rate, thereby maximising the number of hours we could spend on surveillance. Initially Sam baulked at the idea, but I persisted.

'He's a real nice guy and he's totally miserable,' I said. Another reason why I hate matrimonials – I'm inclined to empathise with people in difficult situations instead of being coldly professional.

He agreed in the end, as I thought he might. Accordingly, Mr T's budget would cover, give or take, fourteen hours' surveillance, or four mornings.

I telephoned Mr T, and he told me that he was taking Tuesday and Wednesday of the following week as holidays. We agreed that we would carry out the surveillance on Monday, Thursday and Friday from eight each morning until such time as Mr T went home for his late morning break. I assured him that if 'something' happened during the course of the surveillance, we would not be 'watching the clock' and sign off, we would stay with his wife until she returned home.

The couple lived in a medium-sized council housing estate off the N11 on the south side of Dublin. It comprised six small culs-de-sac off a perimeter road and was bounded on two sides by large green open spaces and playing fields. Their house was near the top of one of the culs-de-sac. As we had a fairly recent facial photograph of Mrs T, identifying her should not present too much of a problem.

On the Monday morning, we drove into the estate at 7.45a.m.

We located the house and noted Mr T's car parked outside and then drove back to the perimeter road and stopped near the entrance to the estate. Mr T would have to pass us on his way to work, as the only vehicular access to the estate was back out onto the n11. At 8.04a.m. he drove past. We moved up closer to the entrance to the cul-de-sac, where we could look across and see the front door of the house. As Mrs T couldn't drive, we had to cover the possibility that someone might call to the house or that she might be collected by car.

It was a cold, wet March morning. To avoid drawing unnecessary attention, you can't leave the engine running to stay warm; to minimise the windows fogging up, you have to leave a couple of windows open a small amount; it is not recommended that you bring a thermos of hot drink with you, in case you need to use the bathroom in a hurry. In other words, static surveillance can be a pretty miserable job on a wet, cold morning.

We didn't have to wait long. It stopped raining just after 9.00a.m. and Mrs T emerged from the house at 9.20a.m.

She was wearing a blue/light grey tweed full-length overcoat and black flat shoes, and she was pulling a wheeled shopping bag behind her.

'Don't think she's going for a fling,' Sam said as we watched her walk to the top of her cul-de-sac. She turned right.

'That's a dead end,' I said.

Sam moved the car forward so that we could keep her in sight while I opened the Dublin street map to the relevant page. Near the bottom of the perimeter road, she veered to her left and into the park.

'I'll go after her,' I said as I pinpointed our location on the map. 'There's another housing estate over there,' I added as I got out of the car.

I kept a good gap between us while we were crossing the park, but I quickened my pace as we approached the other side. I had to close the gap and keep her in my line of sight when we entered the other estate, in case she turned into one of the side roads.

Mrs T plodded on. She stayed on the main road of that estate. I let the gap widen again. There were no other people walking on the road; if she turned around for any reason, there was no doubt she would see me in the distance. As we approached the end of the road, I quickened my pace. She turned left and out of sight. I broke into a run. As I came around the corner, I had to jam on the brakes. Mrs T was standing at the edge of the kerb less than twenty feet ahead of me, looking up and down as if checking for traffic.

The best that could be said of that little episode was that I got a good look at her face. But she had seen me close up, too – not so good.

Sam had driven round and was parked about fifty yards away. I hurried past Mrs T, without making any eye contact, as if I was late for something. As I got into the car Sam said, 'There's a church down there; maybe she's going to Mass.'

Looking round, I replied, 'Maybe she's going over there', pointing to the shopping centre on the other side of the road.

Mrs T crossed the road heading for the shopping centre. This time Sam followed on foot and I drove into the car park.

We always carried a couple of spare jackets on the back seat of both cars. I pulled off my jacket and put on a navy sleeveless fleece. My hair had been tied back in a ponytail so I let it down to make a superficial change in my appearance. I knew that, since Mrs T had seen me quite close up, I would have to avoid a face-to-face meeting with her if at all possible. I ran to the main door of the shopping centre and spotted Sam almost immediately, standing outside a hardware store. I greeted him with, 'This is a flippin' waste of time.'

'Maybe not, she's gone in there,' indicating the coffee shop. Sam had walked past and looked through the shop window. Mrs T was sitting at a table in a corner of the coffee shop, with her back to the window and the door. She was on her own.

Sam took off his jacket, before we went in. I sat at a table with my back to Mrs T. Sam went to the counter and ordered coffees and scones. 'I'll bring them down to your table,' said the assistant. Sam took out his wallet to pay.

'You can pay later,' said the assistant, smiling at Sam.

'Ah, sure, I might as well pay you now,' Sam replied, handing her a fiver.

It is a 'house rule' that we pay up front in these situations. We had learned the hard way. In the early days, one of our surveillance subjects, whom we had followed into a café, had left quite suddenly – nothing to do with us following him. But we hadn't paid for our food. While I followed the subject, Sam had to jump the queue at the counter, thereby drawing attention to himself. Me legging it out of the café after our man hadn't helped the situation. We learned a lesson that day about keeping a low profile and being discreet!

Sam was facing Mrs T's table. She still had no tea or coffee in front of her. Just after ten o'clock, another woman joined her at the table. They had a pot of tea and two pastries. They looked like two middle-aged women enjoying a natter.

The coffee shop was filling up with customers and tables were getting scarce. We were just sitting there with dregs of coffee in the cups in front of us. We couldn't risk having more coffee, which could lead to loo problems later on. A waitress had already tried to clear our table on two occasions and each time, as she approached, I had lifted my cup as if I was still finishing my coffee. We decided to leave. It was 10.45a.m.

We waited near the front door of the shopping centre, where we could watch the door of the coffee shop. Mrs T and the other woman emerged at 11.00a.m. They stood talking outside for another five minutes. Sam took photographs of them as they chatted.

When you're doing surveillance, not only do you have stay focused on the subject, you also have to be alert to other people and aware of your surroundings.

'Bloody security man is watching us,' I muttered to Sam. I knew what was coming next. I hated doing it; I found it embarrassing, but needs must. I moved around so that I was standing between Sam and the two women. Sam pointed the camera in my direction as if taking photographs of me, but in fact continued to take photographs of the two ladies over my left shoulder. I smiled broadly and said through gritted teeth, 'Are you nearly finished?' The security man appeared to lose interest and sauntered off in the opposite direction.

The two ladies parted company. Mrs T headed farther into the shopping centre and her companion turned to go out of the main door. Mrs T headed straight to the supermarket, depositing her shopping bag against the wall of the aisle at the back of the checkouts and collecting a small shopping trolley. Off she headed down the first aisle.

With a grin, I said to Sam, 'Your turn!' He glared at me, shrugged his shoulders, and without a word turned away towards the trolley bay.

Supermarket shopping was a bit of a private joke between the two of us. Sam's mother and mine lived four doors from each other and have been close friends since the early 1960s. (And strangely, even though they knew each other so long, they still addressed each other as 'Mrs Sleator' and 'Mrs Carroll'!) Neither of them could drive so when we were available, either Sam or I would drive them to the local supermarket for their weekly shop. Much as we loved them both, it was torture! They knew the price of everything in the store. Every week, they would check prices, stand and discuss any price increases they had found (whether or not they were buying the items); and their shopping, which should have taken about thirty minutes, could last anything up to an hour and a half. I had taken the mums shopping the previous Saturday, so now it was Sam's turn.

I loitered, without intent, around the noticeboard on the back wall and then around the magazine and newspaper stand. I glanced at my watch periodically and kept an eye out for the store detective and uniformed security man. I felt I had been hanging around for too long. Maybe they would think I was watching the tills or something. I felt 'obvious' and therefore uncomfortable.

Mrs T's shopping bag was still propped up against the back wall, along with another seven similar bags, all neatly lined up. God, what a waste of time, I thought.

It was ten to twelve when she appeared, pushing her trolley towards the checkouts. She had had enough time to shop for an army, but her trolley was less than half full. She got in line at one of checkouts.

Sam appeared, minus his trolley. He went to the express

checkout. In the fifty minutes he had been in the supermarket, he had selected three packets of chocolate chip cookies. He handed me the receipt: tea, coffee, milk – and biscuits – were staff refreshments and therefore tax deductible.

Mrs T headed back in the direction of her home, which was nearly half a mile away. Since Sam had stayed with her in the supermarket, it was my turn to follow her on foot. In any case, a woman walking through a park on her own could be a bit apprehensive if she spotted a lone male walking behind her.

I think I might have spotted the van before she did. Instead of staying on the tarmac path across the open space, where Mrs T was walking, I had moved out to my right onto the grass so I had a more direct line of sight to the main road of her estate. The van was parked on the perimeter road on her estate, near the top of her cul-de-sac. Mrs T was sauntering along and, as she rounded the bend in the path, she must have spotted it. She increased her speed. I could see that she was hurrying. She stepped off the kerb. The shopping bag thumped down onto the road, wobbled precariously and toppled over. She just stood there.

I did something you should never do when carrying out surveillance; make a direct approach to a target. I trotted over to her. She looked as if she was about to burst into tears.

'Let me help you,' I said and bent over to lift the bag into its upright position.

'Thanks very much, dear,' she said.

'You okay?' I asked

'I'm grand, thanks,' came the reply. She hurried off and around the corner into her cul-de-sac.

Sam was parked about a hundred yards up the road. As I got into the car he said, 'What did you do that for?'

I said nothing and stared straight ahead. There was a niggling thought at the back of my mind. Nothing specific. 'There's something not quite right here,' I said eventually.

We had agreed with Mr T that we would maintain surveillance until he returned home for his break in the late morning. He was home now, so we left.

Mr T phoned at four o'clock that afternoon and I gave him a summary of the morning's surveillance.

'She left the house at nine twenty a.m. and walked to the shopping centre; between ten and eleven she had coffee with a woman; then she did her supermarketing and came straight home,' I said.

'That's all? You're sure?' he asked.

'That's all,' I replied.

'You'll do it again on Thursday?' he asked.

'No problem,' I said.

What I didn't tell him was that it was going to be very difficult for me to be near Mrs T for the next few days because of the shopping bag incident.

The surveillance on Thursday was a complete waste of time. We took up our observation position at 7.45a.m. Mr T drove out at 8.04a.m.

'Bang on time,' I said to Sam. 'He left at exactly the same time the other morning.'

Mr T returned at 10.45a.m. in the van. 'Nice job if you can get it – he's done two hours' work,' Sam said.

'Okay, let's go,' I said. But I still had that niggling, apprehensive feeling about this job. I rang Christine so that she could report to Mr T before we got back to the office. 'Three hours wasted,' I told her. 'No one entered or left while he was out of the house.'

The early part of the surveillance on Friday morning was exactly the same as the previous Monday. Mr T headed off at 8.04a.m. and Mrs T came out of the house at 9.20a.m. and headed off across the park. This time we scooted out of the estate, turned left down the N11 and right again up past the church and into the other estate. We could see Mrs T approaching in the distance. We pulled into the car park at the shopping centre and watched her cross the road and go into the shopping centre, where she headed straight for and entered the coffee shop. It was 9.50a.m. The same woman she had met the previous Monday joined her.

Sam bought the *Irish Times* and we sat on a nearby bench reading the paper while keeping an eye on the door of the coffee shop. Just after eleven the two women emerged. They parted company and once again Mrs T went to the supermarket. She headed for home at 11.45a.m.

That day, Mr T didn't appear until 2.20p.m. He was driving his own car, which meant that he had finished work for the day. We had been on the job for eight solid hours that day alone and all our subject had done was have coffee with a friend and buy groceries. I did a quick calculation: apart from the original interview time and administration work, we had been on this job for a total of nineteen hours, five hours over the agreed budget. At that stage Mr T owed us for fourteen hours' work: the deposit he had paid only covered the first five hours at the reduced fee rate.

The photographs we had taken on Monday had been processed and printed, I spent part of the Friday afternoon dictating the report and Christine typed it up. My report could have consisted of two paragraphs but Mr T had struck me as a fussy and obsessive type of person, so I spelled everything out in my report.

Mr T called to the office the following Tuesday. Neither Sam nor I was there so Christine went through my report with him. He was still adamant that his wife was having an affair, despite the lack of evidence. He told Christine he would send on a cheque for the balance of the fees that he owed. I'm still waiting!

———

We managed to avoid matrimonials in the intervening years, apart from two that I recall, neither of which enhanced our opinion of this type of work.

The first involved Doberman dogs – I don't even want to think about it.

The second I had agreed to take because a solicitor, who was one of our bigger clients, asked me to. He acted for the wife, who lived on the outskirts of a city in the south of the country with her husband. The husband spent a lot of time in Dublin, particularly at weekends. The problem was that his wife didn't know what he was doing or where he was staying during these weekend trips. The telephone contact number he had given her was purportedly for the Burlington Hotel, but the number wasn't listed in the telephone directory under the Burlington.

His pattern of movements on Fridays was quite regular. He would come home from the office about one o'clock, have lunch and then head off for Dublin around three or three thirty, supposedly to 'meet the lads'/go to a rugby match on Saturday and/or to play golf. He would return home on Sunday night.

Sam and I set off on a Friday morning. We arrived at 2.10p.m., and I telephoned the wife.

'He went early – he's gone about fifteen minutes,' she told me. The language used in our car simply does not bear repeating.

'If he's really heading for Dublin, maybe he'll take the N9,' I said to Sam. 'Maybe we could catch up with him.'

Sam looked at me and grinned. He really enjoyed driving. I felt safe enough with him driving – well, I had to, I had no option most of the time, and, anyway, he is a far better driver than me, particularly at speed. I'm just too careful at times. He needed no further encouragement and took off.

Sam's job was to drive, mine was to try and spot our friend's car as we overtook traffic ahead. We knew the make, model, colour and registration number of his car.

I had to consciously stop myself from being a back seat driver and watching the road as well as the cars we were overtaking. It was a bit of a hare-brained idea. You couldn't attempt to do it nowadays, what with the Garda Traffic Corps, penalty points and the sheer volume of traffic. Most of the journey was a bit of a haze for me. But we did eventually catch up with him.

We had just passed Crookstown on the N9. Up ahead were three cars and a Guinness lorry laden with kegs. It was a fairly straight stretch of road. Sam said something like, 'Check this lot,' as he moved out to overtake. We passed the first and second cars; I checked the third car, the one behind the lorry.

'That's him!' I yelled.

'Oh, fuck!' said Sam.

A tractor was approaching on the other side of the road.

He had no choice but to cut in, immediately in front of our friend, who blasted his horn and flashed his headlights. He kept his hand on the horn. You couldn't really blame him; after all, we had cut in right in front of his car.

The tractor passed and Sam, this time checking carefully, decided to overtake the lorry, which we did safely. The road was clear ahead.

Next thing, our pal drew level with us and blasted his horn again. Sam looked over, raised his hand in a gesture of apology and mouthed the word 'sorry'.

Our subject drove on ahead and suddenly jammed on his brakes. Sam did likewise. His car gathered speed. Sam kept a fair distance between the two cars. The other guy jammed on his brakes again. Sam braked hard. He took off again. Sam slowed down to about forty miles an hour to increase the distance between the two cars.

We were about six miles from Kilcullen when we came around a bend in the road and there he was. His car was stationary and he was standing at the back, leaning on the boot with his arms folded across his chest. Sam slowed down to a crawl. I think he was trying to decide whether or not to swing out to our right and go past. Our friend walked towards the car. If he was trying to scare us, he was doing a bloody good job!

I had the file on my lap and stuffed it up my jumper. If he saw his name on a file cover, I reckoned he would lose it altogether. Sam hit the central locking on the key fob. He opened the driver's window just a crack. Sam started to apologise, but it was pointless. We sat in silence and took the verbal abuse – including details of what he would have done to Sam if there weren't 'a lady present'. He marched back to his car and took off. I suppose you could describe his behaviour as road rage.

One of the things I really like about Sam is that he usually keeps his cool very well; he doesn't get flustered about things and has a great sense of humour.

He looked at me and, scratching his head à la Stan Laurel, said, 'I guess we've blown that one.'

Our solicitor client was most understanding. I gave him the name of one of my colleagues in the business.

Ray and Liz

Those two cases just reinforced my dislike of matrimonials and my desire to avoid them at all costs.

We did do another matrimonial, though. It was 1996. A mutual friend, Frank, telephoned Sam to tell him about the difficulties another friend of his was experiencing. Frank asked if we would be prepared to undertake some work on the case. My immediate reaction was, No, absolutely not!

That night, Sam met Frank and his friend Ray for a couple of pints. The next day, he told me some of Ray's problems. I eventually agreed to look at the case, but only on the basis that we used technology to gather the initial information.

There have been huge advancements in all sorts of technology since the 1990s. Back then, the first mobile phone we had installed in one of our cars had cost £2,000; there was no such thing as the Internet; our first computer had been an Amstrad which needed five or more floppy disks just to get kick-started. Security devices, such as voice-activated recorders and listening devices, could not be obtained in Ireland, but we had bought a selection of these technical aids at trade shows in the UK.

Ray and his wife Liz had been married for nearly fifteen years. They lived in an upmarket housing estate in north County Dublin. He worked full time and she worked four mornings a week from nine to one. They had two children who attended the local primary school. Their daily routine was just that; routine.

Ray was up first each morning. He brought his wife up a mug of coffee, sorted out the breakfast cereals, made the girls' packed lunch, got himself ready for work, and the family would sit down to breakfast about seven forty-five. He would leave for work just after eight.

Liz would drop the children to school and continue on to the doctor's surgery where she worked as a receptionist. She would collect the girls from school at one fifteen.

The couple's social life was uneventful; they went everywhere together except for once a month when Ray would have a night out with the lads and Liz would have a separate night out with the girls.

'What about your personal – your sexual – relationship?' I asked.

Maybe the bluntness of my question had caught him by surprise. He looked uncomfortable. I hoped he didn't think that I wanted all the gritty details. I didn't: I just wanted an indication that all was well in the bedroom department.

'Grand,' he replied.

I made a mental note to ask Sam to talk to him about that side of his life. Maybe he was the type of guy who didn't blab about his personal relationships, or maybe he didn't like the idea of providing this type of information to a woman.

'At least, that's the way it used to be,' he continued. Based on what he told us, things had changed noticeably in the previous couple of months. His wife's attitude towards him had changed completely. She had become distant and gave him the 'silent treatment'. When she did talk to him she was bitchy and she constantly picked rows with him over simple things. The family breakfast was a thing of the past, now it was just Ray and the girls.

The school had telephoned him twice in the previous four weeks to say that Liz had not arrived to pick up the girls at lunchtime. On each occasion Ray had left work and collected the girls and on each occasion the house was empty when he returned home. When Liz turned up some hours later, she blankly refused to give any explanation whatsoever. She just wouldn't discuss it.

He described the changes in their social lives. They never went out together now. Liz's monthly night out with the girls had increased to at least two evenings a week. She had gone out on the previous two Friday nights and each time hadn't returned home until the Saturday afternoon. Once again, she had simply blanked him, no explanation, feeble or otherwise.

To my mind, either Liz had lost her marbles or she was having an affair. Or both. I suggested that the first step would be to install a listening device (a bug) on his home telephone. This should give us enough leads to work with, depending, of course, on the information obtained during any recorded telephone calls. I explained what would be involved.

We had previously taken legal advice about the use of such equipment in the context of the Wireless and Telegraphy Act, and certain procedures had to be followed. Ray told me that his was the sole name on the account with Telecom. I asked him for a copy of two previous telephone bills to verify this fact, which he subsequently dropped in to the office. Apart from our standard form of contract, he also signed an additional indemnity form relating to the use of the equipment.

Sam always looked after all the technical side of our business: videos, cameras and surveillance equipment. I generally went along to assist with installations. We had arranged to meet Ray at his house at ten thirty on Tuesday morning. Ray's wife was at work until one, so access to the house would not be a problem. On Monday afternoon, Sam checked his 'goodie bag', as I called it. This bag contained various pieces of equipment, tools, electrical tape and all the bits and bobs that we needed to install surveillance devices.

Most people would probably be quite shocked by the number of different types of equipment available, even at that time, the mid-1990s. Take, for example, covert cameras. Pinhole camera lenses were so small they could be hidden in bog standard smoke detectors, the type that are installed in most homes, in small wall-mounted passive infrared (PIR) motion detector units, in operational wall clocks, in men's tie pins, in briefcases.

Audio transmitting and recording units came in a range of sizes and types. They could be fitted in a normal double adaptor that you might use anywhere in the house, or a four-way adaptor, the type that has an oblong block of four electrical sockets with a lead and a three-point plug at one end. Then there are single or double wall sockets, which can be swapped with normal electrical wall sockets. All of these specialist items of equipment, which also contain transmitters, can be used for their normal purpose. You can plug your electric kettle or any appliance into one of these gadgets and it will operate normally.

Bugging a telephone needed more equipment and greater skill. Most homes have a number of extensions around the house. If calls made from or taken on any of the extensions are to be recorded, it is essential that the device is installed at the first point of entry of the phone line into the house: you can't just bug an extension.

We arrived, as arranged, at Ray's house at ten thirty on Tuesday. Even though we knew his wife would be at work and wasn't due home until about 1.30p.m., we are conscious of 'sod's law' – what can go wrong will go wrong – so we like to be in and out as soon as possible.

The first point of entry of the phone line was in the hall. The transmitter had to be installed at this point.

The transmitter was approximately an inch square and half an inch deep. It was a simple matter of unscrewing the cover of the phone connection, inserting the transmitter, connecting up the leads and replacing the cover. The transmitter has a range of up to a hundred metres. The next part of the installation was the receiver and the vox – the voice-activated recorder. This equipment had to be located within the transmitter's range.

We checked the various rooms on the ground floor of the house and decided the kitchen was the best location. Whilst the receiver is only the size of a packet of cigarettes and the vox is the size of a small Walkman, obviously they had to be hidden from view. Ray put the kettle on to make some coffee while we considered the various options. There was a large free-standing fridge-freezer in the corner of the kitchen. Unless Ray's wife was extremely house-proud it was unlikely that she would pull it out to clean behind it, so I suggested that the remainder of the equipment should be taped to the back of the fridge-freezer. The lads agreed and the receiver and vox were taped securely to the back of the appliance.

We spent the next hour testing the equipment, making calls and answering each extension. Everything was being recorded.

We gave Ray a small playback machine, mini-headphones and a box of tapes, which he locked in his briefcase. Each tape would record up to six hours. All Ray had to do was pull out the fridge a few inches, remove the tape, mark it with the date and time and then insert a new tape. He would have to do this each day. We made him practise this procedure until he could have done the job blindfolded and with one hand.

I suggested that he should look after the installation and removal of the tapes and we would listen to and transcribe the tapes, but he was adamant that he would listen to the tapes and pass on any relevant information to us that warranted any follow-up investigations. I think he was reluctant for us to hear at first hand any of his wife's conversations. Not forgetting our previous experiences with Mr T, I did wonder if there was an ulterior motive behind his decision. Still, he was the client: he was paying the bill, so it was his choice.

It was then ten past one; his wife was due home within twenty minutes. We had to get out of there, just in case she returned home earlier than expected.

I didn't expect to hear from Ray quite so soon. On Wednesday morning, Christine told me that he had rung at 9.10a.m. looking for Sam. He didn't want to talk to me. Sam was out on a job, so Christine told him that she would get Sam to call him back. Christine does not give our mobile numbers to anyone. Since Sam was doing surveillance that morning we didn't know exactly what he was up to at that precise time, so I asked Christine to text him to let him know that Ray was looking for him.

Sam phoned at eleven thirty to say that Ray would be calling into the office at half past one and that he would be back in the office before then.

Sam and Ray arrived simultaneously. Christine told me later that they had spoken quietly to each other in the corner of our reception area for a few minutes before coming into my office.

Ray was ashen-faced, clearly upset and apparently very, very angry. He plonked the tape on my desk. I left it sitting there for a while and then picked it up.

'Tell Shirley what has happened since we saw you yesterday,'

Sam said. Obviously Ray had given him a summary while they were talking in reception.

'I can't listen to this stuff,' Ray said quietly.

'That's okay,' I replied.

He told me that when he got up that morning, the first thing he had done was to remove the tape from the vox at the back of the fridge-freezer and lock it in his briefcase. Then he had put in a new tape.

After breakfast with the children, he left for work at the usual time and on arriving at his office he decided to listen to the tape before any of his staff arrived. He had known from the position of the tape inside the cassette that something had been recorded. He listened to the first call, an incoming call from Liz's mother. It was general chit-chat about the kids, Liz's work and plans Liz had made to have lunch with her family the following Sunday. He had known nothing about the Sunday lunch plans and that annoyed him somewhat.

He said nothing more.

'And the next call?' I prompted.

'She rang some bloke called Robert,' he said.

Silence again. He looked as though he was trying hard not to cry.

'Do you mind if I listen to it?' I asked as gently as I could.

He said nothing.

I looked at Sam and hoped that our telepathy was operating as usual. I wanted Sam to do some 'guys together' stuff and keep him as calm as possible. I used Sam's office to listen to the tape. I brought my yellow legal notepad so that I could make notes as I listened. The first call was the conversation between Liz and her mother. It seemed innocuous enough except for one thing. Ray hadn't mentioned it so maybe he had missed the point. The Sunday lunch plan was that Liz would drop the kids off at her mother's at twelve thirty and pick them up around six. Obviously she had some plans for Sunday afternoon that didn't involve the kids.

The second call was an outgoing call to someone called Robert. People doing my job can and do get case hardened. We frequently see the worst of human nature and behaviour. Generally we don't shock easily. But that doesn't mean that we lose our ability to feel sympathy, understanding and concern for other people in difficulty. We just try to keep our own personal feelings completely separate from business. That's the theory, anyway.

As I listened to the conversation between Liz and this chap Robert, I realised that Ray would have been devastated at the content. The bulk of the conversation could be described as soft porn. There could be little doubt that there was a physical relationship between the two. It must have been truly awful for Ray to listen to that stuff. The possibility of finding something like this was why I had originally suggested to him that we do the listening and transcribing of the tapes.

The significant note I made on this part of the tape related to Liz and Robert's plans for the next Friday evening. It seemed that Liz was going to pick up Robert from his home at eight o'clock. I underlined the word 'home' heavily and beside it wrote '?Single – no transport?'

As I walked back through reception, Christine asked me if I wanted some coffee. I merely nodded. Sam and Ray already had mugs of coffee and they had demolished a packet of chocolate chip cookies.

Well, at least he's eating, I thought. I suddenly thought of my mum – her answer to all problems was 'a nice cup of tea and something to eat'. I'm surprised sometimes how one's thoughts and actions are so clearly related to early nurturing.

'Tell me,' I said, 'what are the arrangements for Friday evening?'

'She told me she's going out with the girls,' Ray replied. He seemed calmer now. Sam, who had gone through the trauma of marital separation only a year earlier, had obviously done his bit – man to man, so to speak.

The first thing we had to establish was whether or not Ray wanted to continue with the original plan. He was adamant that he did.

Next, the practical arrangements. Once again I suggested that we should listen to and transcribe the tapes. He agreed immediately. Ray would drop the tape into our letterbox on his way to work each morning. I would give him the 'edited highlights' (minus the gory details) by phone each afternoon. I knew I was giving myself additional work. I would have to do the listening and transcribing personally. Bearing in mind the content, I wouldn't be happy with Christine doing that part of the work; she was only nineteen years old and I didn't want to be responsible for possibly colouring her attitude to marriage and personal relationships at such a young age.

I listened to the Wednesday tape on Thursday morning.

There was the daily call from her mother. Nothing significant. Liz had mentioned her girls' night out on Friday with her friend Rosemary. Two notes went onto my yellow pad: '?Family don't know of marital difficulties?'; and '??Rosemary – ask Ray'.

There was a ten-minute outgoing call to our friend Robert: more graphic stuff, including descriptions of what they planned to 'do' on Friday night.

Another outgoing call, which lasted forty minutes, was to her friend Rosemary. They talked about clothes, shoes, hair, shopping – the usual trivial stuff! Then the topic of conversation turned to Ray. Rosemary asked Liz, 'What are you going to do about Ray?'

From that point I listened particularly carefully, using the pause button whilst I made notes and then letting the tape run on. I was really glad that Ray had agreed that I should listen to the tapes instead of him. Case-hardened as I am, I was frankly shocked at the turn in the conversation. The women were discussing how a barring order could be obtained to get Ray out of the house.

'But he's never laid a hand on me,' Liz said clearly.

'Doesn't have to,' came Rosemary's response. 'You only have to say that you're afraid of him – that you think he will hit you.' She then started to give Liz information about how this could be achieved. Before Liz applied to the courts for a barring order, she should complain about Ray to the local garda station a couple of times. All she had to do was to go into the station 'bawling your eyes out and the gobshites will believe you – simple'. It would be her word against his and the gobshites always believe the woman. The conversation continued in this vein for a few more minutes. Then, just like turning off a switch, they went back to shopping and clothes.

'What are you wearing tomorrow night?' Liz said.

Rosemary described her new clothes, Liz did likewise, and the conversation closed with 'See you tomorrow at eight.'

They appeared to be planning, or at least discussing, ways to get Ray out of the family home, not only by a fraudulent application for a barring order but also by Liz filing a criminal complaint against him. Not once during the conversation was any consideration given as to the affect this might have on Ray; of how he might end up in a holding cell in a garda station; of how depriving the two girls of their father would affect them; how, since mud sticks, the attitude of the 'no smoke without fire brigade' might affect Ray's employment and as a consequence his ability to financially support the children.

In my view, this was a dangerous turn of events and there was no indication of how soon these spurious complaints might be made. I phoned Sam and put him in the picture. I was in a bit of a quandary. Ray had to be informed as soon as possible and he needed to consult a solicitor. I thought about the best way of handling this information, but I wasn't sure how Ray would react; I simply didn't know him well enough.

Two other matters arose from that particular conversation. The first was that Liz should be placed under surveillance on Friday evening with a view to tracing Robert; and the second, merely an aside, Rosemary also appeared to be meeting up with Liz and Robert at eight.

That's what I took as the starting point for my conversation with Ray, suggesting surveillance should be carried out from seven o'clock the following evening. If we located Robert's home address we could make enquiries, which should provide background information on him. Ray readily agreed.

This led me nicely to the next point, the Sunday lunch arrangements with her mother.

'Based on the tape, it seems she's dropping off the girls at twelve thirty and picking them up again around six,' I said.

Silence on the other end of the phone.

I continued, 'So I suggest we should pick up surveillance from the mother's house from about twelve on Sunday? To see what she does for the afternoon.' In between a bit of cussing and swearing, he agreed.

I really wasn't sure how to handle the next bit of information, the conspiracy bit.

'Have you talked to your solicitor about your situation?' I asked.

'Not yet,' he replied

'Well, I think you should, and as soon as possible.'

'I had hoped that maybe we could sort it out and she'd come to her senses,' he said. 'Up to now, she had her head screwed on right.'

I could have said flippantly that it wasn't her head that was the problem, it was another part of her anatomy – but I didn't.

I broached the subject of barring orders and how easily, apparently, they could be obtained. He got the wrong end of the stick. 'I couldn't to that to her,' he said.

'No, but she could do it to you,' I replied.

I had no choice now. I had to warn him of the precarious situation he was in, so I gave him a broad outline of the conversation between Liz and Rosemary. He agreed to phone his solicitor immediately. I suggested that he told his solicitor that he was happy for us and the solicitor to talk about his case. He agreed. He gave the name of his solicitor and the name of the firm, and said he would phone me as soon as he had spoken to him.

I sat staring at the file cover, while I gathered my thoughts. My dislike of matrimonials was reinforced even more, if that was possible. And now, on top of it all, I had to deal with this particular solicitor. He was not a direct client of mine but I had had some dealings with him in the past as he had acted on behalf of one of my insurance company clients in compensation claims.

On the surface, he was a tall, attractive looking man in his mid-forties. However, in my view, his personality didn't match his appearance. He was pompous, arrogant, and rude to boot. I found that he showed 'due deference' to fellow members of the legal profession and to medical consultants; he was reasonably polite to other professionals – accountants, engineers, GPs and so on; he treated lay people (i.e. non-professionals) with a modicum of civility. And, bottom of the pile – his pile, anyway – came the gardaí and private investigators. He treated us like something offensive he had picked up on the sole of his shoe.

Pompous git, I thought, but I knew I would deal with him politely and try not to lose my rag, at least in the early stages.

'I couldn't get to talk to him. His secretary said the earliest he could see me was next Wednesday,' Ray said when he phoned back.

'I'll give him a ring and call you back,' I told Ray. Christine put her head round the door of my office.

'Coffee?' she said.

'Yes please, and can you hold my calls?' I replied.

I don't know why he took my call, but he did.

'Well, Mizzz Sleator, and what can I do for you?'

Not a lot, I thought to myself.

'We have a mutual client, Ray X, who needs to see you today,' I said, trying to keep an even tone.

'I'm very busy. I just can't see people at the drop of a hat,' he replied.

'Ray needs to see a solicitor today. If you can't or won't see him, then I'll get him a bloody good solicitor who will.' I think I probably barked that statement at him. I continued, 'I have uncovered evidence of a conspiracy against Ray, and by the end of the day he could be out of his home or in jail.' I knew I was pushing it a bit, but if that silly cow of a wife did act on her telephone conversation with Rosemary, it could happen.

After some humming and hawing he agreed to see Ray at eight o'clock the following morning in his office.

'Thank you, I'll tell Ray,' I said, and hung up.

I arranged to meet Ray outside the solicitor's office at eight the next morning.

Friday was going to be a long day. I would be meeting Ray at eight, doing the usual day's work, and then Sam and I would be putting Liz under surveillance from seven until . . . whenever.

Outside the solicitor's office, I said, 'Ray, you start by telling him what had been going on before you instructed us and I can deal with the evidence we have uncovered, okay?' He nodded.

Ray pressed the intercom button, the buzzer sounded and he pushed open the door. We walked down the hall and pushed open the door to the reception.

'Well, Raymond, and what can . . .' PG, which is what I mentally call him, stopped mid-sentence.

'Mizzz Sleator, I wasn't expecting you,' he added. The dog-poo expression was on his face.

Bet you weren't, I thought.

We went into his office. Ray started to tell of the events that had led to his instructing us. PG interrupted, 'I personally don't deal with family law matters.'

I touched Ray on the arm and said, 'I have taped evidence of a conspiracy against our mutual client . . .'

He interrupted again. 'Taped evidence is not admissible in a court of law.'

'It is in certain circumstances,' I retorted. 'If you follow the correct procedures, it may be introduced at the discretion of the judge.'

'With respect, Mizzz Sleator, I am the lawyer here', he replied.

This 'with respect' stuff, and even 'with the greatest respect', particularly in the legal profession, is a well-known code; what it actually means is, 'Listen, stupid, I know better than you.'

So I countered with, 'With the greatest respect, I have actually introduced such evidence in court. If this gets to a court situation and you do not know the correct procedures, I will be very happy to explain them to you.'

Steady on, Shirl, don't push your luck, I thought to myself.

In the most civil tone I asked, 'Would you like to hear the tape?'

'Not at the moment,' he said, and stuck out his hand and

gestured. I assumed that he was indicating that I should hand over the tape to him.

'I'll send around a copy and the transcript later this afternoon,' I said.

He stared at me. I think he was somewhat taken aback. I tried to ease the feeling of hostility in the air.

'I like to keep control of the chain of possession of evidence. That way I can categorically state that no one had access to or could tamper with the evidence, should it come to a court hearing. The only person I will give the originals to, be it videos, tapes or photograph negatives, is the judge involved in the case,' I said.

Referring to my handwritten notes, I read out the full details of the conversation between Liz and Rosemary, avoiding looking at Ray throughout.

When I finished I looked over at him and said, 'Sorry, Ray, now you know why I wanted you to go to your solicitor urgently.'

I suppose he could have yelled at me, but he didn't. He squeezed my hand and simply said, 'Thanks, Shirley.'

I stood up and said, 'I'll leave you guys to sort out the legalities. I'll see myself out.'

I stopped at the door and looked at the solicitor. 'I think the local gardaí should be informed,' I said. I checked my mobile phone and wrote down the name and number of the divisional garda superintendent on a page of my mini-notebook. I walked back to the desk and put the page down in front of the solicitor. 'That's his direct line number.' I said.

I tried to remember not to slam the office door on my way out.

Friday Night and Saturday Morning
On Friday night Sam picked me up at six fifteen. We drove straight to Ray's home and checked the driveway. Both cars were there. We re-checked the make, colour and registration number of Liz's car. One of the things we noted was that the offside brake lens was broken. Small things like that make life a little easier for us, as only one brake light would show red when she braked, making the car more easily identifiable.

Liz drove out of the estate at 7.40p.m. and followed the coast road heading for Dublin city. She turned right and continued into Raheny village. She pulled into the garage forecourt opposite St Anne's Park and went into the shop. I hopped out of our car and followed her in. As she looked at the wine display, I looked at the magazines. She approached the checkout with two bottles of red wine.

I left the shop. When I got back to our car, Sam was debating with himself whether to try taking some photographs, but there were too many people about, and, anyway, buying wine didn't in itself prove anything.

Traffic on the Howth Road was fairly brisk, but the phasing of the traffic lights down the road allowed a long enough gap in the traffic flow for her to make it back across the road, with us behind her. She turned left on Sybil Hill Road and then right onto Seafield Road. Just as she reached the school, her right-hand indicator flicked on and the red (and white) brake lights showed.

Sam pulled over to the left, hopped out of the car, crossed the road and headed in the direction of her car. He bent down and pretended to tie a shoelace, just so he could time his arrival beside the house while she was at the front door. As he passed, a woman opened the front door. She had long blonde hair styled in a loose perm. That was all he could see without actually stopping in front of the house. He kept walking.

I climbed over in the driver's seat. I drove up the road past him and pulled over. 'I think the house number is xx,' he said. He checked the number of the house directly opposite our car and then counted back the number of houses to the one Liz had entered.

'Yep. It's definitely xx,' he said.

We always keep a copy of Thom's Street Directory in each car. Thom's directory lists the names of occupiers of property, based on the electoral register. I checked the street listing.

'A Rosemary X is listed,' I said.

At half past eight Sam phoned Ray to see how he was keeping up. He seemed to be okay.

'We've followed her to a house in Clontarf. It looks like it's

Rosemary's house – we don't know about this Robert fella yet.'
Sam told Ray that he might not get a chance to phone again later,
but he would definitely call him in the morning.

At nine thirty Blondie left the house and walked down the
road in the direction of Clontarf Castle Hotel. We settled down to
await developments. We waited. How we waited. Once it got dark,
I was able to hop out of the car for a quick cigarette. Sam is a
reformed smoker and can't abide anyone smoking in his
company, particularly when cooped up in a car. I couldn't really
smoke in peace even outside the car because he was always on the
alert to make sure that the red glow from the top of my ciggie
wasn't visible in the dark.

Nothing of interest, literally nothing, happened until Blondie
arrived home at ten past one. We were debating whether or not
we should leave. Maybe Liz was going to spend the entire night
there; it was unlikely that she would be going on somewhere else
at that late hour. In the middle of our conversation, the porch
light came on.

It was 1.50a.m.

Liz came out of the house. We could see the silhouette of
another person but unless we turned the headlights on full beam,
which obviously we couldn't do, we wouldn't able to identify that
person.

Liz drove away. The silhouette went back into the house.

We followed Liz at a distance. She headed straight home.

It was twenty past two when Sam dropped me off at my
home. I have a policy of doing my detailed file notes immediately
after a period of surveillance, so it wasn't until three thirty that I
crawled into bed. I was asleep as soon as my head hit the pillows.

I overslept on Saturday morning and didn't wake until eight.
I was muzzy-headed and tired but it was my turn to do the
supermarket run with the two mums and I was due to pick them
up at ten thirty. But first I had to make some telephone calls
about Ray's case. The only information I had available at that
time was Rosemary's name and surname, the address in Clontarf
and the first name Robert. Not a lot to go on. I needed to check
the electoral register for the address, but the council offices were

closed for the weekend. I knew a copy of the register was kept in the local public library and in the local garda station, but I was still in my PJS and I was tight for time because of the mums' shopping expedition. So I decided to 'phone a friend'. He rang one of his colleagues based in Clontarf, who checked the electoral register. Rosemary was listed, as was Robert, and interestingly he had the same surname as her. Was he her husband, her brother, a relation? Hopefully I'd know on Monday. I made a few more calls to various contacts, who agreed to see what they could find out.

Both mums lived in Santry and shopped in a supermarket in Beaumont. When I picked them up I told them I had to check something out. As it happens, having two elderly ladies in your car is always good cover . . . who'd suspect you were carrying out surveillance? So we drove from Santry to Beaumont via Clontarf. The mums were quite used to taking the scenic route to destinations. They chatted away in the back seat like long-lost friends, even though they had probably seen each other the previous day.

There was no car at the Clontarf address.

Sunday

Sam picked me up at eleven thirty on Sunday morning. He had driven by the Clontarf house at two thirty that morning. The house was in darkness and there was no car in the driveway.

Liz's parents lived in a sprawling housing estate in Santry. The roads were narrow with mainly on-street parking except for corner houses, which had driveways, and some mid-terrace houses where the front gardens had been converted to off-street parking. So parking could be problematic for us.

Her family lived in one of the corner houses, so we decided to park on the side road. We managed to get a space that would give us a clear view of the front garden and approach to the front door. This was preferable to parking on the roadway at the front of the house, where Liz would have to pass us to get to the house.

She turned into the driveway at 12.35p.m. The girls jumped out of the back seat of the car and ran around the side of the house into the back garden. Liz followed.

At 12.45p.m. he reappeared from the back of the house, minus the kids. She drove directly to the house in Clontarf.

At 1.45p.m. Blondie emerged. She looked to be in her mid-twenties. A young boy of about nine immediately followed her, and behind him came a girl aged about six who was pushing a buggy containing a small child. Bringing up the rear was Liz, and behind her a tall, slim, dark-haired male. I didn't even have to look at Sam; I could hear the camera clicking away beside me.

It became apparent that Blondie and the kids were going out and Liz and the man were staying at the house. The man put his arm around Liz's shoulder, pulled her closer and started nuzzling or nibbling her ear.

'That's Robert, I guess,' I said.

'Take a look,' he said, handing me the camera so I could look through the telephoto lens.

'Bloody hell, he's about ten years younger than her. She's got herself a toy boy,' I said, and handed back the camera.

Liz and Robert went indoors.

By four o'clock, I needed a cigarette and Sam needed the bathroom. Clontarf Castle Hotel was at the bottom of the road, so Sam could have headed off to the hotel bathroom and I could have stayed and smoked as many cigarettes as I wanted while he was gone. That would have been the totally professional thing to do. But we had been there for four hours, any of the neighbours who might have noticed us would surely be getting nosy by now and, in any event, we were bored stiff. As I said before, it was like watching paint dry. We decided to take a chance and leave the area for a few minutes.

'The old pebble job, I suppose?' said Sam.

We got out of the car and sauntered along towards the house. It had a small front garden and the back of Liz's car was level with the front garden wall. As we drew level with the car, oops! I dropped my handbag, which just happened to be open. This was for the benefit of anyone who happened to be looking in our direction.

We both bent down to pick up the bits and pieces from the footpath and Sam took the opportunity to pick up a small pebble and place it on the top centre of the car's rear tyre. If the pebble was gone when we came back, we could reasonably assume that the car had been moved. We continued down the road. Sam went on ahead and I sauntered along, having a nice quiet smoke.

After about fifteen minutes we walked back up the road towards the house. When we got level with Liz's car, we couldn't do the old handbag trick again, so Sam simply bent down, apparently to tie his shoelace. He slipped his hand in under the wheel-arch. As he stood up, he opened his palm and there was the pebble. It looked as if the car hadn't been moved during our absence.

Sam had bought a Sunday newspaper in the hotel. Back in the car, we took it in turns; one watched the house while the other read the newspaper. At 5.25p.m., Liz and Robert emerged from the house. They stood talking and, well, snogging at the side of the car.

Sam had turned on the motor winder of the camera. The clicks were coming in rapid succession. The two changed position slightly and the rapid clicks started again. He used the entire roll of thirty-six exposures in a few seconds.

Liz reversed the car out on to the roadway. She tipped the side of a car that was parked on the opposite side of the road, straightened up and drove away. We followed her. She drove to Santry.

At six thirty, she emerged from the back of her parents' house with an older woman, presumably her mother. The two kids came running out a few seconds later. The girls piled into the back seat of the car, Liz gave the older woman a hug, got into her car and reversed out onto the road. With a beep of the horn and a wave, she drove off.

She drove straight home.

Monday

We decided to concentrate on finishing up Ray's investigation. The first thing I did when I got to the office was to start dictating my report on the case. While I made reference to the taped conversations, I did not quote the content; I would deal with those conversations separately by way of transcripts. I would get Christine to transcribe the conversations with Liz's mother; I would do the others. Sam's priority was to process all the photographs.

By eleven o'clock, I had received information from the various sources I had telephoned on Saturday, so I could then add that section to my report.

I was able to draw up a profile of Rosemary and Robert.

Rosemary was twenty-five years of age; she was a single parent. I had the names and dates of birth of her three children; the eldest had been born when she was just sixteen years of age. She admitted to receiving maintenance or support payments for the two younger children, and the fathers' names (two different men) were on file. She claimed that she did not know the identity of the father of the eldest boy. She had no history of employment. The house in Clontarf was rented and the area health board paid the rent each month. Robert was known to reside in the house.

Robert was twenty-three years of age. (Fourteen years younger than Liz.) His history of employment was chequered, to say the least. It appeared that he got his first job when he was sixteen, and he had held four jobs between the ages of sixteen and twenty. The longest period he had spent with one employer was thirteen months and the shortest four months. He had now been continuously unemployed for twenty-six months, during which time he had attended three FÁS retraining courses.

The report, transcripts and photographs were ready by lunchtime. Sam phoned Ray and arranged that he would meet us in the office at four that afternoon.

I went through the report with Ray. On the surface he seemed calm but withdrawn. None of us could figure out how or where Liz could have met Rosemary or Robert.

He told us that his solicitor had contacted the superintendent of the local garda station, and he had agreed to put the station on notice of the situation in case Liz tried the 'I'm afraid my husband is going to hit me' routine. He confirmed that his solicitor had drafted a letter to Liz but it wouldn't be sent until the solicitor had had an opportunity to read our report. Ray was going to take him the report once he left us.

I went through my itemised bill with him. He gave me a cheque on the spot and headed off to his solicitor. His parting words were, 'I'll let you know how I get on.'

———

We heard nothing from Ray for about seven weeks, when he joined Sam and his friend Frank for a few pints one Friday night.

Bear in mind that, as far as we were aware, he was the innocent party in this marriage breakdown.

He told Sam that he had moved out of the family home and into a rented apartment, as he didn't want to disrupt the girls' routine. Liz had apparently eventually agreed to let him see the children every weekend from three o'clock on Saturday afternoon and overnight until six o'clock on Sunday evening.

The couple's respective solicitors had just about concluded a separation agreement under which Ray would continue to pay the mortgage and utility bills for the former matrimonial home. They were now embroiled in an argument about maintenance for Liz herself. She wanted £2,000 per month, but Ray's solicitor was trying to insert clauses covering a reduction in the amount of maintenance for the wife in the event of Robert or any other man moving in to co-habit with her in the family home. Apparently, Liz felt that this was not reasonable!

Sam told me all this over coffee the following morning. 'Equity and justice, my foot,' was my response.

That was my last matrimonial investigation.

11 IT'S AN ILL WIND

We had been bickering with each other all morning. It wasn't just that it was a cold wet Friday in January; or that we had been cooped up together in the car for hours. In fact we should have been in quite a cheerful mood. We were on a routine insurance claim job. Nothing spectacular: just the same old tune, 'I can't work because of my accident.' But we knew he was doing something.

On three previous occasions, our subject, Larry, had left home at the same time and headed for Dublin, and on each occasion we had lost him. Sam had wanted to throw in the towel at that stage, but I'm stubborn, and we eventually agreed to have one more go. If we lost him this time, I'd admit defeat.

On our fourth attempt, Sam and I had successfully managed to track Larry from his home in Wicklow all the way to his destination in Dublin city centre. It had involved a bit of dicey driving and going through lights on amber, but we had achieved our objective. We had followed him to a run-down amusement arcade in the city centre situated on a narrow one-way street.

We had waited ten minutes after his arrival and then Sam had gone into the premises to see what he could see. It was an oblong-shaped premises with slot machines against the left- and right-hand walls; there was a door at the right-hand side of the end wall and a cash desk/kiosk beside that door. The shop window was blacked out so there was no natural light, and it was as dismal inside as outside. Amusement arcades are not exactly a hive of activity at eleven thirty on a wet January morning. There was one customer playing on a slot machine and a guy in the kiosk, neither of whom was Larry. Sam spent five minutes playing on one of the machines and left.

————

Back in the car we debated what to do next. Sam wanted to terminate surveillance and see if we could get any leads from enquiries; I wanted to stay, in case Larry left and went on somewhere else. Sam decided he wanted to go to McDonald's to buy a take-out meal. 'Will I get you anything?'

My reply was an abrupt 'No, thank you!'

As he was getting out of the car, I said, 'I'm going for a cigarette,' and climbed out. I sat on the side steps of a nearby church and lit up. I could clearly see the door to the arcade so I would see Larry if he emerged.

I knew the tension and arguing that morning were primarily my fault. I was in a foul humour and if I had been honest with myself, I should have stayed home from work that day and have taken out my mood on the furniture or something, but not on Sam. I was really angry with myself. How could I have been so thick, so stupid?

I had been in a relationship with a guy for over a year. We saw each other regularly, but hadn't lived in each other pockets. We saw each other maybe once a fortnight. We went out for a meal, drinks or a movie. Sometimes we stayed in and I would cook dinner. I had really thought our relationship suited both of us: we both worked long and irregular hours; we were comfortable with each other.

I hadn't actually seen Jeff for nearly six months but he phoned me regularly. He had volunteered for UN peacekeeping duties in Bosnia. We had talked on the phone two weeks earlier and told me he would be home within six weeks. Mug that I am, I had told him how much I was looking forward to seeing him.

It was sheer chance that I caught the liar out. I don't often watch television – I am more of a radio fan – so I don't know why I turned on the television the previous night. I flicked over to RTÉ 1 for the nine-o'clock news. I was making coffee in the kitchen when I heard a lead-in to a report about the first of our UN peacekeepers to return home from Bosnia. I went back into the sitting room and watched the guys arriving, still wearing their blue berets. The video clip cut to the waiting families and then there was footage of various guys with their families.

There he was, with a beaming smile on his stupid face. Jeff, with his arm around a pretty dark-haired woman and carrying a little girl of about three in his other arm. The lying toe rag said, 'It's great to be back.' How could I have been so stupid? Why had it never entered my head that he was married?

Sam had been gone about ten minutes and I was on my second cigarette. No one had entered or left the amusement arcade. At least it had stopped raining although I had been a bit hasty in storming out of the car; the arse of my trousers was damp from the wet steps.

Keeping one eye on the door of the Arcade, I amused myself by 'people watching', just watching the world go by. I glanced down the long, straight laneway that led away from the arcade. It was narrow, just about wide enough for one car, if the bins and rubbish bags hadn't been there.

Three young lads had just turned into the top of the lane. I glanced at the door of the arcade again.

I was looking up ahead to see if I could spot Sam approaching. I knew I would have to apologise to him for my bad behaviour earlier.

A thought struck me: in all the time I had been sitting on the steps, no one had entered or left that laneway. I knew I couldn't be wrong, they would have had to pass within feet of where I was sitting. I glanced to my right again. The three lads were about halfway down the lane. Every couple of seconds, one of them would look behind them.

They're up to no good, I thought.

I walked up the steps to the plinth and leaned on the railings. Subconsciously, I think I had distanced myself from the three lads as a safety measure. I glanced in their direction again: they were in a huddle facing the wall. I clearly saw them pulling tights down over their faces. They turned. The tallest of the three was holding a handgun down by his side. I ducked back and flattened myself against the wall of the church.

They came out of the laneway at a gallop. Although my heart was thumping, my reaction was instinctive. I stared at their backs – I was going to have to try and remember what they were wearing. They ran across the road and through the door of the amusement arcade.

My bag and mobile were locked in the car. The nearest premises was a clerical outfitters' shop on the opposite corner of the lane. I barged into the shop and yelled, 'Call the guards! Armed robbery in progress – over there in the arcade!' The elderly man behind the counter stood looking at me with his mouth open. Maybe he thought I was nuts. I didn't care. 'Call the guards!' I roared at him. 'Armed robbery over there,' and I pointes to the arcade across the road.

I ran out of the shop. I didn't know what else to do. I looked up and down the road hoping to see a uniformed garda nearby.

At that, the three yobbos ran out of the arcade. Two ran in the direction of Marlborough Street and the third, the tallest, legged it back up the lane. I watched him. I saw him throw something in the direction of the first pile of black refuse sacks he came to. He kept running, occasionally glancing over his shoulder in my direction.

I stood on the corner of the lane. I was trying to keep one eye on the pile of black sacks and look out for a patrol car at the same time. Two unmarked garda cars arrived within minutes. One came from the O'Connell Street end of the road and the other from Marlborough Street. They stopped with inches to spare between the bonnets of the two cars. One detective ran into the arcade, and another car ran into the clerical outfitters.

I ran over to the parked cars. 'I'm the one who reported it.' The driver looked at me as if I had two heads.

Ah, shit – I can't do any more! I thought as I turned away from the car.

I'm sure I was in shock. I felt like bursting into tears. I saw the elderly gentleman from the clerical outfitters' standing at the door of his shop talking to the detective. He was pointing in my direction. I stood on the footpath and watched the detective approach me.

'Did you see what happened?'

I nodded.

'Can you give me any descriptions?' His voice was quite gentle.

I nodded again.

I grabbed his arm. 'One of them threw, I think it was a gun, up there.' I pointed up the laneway.

'Ger!' he roared. One of the other detectives came running.

'Can you show me where?'

The three of us headed towards the pile of rubbish bags.

I stopped about ten feet from the pile.

'There,' I pointed.

Both detectives looked at and around the pile of bags. Ger ran back to the cars and came back with some sort of a plastic bag. The first detective – he told me his name was Tony – asked me if I would recognise any of the youths.

'I think so.'

'Will we go look and see if you can spot them?'

I nodded again.

As we got to the corner of the lane, the poor old guy from the clerical outfitters was standing at the corner.

'I'm very sorry that I yelled at you,' I said as we approached him.

'That's all right, my dear – would you like a cup of tea?'

I shook my head. 'We're going to see if we can find them.'

I was in the back of the car, Ger was driving and Tony had turned around to talk to me.

'Oh, shit! What about Sam?' I quickly told them that Sam was my partner and had gone to McDonald's. I pointed out our car. Ger beeped the horn and drove forward again. One of the other detectives came over. Ger quickly told him the situation and asked him to keep an eye out for Sam.

'What's his other name, love?'

I told him.

Ger reversed again.

'What did they look like, Shirley?' asked Tony.

I leaned back in the seat and closed my eyes. I have a good memory and excellent observational skills – well, I should, having spent so many years doing this job. I find it really helps when I visualise events, see the pictures in my mind, like watching a movie. 'There were three of them, all mid- to late teens, all skinny.'

I continued with a detailed description of what each of the three yobs was wearing, right down to their footwear. The only thing I wasn't sure about was whether the tracksuit top the smallest fella was wearing was very dark navy or black. One, some or all of the descriptions I provided must have rung a bell with Tony and Ger: I noticed that the siren had been switched on and they seemed to be heading in a specific direction. They drove at speed along Sean McDermott Street and, before turning left into Portland Row, the siren was switched off.

Ger slowed down, and we turned left into Summerhill. Just past Buckingham Street, I saw him. I nudged Tony in the shoulder. 'There's the tall one.'

He was up ahead of us, walking towards Gardiner Street. Ger slowed to a crawl. Tony picked up the radio and when his call sign was acknowledged, he said, 'X has been identified for the arcade robbery.' He gave the location.

They waited until X had crossed the road at the Rutland Street flats.

Good planning, I thought, not that I'm an expert. But there were railings on each side of the road from that point right down to the junction with Gardiner Street. X had nowhere to go except straight ahead, unless he turned back. Ger inched forward and came almost to a stop. Tony eased himself out of the car and gently closed the door. He started walking. Ger took off like a bat out of hell and slammed the car to a stop just ahead of X. He jumped out. X's reaction was instantaneous. He took one look in Ger's direction, turned to run back towards the flats and ran straight into Tony.

I leaned back in the seat. I could feel myself physically relax.

Shit! Maybe Mum was right, maybe I should have joined the gardaí after all, I thought.

Then another thought hit me: we had one car, two detectives and me – where were they going to put that yob? Beside me in the back seat?

I watched Tony approach. He had a big smile on his face.

I'll just tell him I'd rather walk, I thought.

'Well done, love, I've just organised some transport for our friend.' A patrol car arrived about five minutes later and our 'friend' was taken away to Store Street Station.

Back in the car, Tony noted my details and contact number. He told me he would be in touch with regard to obtaining my statement. By way of conversation, he asked what I had been doing in the laneway. 'Did you say something about watching a shop or something?'

I told him about Larry, his claim and the difficulties we had experienced in tracking him this far.

'To make matters worse,' I continued, 'when Sam went into the arcade, he wasn't there.'

Tony got on the radio again. 'Mick, do we have a key-holder for that arcade?' he asked.

After a couple of minutes, the radio crackled into life.

'We've two key-holders: Y and Larry Z, same address in Wicklow.'

'Thanks, Mick'. Tony winked at me and grinned.

———

Sam was standing beside the car when we got back to the arcade. I was really glad to see him. I walked over. 'I'm sorry for being such a bitch.' I was trying really hard not to cry. He hugged me.

I hadn't noticed Tony standing beside us until he said, 'Why don't you have that cup of tea now? I'll see what I can find out over there.' He tilted his head towards the arcade.

Tony went over to the clerical outfitters' and pushed open the door. 'Is that offer of tea still good?'

'Of course, Guard.'

'Can you make it for two?'

He held open the door. Sam and I went inside. I started to apologise again but he interrupted me with a wave of his hand.

The elderly gentleman looked at Sam. 'That's a very cool-headed woman you've got there.'

Sam looked at me and grinned. I hoped he wasn't going to say how 'un-cool' I had been fifteen minutes before the event. 'She always wanted to be in *Starsky and Hutch*.' I glared at Sam and the old man looked at him blankly. He had obviously never heard of *Starsky and Hutch*. He looked as if he might have been a priest, he had that quietly spoken, reserved demeanour. I was tempted to give Sam a dig in the ribs but I didn't want to give the poor old chap another shock. I wasn't going to be responsible if he keeled over from all the excitement.

The old man disappeared out the back of the shop. When he returned, he was carrying a tray with cups of tea, sugar in a bowl and a big plate of biscuits. I would have murdered a big mug of tea, but I didn't have the neck to ask him if he had any mugs; I settled for the dainty cup instead. As we sat and talked, Sam tucked into the biscuits.

'I though you'd eaten already?' I said pointedly to Sam; he was literally taking the biscuits two at a time.

'I have – they're my afters,' he said, grinning.

Tony came back after about fifteen minutes and I walked to the door with him. There was no need for the elderly gentleman to overhear anything. And it's my experience that people are usually more relaxed talking on a one-to-one basis.

'Odd fella altogether, I had to practically drag him out of the office to talk to me,' he said.

When he had gone back into the arcade, only the young cashier was present. He asked to see the owner; the young lad had hesitated and mumbled something like he wasn't sure that he was in. Tony had told the lad that if Larry didn't want to come out of the office he would have to wonder why he was avoiding the gardaí, particularly in view of the fact that he had just been robbed. The young lad picked up the phone. Larry eventually appeared and said something about having been on the telephone. Tony didn't believe him.

Then Tony hesitated, as if he was thinking things through. I felt that while Tony wanted to do what he could to help me with my job, he was only prepared to give me information he felt was relevant to my enquiries.

I had no problem with that; I couldn't ask for any more.

Checking his notebook, he confirmed that Larry was the owner of the business and provided me with details of the date he had opened. He said that Larry had stated he generally works four days each week, sometimes at weekends, and that he had no other business interests. He also told me the name of the insurance company.

Bingo, I thought.

Tony told me he would let me know if he got any further information that might help. I thanked Tony for his help and he left.

I went back to the counter and once again thanked the old man for the tea, and Sam and I headed back to the office. We discussed the information I had received from Tony. Sam was more interested in hearing about the robbery than doing any planning on the Larry job. I gave him a brief run-down and we returned to planning our next steps in the job that pays our bills.

Tony phoned later that afternoon. He told me that the gun was in fact a replica, but the yobbo's fingerprints were on it. He had also admitted to the offence and had confirmed the names of his two associates in the crime. The guards had lifted his two friends for questioning. Tony said that he wouldn't need a formal written statement from me unless the guy changed his plea to not guilty. He thanked me for my help, and told me again that he would call if he found more information that would help me with Larry.

I now had some good information, but apart from the fact that we had followed Larry to the arcade, all the rest was hearsay. I needed evidence that could be produced if the claim ever came to a court hearing, and I thought my best bet was to follow the property trail. I decided to allocate an entire day to making enquiries in the city centre.

It was just after nine in the morning when I left my car on a meter in Marlborough Street and walked down to the arcade. The amusement arcade was closed and its graffiti-covered shutter pulled down. The shop next door had just opened, so I went in. The man behind the counter looked to be in his early sixties. He was immaculately turned out in a dark grey three-piece suit; the word 'conservative' immediately sprang to mind.

'Good morning,' I said with a 'nice' smile on my face.

'And good morning to you, madam. How can I help you?'

I told him a story (which I made up as I went along).

I wanted to open a small boutique in the centre of town but couldn't afford O'Connell Street rents. I just happened to notice the premises next door, which looked empty and semi-derelict and would he know if that shop was to rent. I couldn't have offered that story if the assistant had been a woman. She would have known instinctively that a boutique in this area would be a trading disaster.

Over the next ten minutes he told me all about his problems with next door; the problems he had with the clientele – he actually used that word to describe the young lads who hung around amusement arcades; the lack of co-operation from the tenant in his efforts to keep 'their clientele' from loitering around his shop front, etc., etc.

At the end of the conversation, I came away with one piece of useful information – the name of the landlord/owner of the property. The pub farther down the road owned it.

The pub hadn't yet opened for the day, so I headed off to the

Council Rates Department in Dublin Castle. I had dealt with that department on a number of occasions and was on first-name terms with one of the girls in the general office.

'Hi, Annie, which inspector looks after O'Connell Street.'

She went to check her list.

'It's B, I'll ring up and see if he's still here.' He was.

I climbed the main stairs and went into the inspectors' office.

'Mornin', Shirl, what can I do for you?'

'Hi, B, need to know who pays the rates on the amusement arcade near O'Connell Street'. He rolled his eyes to heaven. With B that meant one of two things: either he's fed up with me coming in looking for information; or he's had some grief from the occupiers of the premises. I hoped it was the latter.

He pulled down one of the big registers off the shelf. 'Do you know the number?' he asked.

'Sorry, no. It's across the road from the church,' I added helpfully.

'Ah, yeah. Had a bit of a ding dong with them over vacant dates.'

Thank God for that, I thought. This meant that he would remember some detailed information, not just the basics.

He told me that the pub had originally used the premises as an additional storage facility. He had been on his rounds, checking properties, and had noticed that the use of the property had changed to an amusement arcade. When he called in he had been told that they had 'just opened for business'. He then checked with the pub and found that they had rented out the property nine months previously. He had gone back to the arcade a few times and eventually met the tenant in person. When he challenged him about the earlier statement regarding the date he had opened for business, the 'tenant' (my word, not his), had tried to convince B that he must have misunderstood what had been said.

He still hadn't told me the name of the rated occupier, but B is not the kind of person you can push for information. He will give the details in his own good time.

'Ah, yeah! His name . . .'

Bingo again – it was Larry.

B also gave me the relevant dates. As I was leaving, I leaned over and gave him a peck on the cheek. 'You're a little treasure,' I said.

As I walked towards the door he shouted, 'And you know what they do with treasure!' I turned to look at him, gave him a grin and left.

I stood waiting at the main reception desk in the foyer of the insurance company. I watched the young woman behind the desk. She had a bit of an attitude problem; at least I thought so. She looked about twenty, maximum. She hadn't yet learned the necessity of making eye contact or smiling when speaking to visitors. In fact, she barely raised her head when she was approached. It wasn't just me; she was like that with all the visitors who stopped at the desk. I had been very pleasant to her when I asked for Tony, the claims manager.

'Have you an appointment?'

'No, but tell him I'll only take a few minutes of his time.'

'You can't see him without an appointment.'

During this short conversation, she continued tapping away on her keyboard. Her attitude was beginning to grate on me. This company had been clients of mine for over ten years and I knew Tony would see me if he was in the building, even if I had to wait a while. I wasn't going to start explaining this to the young whippersnapper in front of me. I leaned on the counter and spotted the name tag pinned on her uniform jacket.

'Carole, my name is Shirley Sleator. Ring Tony and ask if he has time to see me.' I sounded as pissed off as I felt.

Oh, yippee, I had managed to awake a response. Glaring at me was better than nothing.

'Take a seat.'

I continued to stand at the desk until she picked up the phone.

Finally Tony emerged from the lift. 'Hi, Shirl, how are things?'

I explained about the robbery and that I had been told that his company insured the business. 'Come on up,' he said without hesitation. He checked on his computer and confirmed that they did insure Larry's business. He had not reported the robbery, so no claim had been filed. Tony gave me the date the cover had commenced. It was three months after Larry's accident, which meant the maximum period he could claim for loss of earnings was three months. The date also tied in with Dublin Corporation's rates register.

I stood to leave his office. 'Tony, can I ask a favour?' I told him my next port of call was to the pub that owned the premises. He agreed that I could say that I acted on behalf of his company. I wasn't planning actually to say that a claim had been filed; I intended to simply state the facts, that I acted for such and such insurance company (true) and that there had been a robbery at the arcade (also true). After that it was in the lap of the gods as to how much information I could get.

He wished me luck and asked that I should keep him in the picture. After all, he was the claims manager and one of his insured had, on the face of it, filed an exaggerated claim for compensation even though it was with another insurance company. It would be a handy bit of background information to be filed away in the event that Larry should make a claim against his company at a future date.

On my way out, I stopped by the reception desk: I couldn't stop myself. There was no one around. I leaned on the desk. 'Carole, are you happy in your work?' I asked gently. She glanced up at me with a puzzled expression. ''Cause if you're not, you should get yourself another job. But if you are, get Tony to send you on a training course on how to deal with the public.'

I looked back at her as I went out through the glass doors. She was still staring at me. I wasn't being bitchy, in fact I felt sorry for her; it was probably her first job, and they should have trained her properly before putting her on the front desk.

I like to talk to people face to face. If you phone looking for information they can put you on the long finger, forever. Depending on the approach you make, most people are uncomfortable with the idea of telling you 'no' or 'get lost' when they're looking you straight in the eyes. So I decided to go back to the pub rather than phone them. I had to get the timing right, though, there would be little point in trying to talk to staff if the place was packed with lunchtime customers.

It was ten past twelve by the time I got back to the pub. There were about half a dozen customers. I picked the oldest of the four barmen to approach, hoping that he might be the manager. 'Hiya. Could I have a quick word with the manager? I'll only keep him a few minutes.' I hoped I hadn't put my foot in it – the bar manager could have been a woman for all I knew.

'Sure,' he said, and disappeared through a doorway at the far end of the bar.

I caught another barman's eye. 'Cup of coffee, please.'

I took the coffee and sat at a table away from the bar and waited. A pleasant-looking chap in his mid-forties approached my table.

I stood up and stuck my hand out – most people automatically accept the offer of a handshake – and we shook hands. I told him my name and that I represented such and such insurance company. 'Did you hear about the armed robbery in the arcade down the road last Friday?'

'Yeah. They got them, didn't they?'

I nodded and continued, 'I understand that the pub owns the premises, is that right?'

He was looking at me as if to say 'Yes. And . . .?'

'It's just routine: I need to confirm details of the tenancy.'

He told me that the 'office' looked after lettings and gave me an address in west Dublin. We chatted a while about this and that. I thanked him and, having finished my coffee, I left.

I timed my arrival at the office for just after two o'clock, in case it was closed for lunch.

I buzzed the intercom and a male voice said, 'Yes?'

'Hi, I'm from such and such insurance company. It's about the robbery.'

'Robbery, what robbery?' said the voice.

At the same time the front door clicked and I pushed it open. There was a staircase at the end of the hallway. As I approached the bottom step, a man appeared at the top of the stairs. 'Come on up,' he said and led the way to a small office.

To say it was cluttered was an understatement. There were heaps of files on the floor next to the desk. Well, I assumed it was a desk. It was flat on top and had four legs, but the surface was completely covered with papers.

Four old metal filing cabinets ran along the length of one wall, complete with an old electric kettle, a couple of mugs and a carton of milk on the top of one of the cabinets. A smell of stale smoke hit me as soon as I walked in. God only knows when the windows were last opened.

As he settled himself behind the desk he said, 'Nobody told me that we'd been done.' His resigned tone of voice seemed to suggest he was thinking nobody tells me anything around here. He had a harassed look about him that seemed to match his chaotic surroundings.

'I'm sorry if I confused you – it wasn't your place, it was the amusement arcade, your old storerooms.' I wasn't a bit sorry; I had deliberately phrased my initial approach in a way that would get him to see me.

I went on to explain that I had called into the pub and the manager had referred me to him.

'I'm sorry, I didn't catch your name.'

'I'm Shirley Sleator,' I said, sticking out my hand for a handshake (again).

'Tom X, nice to meet you,' he said.

I gave him some of the details of the robbery (leaving out my part in identifying the yobs). 'I just need to confirm a couple of things, pure routine, just tying up some loose ends, you know yourself.'

He had to check three drawers of the filing cabinets before he found the right file, and then cleared a space on his desk to make room for the file.

'The insured seems to be a little unsure as to when he actually commenced trading,' I ventured.

He rooted through the file and extracted a document. Having glanced through it, he told me that it was a five-year lease, with a rent revision clause in the third year. The first six months had been rent-free to give the tenant a chance to get on his feet. The lease had been signed ten weeks after the accident. I made a mental note: Larry's potential loss of earnings claim had now been cut down from three months to ten weeks.

Tom offered me some tea. I shuddered inwardly and hoped it didn't show. Tom was a very pleasant man and in other circumstances I would have enjoyed chatting to him over a cuppa; but bearing in mind the state of his office, I declined gracefully, saying that I had another appointment to get to across town and I was already running late. I thanked him and shook hands again.

'Drop in next time you're passing,' he said.

I smiled and said I would.

————

While I couldn't actually observe Larry 'working', I had established that he had opened a new business ten weeks, at the latest, after his accident. I prepared my report and included a list of names of potential witnesses necessary to prove that fact, including B from the rates office and Tom who looked after the property portfolio for the pub owners. I thought about Tom, his dishevelled appearance and the state of his office. I reckoned he'd scrub up well if someone took him under their wing. He'll probably have a heart attack if he has to spend a day in court, I thought.

It could take anything up to five years from the date of filing the statement of claim (the originating document) to get a hearing of a personal injury claim in the High Court, but the average was about three and a half years.

'Settlement consultations' were held periodically in the Law Library at the Four Courts in order to see what aspects of the claim could be agreed between the parties and if possible to agree the amount of compensation. Once the original accident was presumed to be genuine, the insurance companies liked to try and reach a settlement figure at these meetings; not because they wanted to limit the trauma of Joe Public having to give evidence in open court, but from purely economic motives. How much would they save in legal fees, if they settled early?

I attended Larry's settlement consultation, which took place in April. The circumstances of the accident were agreed, as were the preliminary medical reports. The stumbling block to settlement was his claim for loss of earnings to date and into the future. His legal team were told in no uncertain terms that we had evidence of his opening and carrying out the day-to-day running of a business ten weeks after the accident. No further details of the business were provided. The insurance company was prepared to offer ten weeks' loss of earnings, no more. They adopted a 'take it or leave it' attitude.

Larry's legal team returned twenty minutes later. They accepted the offer.

12 | COURTEOUS BEHAVIOUR

A high proportion of our insurance claims investigations ended up in court. Most claims are made on foot of actual accidents, though we have uncovered some that were staged or never occurred at all. Most claims of resulting injuries are genuine, but there is a very high level of exaggeration.

Genuine claimants are of course entitled to compensation, and through our investigations we were able to assist many of these people in confirming and supporting their claims, getting them quicker settlements, and helping them avoid the added distress of arguing their case in court.

On the other hand, many honest insurance customers were paying over the odds for insurance premiums to support the scallywags making fraudulent claims (and the legal professionals who made buckets of dosh out of these scams). It is a business where there is money to be made and money to be saved . . . and we often found ourselves caught between these two competing forces.

The very heart of civil law proceedings in Ireland is the Four Courts; a magnificent building that overlooks the River Liffey in Dublin. The central rotunda, which is known as the Round Hall, is its hub.

I feel a personal affinity for the place; I remember my dad taking me to the Round Hall when I was a child to show me the work he had completed; refurbishing the interior of the domed ceiling. It was a beautiful pastel shade with gold edging. He swore to me that it was real gold he had used. For some reason, I always felt comfortable when I was in the Four Courts.

During the working day, barristers, solicitors, plaintiffs, defendants, witnesses, gardaí, and even overseas visitors, are all milling around. Periodically, High Court judges, kitted out in their robes and wigs, cross the public area, with their tipstaff walking in front, tap-tapping the marble floor with his staff to clear the way through the throngs of people. This is just one example of the many quaint practices still carried on in court to this day. In colloquial language, I suppose the tipstaff could be called the judge's 'minder'. I like the idea that our judges can wander around in public, particularly when you look at the security measures that have to be taken to protect senior legal personnel in other jurisdictions.

Sam and I always worked on the principle that every case we handled could end up in a court hearing, in which we could be held to account for every action we had taken, so integrity and professionalism were absolutely essential in our work. We drummed those requirements into every member of our staff, operatives and administrative staff alike. In spite of all the tradition, the superficial pomp, ceremony and ritualistic behaviour, the wigs and gowns, the reality is that court hearings amount to wheeling and dealing – horse trading. And sometimes double standards are concealed in all the activity, though only by a minority of those in the legal profession.

Only once in my twenty years working as a private investigator was I challenged during a hearing as to the ethics of my behaviour. Our subject's senior counsel objected to the inclusion of my evidence, standing and interrupting our counsel as I started to speak.

'M'Lud, I am *outraged* at the invasion of my client's privacy . . .'
Outraged my foot!

It was a lame attempt by our subject's barrister to introduce a 'breach of privacy' with a view to excluding my evidence. It didn't work: we don't have privacy laws in Ireland. The judge did go through the motions of asking me my exact physical position when the various photographs and video evidence were taken.

'On the street, Your Honour.' That was the end of counsel's challenge.

What the judge didn't know, and obviously I couldn't say at the time, was that a few weeks earlier that same barrister had acted for one my clients on another case in which I had given evidence. He had no problems whatsoever with including my evidence on that occasion. We had won the case and had adjourned to the bar in the basement of the building for a celebratory drink. He had come with us, had shaken my hand and congratulated me on the 'wonderful job' (his words) I had done.

I accepted the guy had a job to do, that one day he might be representing a plaintiff and the next day a defendant, but there was no need for him to adopt such a pompous manner and tone. For me, it begged two questions. Whose double standards? Whose unethical behaviour?

There is a saying that 'he who pays the piper calls the tune'. Not true in our case. A fundamental, non-negotiable principle of our business ethics was simply that our reports contained every fact we had established, every detail of what we had observed. Nothing was omitted. Whether our report supported or undermined our client's position was immaterial to me. Our regular clients were aware of this fact; new clients were clearly told that this was the way we did business, they could take it or leave it. However, there were two occasions when members of the legal profession had suggested or asked me to engage in what I considered to be unethical behaviour. On both occasions they were told, quite bluntly, one word comprising the greater part of my reply, 'No!'

Susan

Susan had sued her employer in respect of an alleged accident that had occurred one month after she had returned to work following a period of maternity leave. Unfortunately for Susan, none of her co-workers who were on duty with her on the night of the alleged accident had witnessed anything untoward. Furthermore, she had not reported any accident or incident to her duty supervisor, nor had she mentioned anything, even in passing, to her fellow employees. Two days later she rang in sick. A couple of weeks after that, her employer received a letter from Susan's solicitors, alleging an unsafe system of work, requesting them immediately to admit liability and also notifying them that Susan was going to sue. Apparently the consensus of opinion in the workplace was that Susan had decided to stay home and look after her new baby.

We carried out surveillance from time to time over a period of eighteen months. Susan was a creature of habit; her routine rarely varied and, more important for our client, we had found no obvious signs of disability or restrictions in any of her movements.

Her claim wasn't settled and on the due date, Sam and I attended at the Four Courts for the hearing. Apart from our reports, we had six folders containing copies of eighty-four photographs we had taken over the eighteen-month period. All the photographs were numbered sequentially. At the start of each section of the photographs we had inserted a sticker specifying the date the photographs were taken.

The usual procedure when entering photographs into evidence is that one folder is given to the judge, two folders passed over to the plaintiff's legal team, two retained by our legal team and I take one folder into the witness box with me. All this handing out of folders would take place when our counsel said something to the effect of, 'and, Ms Sleator, photographs were taken . . .'

The case was fourth on the list, so we had plenty of time for a pre-trial consultation. Senior and junior counsel, the solicitor and his clerk, the claims manager, Sam and myself sat around the table in the consultation room. Counsel had gone through the medical evidence with the consultants and had spoken to the various employees of the company who were required to give evidence. All these witnesses had been dispatched to the coffee shop in the basement to wait until the case was called. The six folders of photographs were stacked in a pile on the centre of the table.

As we sat around chitchatting, junior counsel picked up one of the photograph folders and glanced through it. Sam nudged me and nodded in the direction of the junior counsel. He had flicked through the book of photographs and appeared to be studying one photograph in particular, which was towards the back of the folder. He leaned over and whispered something to our senior counsel, who in turn picked up one of the folders from the table and appeared to be examining one photograph closely. They walked to the corner of the room, turned their backs and had a whispered conversation.

I looked at Sam and shrugged as if to say, 'I don't know!'

We both knew exactly what was in the folder. We had, after all, stuck all 504 photographs onto the pages, numbered them and labelled them with the relevant dates.

Curiosity got the better of me. I started at the back of my folder and, going forward, checked the photographs. They were all run-of-the-mill stuff; Susan bending and stooping, doing some gardening, jogging, doing her shopping, lifting her child and pushing him in his buggy (we had made sure that the child could not be physically identified in those photographs), getting in and out of her car – there was nothing controversial or mind-boggling. So what was the problem?

I started at the front of the folder again and went through the photographs again.

I stopped at number sixty-two. I wonder? I nudged Sam and pointed to that photograph. He checked and whispered, 'What?'

'Look at her face.'

The photograph was one of a series we had taken of Susan as she loaded her supermarket shopping into the boot of her car. She was in the process of straightening up from the boot. She had a slight 'grimace' on her face and her right hand was resting at the back of her right hip.

For all we knew, her back might have been giving her gyp, or she might simply have been thinking about something she didn't particularly like. Who knows?

Both counsels sat back down at the table.

Junior coughed, tapping the photograph. 'Shame about number sixty-two.'

I looked at him with a blank expression.

'Could she have been aware of your presence?' senior counsel chipped in, looking at Sam.

'No, I was in the back of the van – to all intents and purposes it looked empty.'

'Hmmm, could be construed that she was in pain.'

Neither of us made any comment.

Someone suggested coffee. Sam and I were at the end of the table farthest from the door, so we would be last out of the room. The others left while we were gathering up our files and paperwork. Junior popped back into the room.

'I suppose it would be an awful lot of work to renumber the last couple of dozen photographs in all the photograph folders?' he said.

Instinctively, I knew what was coming next. 'Sorry?' I said as if I didn't understand.

'They'd have to be renumbered if we took out number sixty-two.' I suspected the 'we' he was referring to was Sam and myself.

I could feel my jaw clamping tight in anger.

Don't yell at him, Shirl, I thought.

Looking straight into his eyes, I said, 'No! Don't even think about it, mate,' and pushed past him out into the corridor.

I don't know whose idea it was to make that suggestion, but I wasn't having any hand, act or part in that scheme. It was tampering with evidence. If the idea had been pushed, I would have withdrawn from the case and they would have had to subpoena me. Then I would have been a 'hostile witness'.

The subject was never mentioned again.

Another member of the legal profession put a similar suggestion to me on another occasion. Once again it happened in a consultation room in the Four Courts. This time it came from a solicitor.

Joanne

Joanne was a housewife we had placed under surveillance on a number of occasions. We had obtained no evidence whatsoever to counter her disability claim. On the other hand, neither had we obtained any evidence to support her claim. In effect, all we had observed was Joanne driving her car and doing some light shopping locally. She wasn't claiming that she had problems driving or shopping.

It was becoming common knowledge in the legal profession that insurance companies sometimes used private investigators to investigate claims. This often made our job more difficult, as a claimant could be alerted to the possibility. Perhaps this claimant's solicitor had warned her that she could be placed under surveillance and she was keeping a low profile until the case settled or was heard in court. For all we knew, perhaps the woman engaged in very little activity before her accident.

Sam and I were attending a pre-trial consultation in the Law Library. The usual crew were in attendance. Apart from the two of us, there were senior and junior counsel, the solicitor and the claims manager. We were discussing where we should go and what should be done next with regard to this claim.

'Maybe you're grasping at straws; maybe you should try and settle the claim,' I ventured.

The discussion continued. Then the solicitor looked directly at me: 'Why don't you let the air out of one of her tyres when she's at the shops and see what she does then?'

I was quite taken aback. 'You're joking!'

He looked at me as if I was on another planet.

'No, sure if she tried to change her wheel, we'd have her.'

I could feel myself clenching my fists. I find that digging my nails into the palms of my hands stops me from losing my temper.

'That would be entrapment,' I said, keeping my tone of voice as even as possible.

There was silence – it was if everyone was holding their breath and waiting. He didn't let it go at that. Looking around the table, he gestured with both hands as if to say, 'What?'

'So, we'd know if she was able to change a wheel.'

I looked at Sam.

'Let's go.' I gathered up my papers and looked at the unscrupulous twit.

'*You* can let the air out of her tyres and see what she does then. We're not going to be part of a set-up.' I glanced at Frank, the claims manager. 'Give us a ring later.' Sam and I walked out.

Once again, the matter was never raised in any subsequent conversations.

Without offering any explanations, I simply told Frank that in the future, I would deal directly with him and not through that particular solicitor.

————

It's a fact that some people, from all walks of life, have attitude problems and at one time or another we have all come across such people. Some people's attitude problems are particularly pronounced when dealing with private investigators, and this may not necessarily be connected to the actual work or job we do. Surprisingly, some members of the legal profession can be included in this group. Lawyers are well educated and should have excellent communication skills. Maybe some of them had slept through or missed that part of their studies that dealt with 'common courtesy and respect' towards others. Or perhaps the Bar Council exam syllabus doesn't cover the topic. Maybe it would be a good idea to have a question in their finals: 'Respect others as yourself. Discuss.'

That maxim formed part of my rearing. My dad's interpretation was slightly different: he always added the proviso, 'Well, only until they do something to lose your respect.'

In my early days as a PI, I used to react to discourteous or disrespectful behaviour with some smart-ass response, but I quickly learned to file it away at the back of my mind for use on some future appropriate occasion. Sometimes, however, I found the behaviour so unacceptable that I did have to respond, there and then.

We were in a consultation room in the Law Library on the morning of the start of a case. Crammed into a room that would normally accommodate six were ten people: two each from the solicitors and insurance company; two medical consultants; three professional witnesses; and myself. We were waiting for our senior and junior counsels to arrive. The usual procedure was that counsel would run through the evidence with the doctors and professional witness and each would leave the room in turn. I would be dealt with last.

The solicitor stood: 'I'll see what the delay is.' The doctors were anxious to get back to their respective practices. When counsel had spoken to them, each would be on standby for a phone call asking them to get back down to the Four Courts. I glanced at my watch. The man was twenty minutes late already.

The door was flung open. There he was, a well-known and highly respected member of the Bar. The phrase 'making an entrance' came to mind. Junior counsel followed him into the room. He glanced at everyone crammed around the table; his eyes rested on me for a split second and moved on. 'Good morning, gentlemen.'

Two things flashed through my mind: how rude, not a word of apology for keeping everyone waiting; and second, 'Hello, there, I'm a woman!'

I was sitting in my usual position at the far end of the table beside the window. Everyone was shuffling around to make space at the table for the two barristers. The solicitor stood to give him his chair. He settled himself and glanced around the table again. It was if he was checking everyone's face. I was sitting directly opposite him at the far end of the room. He turned his head back in my direction and stared at me. I could feel the hostility in the air. The room was so quiet you could hear a pin drop.

Hell, what have I done to him? I wondered.

I leaned my elbows on the table and, resting my chin on the back of my hands, said, 'Morning.' I stared back, wanting to see who would break eye contact first.

'I don't have time to waste on you. What witnesses have you brought along?'

No 'good morning', no common courtesy, not even a hint of respect.

'None.' I had maintained the same physical position. The only thing that had moved was my mouth when I spoke.

'None? What about Social Welfare, what about your operatives?'

I continued to stare at him. 'That's your job, I provide the information, and you're supposed to decide what witnesses to call.' I could feel the knot at the pit of my stomach starting to grow. Don't blow it now, Shirl.

He looked away as he threw my report onto the table. 'Rubbish,' he said.

I don't know if he was referring to the contents of my report or to the statement I had just made, but either way, the knot had moved up to the back of my throat. I felt my cheeks burning. I had had enough of this little . . . whippersnapper!

I stood up, excused my way past the people sitting along the left-hand side of the table and leaned over the corner of the table; my face was only inches from his. 'I'd like a word outside, please.' I kept my voice as even as I possibly could and never took my eyes off his face. I stepped back.

I judged he wouldn't want to lose face in public; he only had to look at me to know that I was very unhappy at the way he had spoken to me. I calculated that he was too arrogant to allow me the opportunity of cutting him down to size in public. I had calculated correctly. Without a word, he pushed back his chair and headed out of the room. I followed, taking great care to close the door gently behind me.

He turned and looked up at me.

'Well?' he said in his haughty voice.

I looked at him. In a way I felt a bit sorry for him: he had been through some traumatic experiences not of his own making; the rug had been pulled from under his feet career wise; maybe he was resentful towards the world in general and not with me in particular. At least I was prepared to give him the benefit of doubt on that last bit. But more important, I remembered something I had been taught as a child: never, ever row in public. I relented a little.

'Well, I don't know if you got out of the wrong side of the bed this morning, or what your problems may be, but I have a problem with your tone, your manner and your attitude.'

He looked at me but said nothing.

'If you ever want to say one word to me again, you keep a civil tongue in your head.'

I didn't know if he just wasn't listening or was in shock at the idea that someone would dare to challenge him. He just stood there. No apology, nothing. I couldn't be bothered with him any longer. 'You're a disgrace to your profession.' I turned on my heel and walked back into the consultation room.

Everyone turned to look at me as I entered. I shrugged my shoulders and made my way back to my seat. There was an embarrassed silence. Someone coughed.

Frank, the claims manager, caught my eye.

'I'm sorry, Shirley'

'It's okay, done and dusted.'

Gordon, who was an actuary and one of the professional witnesses, leaned across.

'Did you deck him one, Shirl?'

'Of course not,' I replied. The relief was palpable. Everyone started talking at once.

The door opened and in he came. I followed his every move. Silence descended like a ton of bricks. He looked directly at me and gave a barely perceptible nod. Truce? I wondered.

'I've checked, we're now third on the list,' and he glanced around the table.

'Now where were we . . .? Ah, Shirley, would you mind if we go though your evidence last? It would be helpful.'

I'm not sure what response he expected from me.

'No problem', I said.

Peace had broken out again, for the moment.

13 | I'M NUN THE WISER

Some cases caught my interest more than others. Generally the more interesting ones were non-routine, with features somewhat out of the ordinary, and had some scope for lateral thinking and innovation.

The function of a PI is to gather and report accurately on information received as a result of investigation and enquiries. It is not our role to reason through the whys and the wherefores, we just have to get out and do the job, gather all the information we can and report back to the client. It's a bit like collecting pieces of a jigsaw and putting them together. Sometimes it can be a little frustrating: you don't always manage to collect all the pieces, which leaves gaps in the overall picture. Sometimes you know there will be no logical conclusion at the end.

This was such a case.

On Monday, 18 July 1988, I received a call from a client, a solicitor who wished me to carry out enquiries with regard to a woman. For the purpose of this story, I will call her Ann Smyth.

Ann, who was in her sixties, was the beneficiary of a large trust fund amounting to £90,000 sterling per year. The trustees of the fund had become somewhat alarmed at the level of her expenditure – some £20,000 sterling per month on her American

Express card alone. Their concern was heightened when they received a telephone call from their bankers requesting funds to clear a cheque drawn on an Irish bank account which was in the joint names of Ann and an identified male, Frank. The cheque in question represented quite a substantial deposit in respect of a large property in the Leitrim/Roscommon border area. The trustees tried to communicate with Ann, who refused to take their calls, so they declined to release the funds.

The trustees were concerned that Ann might have come under undue influence or duress from her male companion. They had been able to obtain some limited information with regard to Frank's background, which, apparently, compounded their worries. They wanted us to make enquiries to see if we could establish her current state of mind, her living arrangements and any other relevant information as to her relationship with this man.

They did mention that Ann passed herself off as a nun and that she often stayed around the town of Knock. As UK solicitors, I don't think they fully appreciated the religious significance of Knock and the number of nuns who were likely to be in that area. However, our prospects were helped somewhat when my client advised that Ann always wore a traditional habit like the nun in the old movie *The Nun's Story,* unlike the 'trendy' habits now adopted by contemporary nuns. That at least, should help us to identify her. The last address the trustees had for Ann was in a town in County Longford.

Sam and I discussed the file and decided to start this investigation on Thursday. We spent Tuesday and Wednesday that week tidying up some other cases and I made some preliminary calls to some of my contacts in the Longford and Castlerea areas. Our first appointment was fixed for half past eight in Longford Town.

Sam picked me up at six on Thursday morning. I threw my holdall in the boot but kept all the paperwork inside the car. Sam had brought his collection of large-scale local maps of the Midlands and West of Ireland. These are some of the essential tools of the trade, particularly in rural areas, as they show small townlands that are not included on the usual road maps. Traffic was very light at that time of the morning. We made excellent progress and pulled in at the Longford Arms Hotel at twenty past seven, so we had time for breakfast before meeting my contact.

Tom arrived early and joined us for coffee. He had made some enquiries and had checked out the Longford address. He told us that Ann and Frank, together with 'an elderly lady in a wheelchair', had visited the property in question on three occasions with a view to renting the lodge, but never actually moved in. They were travelling in a UK-registered Toyota, driven by their 'chauffeur', a young Irish lad from Cavan Town. However, Tom had received information to the effect that Ann, dressed in her nun's garb, had led the St Patrick's Day Parade in Castlerea, County Roscommon, so there was a possibility that she was living in that area.

By nine o'clock we were on the road again, heading towards Castlerea. We stopped off in a town approximately ten miles west of the Longford address. I always like to double-check information received from third parties, and given the 'religious' aspect of this case, who better than a member of the local clergy?

We had to wait until Mass was over before I could get to talk to the local priest. When I'm trying to get information, depending on the person I'm talking to, I usually find that it is best to stick to the truth, or a version of the truth, but in any event I don't think I could look a priest in the eye and lie. So I simply asked if he could help me find a woman who dressed like a nun, but wasn't really a nun, who might be living or have lived in the area.

He leaned back in his chair, looked me straight in the eye and asked me why I wanted this information. I told him I was acting on behalf of UK solicitors; that the woman wasn't in any trouble and that her family were extremely concerned about her well-being, personal safety and, in fact, her mental state.

He didn't tell me very much, and maybe he didn't know a lot. He said she had never lived in the area but she was living in a small townland just outside Castlerea. He added that according to some of his colleagues, she spent a considerable amount of her time at the Basilica in Knock trying to 'recruit' people. It was obvious from his tone and demeanour that he didn't think highly of Ann's activities. With nothing more forthcoming, I thanked him and took my leave.

Back in the car, I filled Sam in on the latest information. We decided to head on for Castlerea and Knock.

Sam drove, and I made some file notes and checked the large-scale map of the Castlerea area. I found the townland without any difficulty and gave Sam the directions.

We found the property easily enough. (At least, we initially assumed it was the property occupied by Ann and Frank, and this was subsequently confirmed.) It was a bungalow set back a little from the road. There were religious statues on every flat surface visible from the road; on every inside windowsill and behind the glass panel over the front door.

Sam pulled over about a hundred and fifty yards from the entrance to the bungalow. I walked back and approached the house. I wanted to get a better look. I decided I would knock on the door, and if someone answered, I would make some fake enquiry or other.

There was no reply to my knock, and there was no car to be seen, so I decided to take a quick look through the windows. There were statues of Our Lady on every flat surface I could see. Large, medium and small statues, holy pictures, blue votive light holders, some lit, on tables, sideboards, on an old-fashioned china cabinet. Either we had found the right house or there were two religious zealots living in this small townland, which somehow I doubted.

Not wanting to push my luck too far, I returned to the car, told Sam what I had seen and made some file notes while Sam discreetly took some photographs. It was Sam who noticed the silver car approaching from the direction of Castlerea. As he held the map up to partially hide us from the occupants of the car as they passed, I took a quick look. It was a large Mitsubishi driven by a male in his thirties. There was only one passenger, a man in his late fifties or early sixties, with dark hair balding on top. As the car turned into the driveway, Sam got out of our car and, resting the map on the roof, he watched the passenger alight from the silver car, approach the front door and let himself into the bungalow. The driver stayed in the car.

'Frank, I presume,' said Sam as he got back in the car.

We headed off to Castlerea. I telephoned my contact Alan from Tully's Hotel on the square in Castlerea and we agreed to meet for lunch at one. Over a quick lunch I told Alan what we had seen out in the townland. He confirmed that the bungalow was indeed the current residence of Ann, Frank and Frank's elderly wife, who was in her nineties and in a wheelchair. He confirmed from my description that the man we had seen at the bungalow was indeed Frank, although he had heard that he had left, or was about to leave, for the UK to order a new car. Apparently the Mitsubishi was only about six months old but they changed their car every year. Alan had been told by some of his colleagues that Ann and Frank's wife were staying in Knock while Frank was in the UK. Alan was surprised that Ann was the 'wealthy party' – local gossips seem to think that it was Frank's wife who had all the money!

As Alan headed back to work, we set off for Knock.

Knock, County Mayo

Neither of us had been to Knock before. The extent of our pooled relevant knowledge comprised: the Pope's visit in 1979; Monsignor Horan and his success against all the odds in achieving the building of Knock International Airport; and that was it! We had no contacts who could be of use in the investigation. There were only a couple of points that could be in our favour: first, because we were not checking out any locals information may be a bit more forthcoming; second, Ann was such an unusual character that literally everyone in the town should know her by sight and some might possibly have some relevant information.

When we spotted the spire and the large cross we knew we were approaching Knock. The town was small – very small. Our first impression was that it consisted of one main street, which was bustling with activity. Two large tour buses crawling down the street slowed down our progress towards the town centre. I took the opportunity to have a look at the businesses as we drove along – a couple of fast food restaurants/chippers; a number of souvenir shops displaying bottles of holy water, religious pictures and statues; a post office; the garda station; and a number of other small stores. The basilica dominated the town, as did the large cross. The cemetery was next to the church area. I also noticed a pub, named after a saint: a bit of a contradiction, I thought – where else but in Ireland?

The tour buses ahead came to a halt in the middle of the street to allow the passengers out. Obviously the visitors/pilgrims take precedence over regular traffic in Knock. When the buses moved off, Sam found a parking space and we walked over to the church. What struck me forcefully were the hundreds of people all walking uniformly in an anti-clockwise direction right around the perimeter of the church. They were reciting the rosary out loud. Most were middle-aged and older women; there were some nuns and a few men but virtually no teenagers or younger people. I was taken aback by this scene; it looked like we had stepped into a 1950s movie.

We decided to make one lap of the basilica before we would go in, just to get a feel for the place. We joined in and walked with the crowds, who were doing the stations of the cross. An elderly woman beside me, with a glow of joy on her face, said, 'Isn't it wonderful to be here?' I don't know what it was, but a sense of good was palpable from this dedicated throng. I could see how you could be seduced into having an epiphany in such an atmosphere and wondered if Sam was having similar thoughts. He seemed to enjoy his stroll among these gentle people and being away from the 'gougers and gurriers' we saw so many of in Dublin.

On entering the building, there was an internal corridor leading to the doors into the basilica itself. This too was a hive of activity. There was a fully fitted-out gift shop selling souvenirs and religious books.

'Wasn't there an old story, something to do with traders inside the temple?' I asked Sam as we made our way into the church itself. There were thirty or so people sitting in the pews. We approached a couple of young altar boys who were nearby. 'I'm going to be quite direct' I said to Sam as we got close to the young lads.

'Hiya, I'm looking for a nun who dresses like the nun in *The Sound of Music*,' I said. 'Have you seen her around?'

They looked at each other and grinned. The taller of the two said, 'Yeah, she comes to the three o'clock Mass.'

The younger lad added, 'She usually sits over there', and pointed to the opposite side of the church.

'Does she usually have anyone with her?' Sam asked.

'Don't think so,' came the reply.

The two lads headed back towards the altar and Sam and I left the church. It was twenty to three. Sitting on one of the benches outside, I had a cigarette while Sam checked the camera. 'I'll go in and you wait near the main entrance,' he said as he loaded film into the camera.

I lit another cigarette as he went into the church. People were arriving for the three o'clock Mass. At five to three I went and stood beside the main entrance.

This has got to be her, I thought as I noticed a thickset woman approaching. Well, you couldn't miss her.

All the other nuns who had passed me had been wearing the usual uniforms. This lady was wearing a long black cape, crossed at the front and secured by a belt. She had a white scarf over her head, crossed at the front and tied in a knot at the back of her neck. On top of the scarf she was wearing a black fur headband, pulled down on her forehead. The cross she was wearing on a long chain around her neck was big, at least three or four times larger than the crosses I had seen around the necks of the real nuns. As she passed me on her way in through the entrance, I realised she was wearing full make-up – the works! It was only when I fell in behind her that I made another discovery: she was wearing high-heeled shoes!

I took a seat two rows behind her in a spot where I would be able to observe her actions and demeanour. I glanced around and eventually spotted Sam leaning against the wall across the basilica directly opposite where we were seated. I kept an eye on Ann during the Mass and periodically I glanced over in Sam's direction. Each time he had the camera, complete with a large, and I thought very obvious, telephoto lens pointed in Ann's direction. Still, he is generally right in his view that no one pays a bit of attention to cameras being used openly, particularly in a crowded situation. As to Ann, she participated fully in the Mass and appeared to be very devout.

After Mass ended, Ann left the church and went into the bookshop with me not far behind her. I wouldn't normally get that close to a subject, but I wanted to observe her manner, actions and reactions, overhear any conversations she may have. After all, the trustees were concerned that she may be under some form of undue influence or duress or that she might be somehow restricted in her ability to travel freely. I also wanted to engage her in conversation. I had to make a judgement call on her current situation and, if possible, try to evaluate her mental state.

Having picked up a couple of religious books, Ann then approached two elderly women and engaged them in conversation. From what I could overhear she was offering the ladies some form of moral support. She moved away and approached another group of ladies with whom she appeared to be discussing St Brid. After making her purchase, Ann left the shop. I stood in the passageway pretending to look at some postcards on a stand outside the window of the shop. Out of the corner of my eye, I saw Ann look up and down the passageway. She obviously saw me, a lone woman, and immediately made a beeline in my direction. Bingo, I thought.

I glanced in her direction when she was about ten feet away from me. With a smile, I said, 'Good afternoon, Sister.' During the next thirty-five minutes, with the help of a few leading questions from me, she told me her full name, including her baptismal name; where she came from originally; where she was living, and with whom – Frank and his wife – and how she met them. She also told me that they were staying at Knock International Hotel during their visit to the town. She spoke with a well-educated, refined English accent. Up to this point, she was very lucid.

I couldn't resist asking her about her 'habit'. 'Your habit is most unusual,' I said, 'I don't think I've seen one like it before.'

She was off again without any further prompting. 'It is a mantle,' Ann said. 'I bought it in a shop in Dundee and adapted it to make it into a habit.' She continued, 'I am a convert, I have taken vows of chastity, virtue and modesty. I am following in the footsteps of St Brid – although her habit was white. I am going to form a closed order of nuns.'

I watched her face closely – frankly I don't know what signs I was looking for – but her demeanour had not changed at all. Her tone of voice was the same; her facial expressions, the smiles, the nods and the gestures, were the same as before.

She went on to tell me of her 'visions of St Brid' and 'the physical signs and events' that had happened to her over the previous two years which had convinced her that her decision to form the order of nuns was the correct one.

Okay, I thought, she's a bit of a religious fanatic.

It was only after she described an attempt on her life by a hired killer the previous year and how Frank had saved her life that I thought, The lift isn't going to the top floor here – I really need a cigarette! I started edging towards the entrance and Ann made her way to the shrine.

As soon as I was two steps out of the doorway, I lit up.

'She's not the full shilling,' I said to Sam as soon we sat down on one of the benches. 'I'm knackered – I have to make some notes.'

I filled Sam in on the significant points as I made my notes. We agreed that we would not return to Dublin just yet and decided to stay in the Knock International Hotel to see if we could get any further information.

It was a small, ten-bedroomed, family-owned and run hotel on the main street. The daughter of the family was on reception when we checked into our rooms. Sam suggested that we meet in the lobby at seven, and we headed off to our respective rooms. I had a quick shower and started writing. Sam phoned the room at ten past seven – I had completely forgotten about the time. We met up in reception area. We really need to know if Ann had returned to the hotel, so we chatted to the receptionist.

I mentioned that we had met this nun who looked like she was out of *The Sound of Music*. We quickly established that the party had one room in the hotel. Ann and Frank's wife shared a room. Frank, we were told, was staying in Castlerea, even though they could have accommodated him in the hotel. They had not returned at that stage.

The dining room windows overlooked the car park and entrance area. We had a quick meal while keeping one eye on the car park. We had the advantage of knowing the make, model, colour and registration number of Ann's car. They eventually arrived at nine fifteen. The driver was the same lad we had seen earlier, and the front seat passenger was the balding man. Ann and an elderly lady were in the back seat.

Frank got out of the car, followed by Ann. As Frank removed a wheelchair from the boot, Sam and I separated again. At this stage, Sam was staying in the background in case close surveillance was necessary. We didn't want him 'associated' with me yet. I strolled out of the main doorway and sure enough (as I had hoped), Ann spotted me. She called out to me and beckoned me over to the car. There she introduced me to Frank's wife, Gertie, and to Frank. Some of my first impressions of Frank have stuck with me: his very limp handshake – it was like shaking hands with a dead fish; his breath reeked of whiskey; he was sweating profusely, though it wasn't that warm an evening; and finally his attitude. His accent, in contrast to the two ladies' 'refined' English accent, was very coarse. Somehow he seemed out of kilter with the kind of person one would image as a companion to the two ladies. He seemed distant and appeared to be none too happy at the fact that I had joined their company and disappeared into the hotel at the first opportunity.

Gertie, on the other hand, was very chatty. She seemed to relish the attention of a stranger. I invited them to join me for coffee in the lounge, and they readily agreed. Over the course of the next hour or so, Gertie told me practically her life story. She was ninety-two years of age. Frances, as she called him, was her second husband and they had been married for twelve years. I made a mental note that at the time of the marriage, she would have been eighty and Frank would have been in his late forties or early fifties. (Certainly worth digging around that bit, I thought.) She had suffered a stroke in 1987 and had been in a wheelchair ever since.

When someone's so open and talkative it's seldom a problem asking apparently innocuous questions.

'What part of the UK are you from?' I asked.

'The Wirral, near Liverpool. I'm one of the Lever family.'

'You mean Lever Brothers, like Sunlight soap?' I asked.

'Yes,' she replied and then started to tell me stories about Lever Brothers' operations during the course of the Second World War.

Whilst Gertie seemed to love being the focus of attention, Ann was getting irritable, making asides to me to the effect that it's a pity Gertie wasn't involved with soap on a daily basis. Her mask is slipping, I thought, and continued prompting Gertie for information. Quite abruptly Ann announced in a loud voice, 'I'm going to spend a penny,' which sounded a little out of character for a 'nun', but she didn't seem to care, or notice, that we were in a public place. She headed off to the ladies.

Gertie watched Ann as she walked away. She clenched her jaw, scowled and then turned to me. With her head tilted to one side she said, 'They make me take pills I don't want.'

'What?' I asked.

'Every day and every night they make me take pills I don't want,' she repeated.

They are all nuts, I thought as I tried to formulate another question, lighting yet another cigarette to give myself time to think. I started to say, 'What do you mean?', but Gertie's face had changed. The smile was back.

'Ah, Frances!' she said loudly.

The bold Frank was crossing the room in our direction. 'Time for bed, dear,' he said. Nodding to me, he simply said, 'Good night' and pushed Gertie in her wheelchair out of the room.

I checked the bar and found Sam nursing a pint.

'They're all bloody mad,' I said as I plonked down into the armchair opposite. 'I need a drink.'

Sipping my Scotch and Coke, I filled Sam in on my conversations.

'Well, they might be mad,' Sam said, 'but is there any evidence that Ann's being held against her will, or under any duress?'

We went over the information we had gathered so far – her apparent freedom of movement, the length of time she spent out and about on her own – and concluded that she might well be somewhat eccentric and a religious fanatic but she didn't seem to be acting in any way against her will.

'Could well be that she feels indebted to Frank for saving her life,' I added.

'Could well be that Frank has an unpaid minder for his invalid wife,' Sam replied.

We finished our drinks and agreed to meet in the breakfast room at eight thirty the following morning, Friday.

On my way into breakfast, I checked the car park. There was no sign of the Mitsubishi. There were three other guests in the breakfast room but no sign of Ann, Gertie or Frank. At nine thirty-five Sam spotted her walking towards the front door of the hotel. Within minutes she had entered the dining room and as soon as she saw me she came over to our table. After I had introduced her to Sam and we made the usual small talk about the beautiful morning, she told us that she had gone to eight o'clock Mass as usual and that she had been so engrossed in her prayer book that she had sat through a second Mass. She said she was going to organise Gertie's breakfast to be taken up to her room. 'She will not be pleased,' she said.

Ann talked to the waitress and left the room, but she was back again within five minutes, pushing Gertie in her wheelchair. As they settled at one of the tables, Gertie looked round and asked, 'Where is Frances?' She could have been asking anyone in the room. Ann replied very sharply, 'In Castlerea'. I was quite taken aback at her tone.

On our way out of the dining room I stopped off at their table to say good morning to Gertie.

'When I got back to the room, she was fully dressed and insisted on coming here for breakfast,' Ann said in quite a belligerent tone.

Oops, I thought, the mask is slipping again.

While I was checking out at reception, I couldn't resist having a go at obtaining more information. This time it was the owner's wife who was on duty.

'You must meet all sorts,' I said as we were paying our bills.

'Ah,' said Mrs Curry with a knowing smile. 'You must have met our nun?' she continued.

The consensus of opinion of the family and the hotel staff, based purely on their observations and, of course, gossip, was that Frank had married Gertie for her money: Gertie was extremely wealthy in her own right and employed a chauffeur and a bodyguard. Initially they had thought that Gertie was Ann's mother, but subsequently had come to believe that Ann was Gertie's paid companion. Ann wasn't really a nun and this was the source of some embarrassment to the hotel as many of their guests, particularly religious, would ask the staff which order of nuns she was attached to.

One other piece of information, which confirmed my conclusion that Ann was, to say the least, a bit odd, was that even though there were two beds in the room that Gertie and Ann shared, Ann insisted on sleeping on the floor. Every night, she removed the pillows and bedclothes, but not the mattress, from the bed and camped out on the floor. Every morning, the room attendant would have to make up the bed again. Very odd.

Sam and I returned to Dublin. I submitted my report and bill to my clients in Scotland. In summary, I told them that in my view, Ann's behaviour and some of her statements appeared somewhat eccentric, but I could find no evidence of duress, depression, anxiety, nervousness or fear.

That was the end of that case, I thought. Little did I know then that, within a few weeks, we would be back in Knock.

Knock II

On Saturday, 20 August, I received a call from Alan, my contact in Castlerea. He had just heard that Gertie had died earlier that week. He agreed to make a few discreet enquiries and call me back.

He phoned again on Sunday morning. He told me that the funeral had initially been planned for Monday but had been put back until Tuesday. According to local information this was to enable relatives travelling from the UK time to get to the funeral. As far as he had been able to ascertain, Gertie's death, bearing in mind her age, was considered 'normal', although quite sudden. Frank, Gertie and Ann had apparently spent a week in the Isle of Man and had returned to the rented bungalow the previous Thursday.

The announcement of Gertie's death appeared in the *Sunday Independent* and ran again in Monday's paper. What caught my eye in respect both death notices was that Ann was described as Gertie's sister. Initially I thought that it was a simple misunderstanding on the part of the newspapers, arising from the repetition of the word 'sister' (the notice read ' . . . and her sister Sr Ann . . .' I phoned a contact in the *Sunday Independent*, who checked the records and confirmed that it was Frank who had placed the death notice and there was no mistake on their part: he had definitely described Ann as Gertie's sister. I wondered why Frank should pass Ann off as a member of the family, but nothing was straightforward in this case.

On Monday morning I telephoned my clients in Scotland and advised them of Gertie's death and the information I had received from both the *Independent* newspaper and my contact in Castlerea. They asked if I would go over to Knock and keep what they called 'a watching brief' while seeing if I could dig up any more information.

Sam and I headed off to Castlerea. We called in to see Alan, who confirmed that he had made some further enquiries since speaking to me the previous day. The first thing he had found out that they had replaced the silver Mitsubishi with a new wine-coloured Toyota Camry and he gave me the registration number. The second item was that no death certificate had been issued at that stage. Finally, according to information Alan and his colleagues had received, but which still needed to be verified,

Frank had ordered the coffin some weeks prior to Gertie's death.

We discussed this latter point. There were two possible explanations that we could think of at the time. First, Gertie was ninety-two years old, had apparently suffered a stroke in 1987 and was confined to a wheelchair. According to her conversation with me she was on some form of medication so there were apparently some health issues. Her husband Frank could just have been so well organised and practical that he thought it prudent to prepare for her death at some time in the not too distant future.

The other alternative? Well, we did discuss it briefly. Gertie was some thirty years older than Frank; she was, supposedly, very wealthy; and she had said to me, 'They make me take pills I don't want – every day and every night, they make me take pills I don't want.'

We decided to file away both possibilities for the time being and carry on with the watching brief.

Finally, Alan told us that a neighbour (from the townland) had been in to his office and had mentioned that Frank had told her that the funeral, which was now due to take place after eleven o'clock Mass the following morning, had been delayed to enable the Bishop of Liverpool and the Duke of Edinburgh sufficient time to travel to Knock for the funeral. Whether or not the Bishop of Liverpool was going to be there, there was no question of the Duke of Edinburgh visiting: Alan would have been formally notified of such a proposal because of security implications.

We agreed to keep in touch, and Sam and I headed on to Knock, where our first port of call was Knock International Hotel. The owner's wife was on reception. She remembered us from our previous visit and greeted us with a smile. 'Here for the funeral?'

I avoided giving a direct reply.

After checking in and leaving our bags in our rooms, Sam and I met back in reception and headed off to the bar to see what information we could pick up. We overheard – frankly, we eavesdropped on – conversations between the barman and some locals who were in the bar. It was obvious that Gertie's death and the funeral arrangements were the talk of the town. This simplified matters somewhat for us because we were able to join in and ask questions. To encourage the flow of conversation, over the next couple of hours, we stood a couple of rounds from the bar.

There was some speculation about why the remains were not being returned to the UK for burial. One thing that genuinely seemed to shock the locals was the fact that Frank had tried to employ a local photographer to photograph Gertie's remains as she was laid out on her bed, but before she was placed in the coffin. Apparently the local guy refused point blank to undertake this assignment. Frank had to go farther afield and eventually had found a photographer willing to do the job. After the photography session, Gertie's remains were placed in a coffin, which apparently was then placed in the hallway of the bungalow at Cooleen.

Another topic of conversation was that no extended family members had attended the removal on the Sunday evening. Quite a number of local residents had turned out, more out of curiosity than sympathy. Apparently, they were hoping to find out some more information about Gertie, Frank and Ann during the eulogy. They were disappointed as the priest merely said a few prayers and announced the funeral arrangements for the following Tuesday morning.

I left Sam talking to the locals as I went across to the basilica. I was hoping that there might be a book of condolences from which I might glean some further information, but none had been left out.

Tuesday, 23 August was a beautiful sunny day. Sam and I arrived over at the basilica at half past ten. We wanted to mingle with the congregation, in case we might overhear any relevant conversations.

At a quarter to eleven a limousine arrived containing eight mourners. Based on the comments made by people close by, the eight comprised previous chauffeurs and immediate neighbours from the townland. Not one family member.

A little later, the Toyota Camry arrived, driven by a young

man who was identified as 'John from Cavan'. Frank was in the front passenger seat and Ann in the back of the car. The Camry was parked immediately outside the front door of the basilica. Ann had changed her 'habit' somewhat. The white scarf and fur headband had gone, and in their place was a wimple and a black veil. The black mantle appeared to be the same. She was wearing full make-up, complete with blusher, and black high-heeled shoes.

The party entered the church, followed by the other mourners and locals. 'We'll take a closer look at the car,' Sam said. The car bore small CD (corps diplomatique) plates on both back and front, and the rear number plate identified a garage in Edinburgh as the supplier. As we casually walked around the car, I noticed that it wasn't locked – at least the door buttons were in the up position. I also noticed some documents thrown on the front dashboard of the car. One appeared to be a UK passport. Glancing around, no one seemed to be paying any attention whatsoever to us or to the car. There were two gardaí in the vicinity but they didn't appear to be paying any attention to us either.

I nudged Sam and nodded in the direction of the documents. 'I think the car is open,' I said. We glanced around again. 'Hope the bloody alarm isn't on,' I said as I sidled up to the driver's door.

I took a deep breath and opened the door. Silence. Thank God, I thought, and slid into the driver's seat. Sam stood by the side of the car so he could warn me of any possible problems – like Frank or Ann appearing unexpectedly.

The first document I looked at was a navy UK passport, which was inside a red leather holder. It was issued to Joseph Frances G. I noted the number on the back of my hand. The photograph in the passport was our Frank. The second document was similar in size, shape and format, except it had a light blue cover. Inside, under a seal, were the words 'Department of Trade'. I had never seen a document like this before. I noted its number on the back of my hand and glanced at the photograph. It was Frank's picture.

I was starting to go through a third document, a navy folder with the title Securicor on the front, when something clicked in my mind. Picking up the passport and the Department of Trade identification booklet, I looked again at the photographs in each document and checked when each document was issued. There was some five years between the dates of issue, but Frank looked exactly the same in both photographs, even down to the suit and tie he was wearing. This struck me as odd. It was possible that he had owned only one suit and tie over the five years: maybe it was his 'best' suit and tie. After all, some men, particularly casual dressers, have one suit and drag it out for every wedding, funeral and formal occasion. But Frank was not one of those. Every time we had observed him, he was always immaculately turned out, a formal suit and tie type of guy. The other possibility, of course, was that the two photographs came from the same series or run of photographs taken at the earlier date. How many people keep small passport-sized photographs for five years – and can find them after that length of time? I thought. And issuing authorities always stipulate a 'recent' photograph for documents such as passports. I filed this point away at the back of my mind, in case something arose at a later date.

I had just opened the Securicor folder when Sam tapped on the window. I looked up, and he nodded his head slightly in the direction of the main door. I put the documents back on the dash, slid out of the seat and gently closed the driver's door. Two men walked past. They didn't appear to be paying any attention to us.

We went in to the funeral Mass. The photographer was taking photographs at various times during the service, which I found a little disconcerting. 'I thought they take photographs like this during weddings. Never seen it done for funerals before,' Sam said as we observed proceedings from the back of the church.

Some of the congregation left as soon as Mass was over, leaving the handful of mourners in situ. Further prayers were said, but there was no eulogy, no mention of Gertie's background or any other personal information, no reference whatsoever to the grieving husband Frank or the deceased's 'sister' Ann.

Gertie was buried in the adjoining cemetery. Frank, Ann and

the eight mourners left as soon as the formalities were completed and headed straight to the bar in the nearby Knock International Hotel.

We gave them a ten-minute head start and then Sam and I returned to the hotel and checked out. I rang Alan and arranged to see him in Castlerea on our way back to Dublin.

Castlerea

Alan had been busy since we last met, getting information from various sources. I treat all information I receive during the course of an investigation as individual pieces of a jigsaw puzzle; it is up to me to put all the pieces together and arrive at a complete picture or, in some cases, identify the gaps and go after those missing pieces so that the picture can be completed. The number of pieces in this particular jigsaw puzzle was increasing by the day, and Alan provided us with even more.

Apparently, Frank had been apprehended in Knock for a minor traffic violation. He had become very angry with the garda officer concerned, not generally a good idea, with the result that he had been brought into the local station, at which he became even more irate and then claimed 'diplomatic privilege'. He had made a telephone call to a Dublin number – Alan wasn't sure if the call was to our Department of Foreign Affairs or the British Embassy – but as result of the call he was allowed to go free.

The behaviour and movements of Frank and, by association, Ann and Gertie were the cause of some concern to the authorities. They had visited Lough Derg, and appeared to have spent quite a considerable period of time in areas bordering Northern Ireland, including Pettigo in County Donegal, and Cavan.

After Frank had come to the attention of the gardaí, they made routine enquiries of their counterparts in the UK. They were told that Frank, Ann and Gertie were 'not known' to them, but the Liverpool address they had provided was located in a very prosperous area. It seems there was a marked reluctance on the part of the Liverpool police to provide any further information.

Finally, Alan had been able to obtain some background

information on Gertie. Apparently, she had been married twice before; and he gave me her two previous married names.

We were approaching Mullingar when I asked Sam to stop for a break. We had been discussing non-stop all the information we had gathered on this trip once we left Castlerea, trying to make sense of it, trying to identify the gaps in the big picture and where we needed to go with this investigation. I really wanted a cigarette and a large mug of coffee, just to clear my head. Over coffee, we went over it all again. As Sam listed the various aspects of the investigation, we discussed possible follow-up enquiries, and I made notes. After two mugs of coffee each (and three cigarettes for me), Sam paid the waitress and we left.

It was just after six o'clock that evening when Sam dropped me off at my house. I felt mentally exhausted. I poured myself a large Scotch, topped it up with a diet Coke and settled down to prepare a summary of what would be my full report to our client. By nine thirty I had given up and headed for bed.

I was in the office at six forty-five the next morning. When I'm based in the office, the first job of the day is to brew the coffee. Whilst it was percolating, I checked the fridge. The milk had gone off and the local shop didn't open until eight. I found the tin of Marvel tucked away at the back of the cupboard – it was a bit lumpy, but it would do for the moment.

I settled down at my desk and reviewed the summary I had started the previous night. Christine appeared just before nine. Bless her; she had remembered to buy some milk on her way to work. I filled her in on the events of the previous two days and asked her to try to get hold of our client on the telephone at about ten. I asked her to tell his secretary that we would need about thirty minutes to run through the current position. Christine came back with the news that our client would ring at eleven. That gave me another hour to put some shape on the information we had obtained to date.

My client and I ended up talking for over an hour. I agreed to fax over my report later that day. He would talk to the other trustees and they would decide what other enquiries they wanted us to make.

When Sam arrived, all incoming calls were diverted to his extension and Christine and I settled down to prepare the report, she typed as I dictated. She faxed over the report at two thirty. At four that afternoon we had what you would describe nowadays as a conference call. My client and the other trustees were in his office, and Sam and myself were at our end of the phone.

I clarified a few points they raised about my report, and we agreed that I would identify areas that could potentially be investigated further and fax the list to Scotland the following morning. What had started out as a specific line of enquiry, i.e. possible duress or restraint of Ann by Frank, was to be extended. Some fears were now expressed about Ann's safety.

Another lengthy telephone call ensued the following morning. The bottom line was that I should carry out whatever enquiries I deemed appropriate, in particular relating to Frank and Gertie's background and their activities while they had been in Ireland.

The points that came to mind immediately were: they had spent some time in Pettigo, County Donegal; there might be some connection with Cavan Town; they had made a trip to the Isle of Man immediately before Gertie's death. There was also the matter of the two passport-type documents we had seen on the day of the funeral; and Gertie's claim that she was a member of the Lever family.

Donegal

Pettigo is a small village smack on the border with Northern Ireland. In fact it straddles the border. On the Irish side, the wee village is called Pettigo, and the other bit of the village, which lies in County Fermanagh, is called Tullyhommon. About six miles to the north is Lough Derg, where Ann met Frank and Gertie for the first time in October 1987.

Depending on the approach I took, and assuming they had lived in the area for a reasonable length of time, I didn't envisage that we would have many problems in getting information. They were outsiders, and Gertie being in a wheelchair, the age difference between Frank and Gertie, and Ann's mode of dress would all have made them somewhat conspicuous. We spent less than a day in Pettigo and the local people I spoke to were very forthcoming with information.

Frank and Gertie had arrived in Pettigo in February 1987 and had called themselves Mr and Mrs Lloyd. That was a new piece of information, and I filed away the surname Lloyd for future checking. They rented a cottage on the outskirts of the village. Very little was seen of Gertie but Frank had quite a high profile. He regularly frequented one of the biggest pubs in the village, usually for hours each time. He drank heavily and on a number of occasions had to be escorted home.

Frank told the locals that he was ex-FBI. He told them that he was writing a book on FBI activities and that he and his wife had moved over temporarily from London. He said he wanted peace and quiet to continue with his writing and that, owing to the ill health of his wife, the environment in Donegal was far preferable to the pollution in London.

He also told them that he was Greek and of the Greek Orthodox Church. What he didn't bargain for was that the daughter of the publican had worked in Greece regularly and could speak Greek fluently. When she tried to engage Frank in conversation in Greek, it was obvious that he didn't know the language at all, not even *yassou* or *kalimera*. Frank merely replied that they had misunderstood him – it was his father who was Greek. (I'm not sure how many Greeks have the surname Lloyd.)

Frank and Gertie had no means of transport during their stay in Pettigo and didn't travel outside the village. It appeared that they had intended to stay in Pettigo for some time – they had indicated to the owners of the cottage that they were interested in a long-term rental. However, they disappeared overnight. As one local said, 'They were here today and gone tomorrow.' A number of cheques Frank had written bounced, leaving local businesses out of pocket. None of the people I spoke to had any idea where Frank and Gertie had moved to when they had left Pettigo.

Cavan

At this point, we had no idea of the extent of the connection with Cavan Town. We knew the chauffeur had been described as 'John from Cavan' and Alan and his colleagues had mentioned sightings of Frank, Gertie and Ann in Cavan.

Sam and I drove up to Cavan to meet with one of my contacts. Over an early lunch, I explained some of the background to this investigation and Joe agreed to help me obtain any relevant information.

There was an unexpected twist to this part of the tale. Frankly, at that stage, there were so many different lines of enquiry going on, all at the same time, that I was beginning to doubt that I would ever get to a logical conclusion.

The new Toyota Camry, which we had noted at Gertie's funeral, was registered to Ann at the UK address in Wirral. It had been involved in a road traffic accident less than one week after the funeral. Our friend 'John from Cavan', who was a UK citizen, had been driving. Ann had given a statement immediately following notification by the gardaí of the accident. John apparently went AWOL for three days before he eventually gave his statement.

Most of the non-life insurance companies based in Ireland were clients for whom I investigated the validity (or otherwise) of claims for compensation arising from accidents, fires, theft, medical negligence and so on. The car was insured by one of my clients through a broker based in Angus in Scotland. When we got back to Dublin, I contacted the claims manager at their Dublin branch and he agreed to get whatever information was available from the UK office.

From the information I obtained in Cavan and from examining copy statements, it would appear that the accident had happened at 3.15a.m. on Sunday, 28 August 1988. At about 10p.m. on Saturday, 27 August, John had driven Ann home to the bungalow near Castlerea. He was due to collect her at 4.30a.m. on Sunday morning to drive her and 'a friend' to Dublin Airport. After dropping her off, John decided he would go to Cavan to meet some friends. He and his pals visited a number of pubs in Cavan and ended up in a disco in the town. The disco finished at two o'clock and John dropped four of his friends off at various addresses in and around the town. He stated that, to the best of his recollection, he left the town just after 3a.m. to return to Castlerea to collect Ann and her friend at four thirty. It goes without saying that this was totally irresponsible behaviour on John's part. It was sixty-two miles to Castlerea, twenty-seven miles of which was cross-country on minor roads; he hadn't been to bed since the previous Friday night; and on top of all that, he had been drinking.

The accident happened just outside Cavan town. According to John, the car 'went out of control on wet gravel and somehow hit a wall' (neither the fact that he hadn't been to bed for over twenty-four hours nor the fact that he had been drinking appear to have entered into his version of events). After making a cursory examination of the damage, John decided to drive on. The car 'packed up' shortly thereafter. It is not clear who called the gardaí, but they arrived on the scene and brought John back into Cavan Town.

John produced his driver's licence and a copy was made.

He had an address in Cavan Town and another in central London. Leaving aside the culture of the time with regard to drink driving, John was only nineteen years of age at that time and had obtained his first driver's licence just three months previously, in May 1988. In my mind there had to be a question mark about the naivety or lack of foresight on the part of Ann and/or Frank in deciding to employ a youngster such as John in the role of chauffeur.

—

On our return to Dublin, I contacted Alan in Castlerea. I filled him in on the latest information from Cavan and asked if he could find out the details of the car currently being used by Ann and Frank. He called me back the next day. Not only had he obtained the registration number of the current vehicle, but he had also checked its ownership details and had established that it was registered to a garage/car showroom in County Roscommon. This looked like being our next port of call.

Roscommon

We took the Cavan to Longford road and at Drumlish cut cross-country to Roosky and down into Roscommon, arriving just after one o'clock. The garage was closed for lunch so we hung around waiting for it to reopen and discussing what approach we would take.

Whenever possible, I stick close to the truth in the process of obtaining information. In 'normal' cases, which might end up in a court hearing, I never want to give the opposition the opportunity of discrediting my evidence on the basis that I had obtained it by lying. In this case, Ann's car had been involved in a road traffic accident; her insurers were clients of mine; and I was, in a way, investigating the accident. So I decided that was the approach I would take.

The owner of the garage was around when I approached to the young receptionist and she called him over to her desk. I repeated my opening speech. They were very forthcoming with information and produced the car rental file. They had no difficulty in recalling details of the transaction.

On 8 September 1988, Frank had personally attended at the garage to rent out the car. As he filled in the necessary documentation, he told the receptionist of the recent death of his wife. The young girl was quite upset when Frank produced photographs of Gertie laid out in the house at Cloonard and of the funeral service and lowering of the coffin into the grave at Knock. At that stage of the transaction, the garage owner had taken over the formalities of the rental paperwork. A photocopy of the main section of Frank's driver's licence had been taken. Another complication arose here. The photograph matched Frank, but the wording printed on the licence was in French. Bloody hell, I thought, not more bloody lines to investigate. The licence was in the name Francis Lloyd. It gave Birkenhead as his place of birth and his date of birth as 1934 (which would make Gertie thirty-eight years older than him); and an address in Barnstable, north Devon.

The only other piece of relevant information we obtained was that on 10 September, Frank had telephoned the garage to advise that the rented car had been stolen. The garage had of course informed the local gardaí of the situation. However, the next day, 11 September, Frank called again to say that he had been mistaken, the car had in fact been 'borrowed by a friend'. The garage informed the local gardaí of the details of the latest call from Frank.

———

Sam and I returned to Dublin and the next day we reviewed all the various strands of information we had gathered during the latest part of the investigation. We eliminated the Barnstable address as a possible lead quite quickly; it was a bed and breakfast establishment.

Frankly, we were not clear as to where all this was leading, in the context of our original instruction from our clients. While we were getting background information on Frank and Gertie's activities in Ireland, we didn't seem to be any closer to establishing the position with regard to Ann's personal safety or whether or not she was being conned.

Following another lengthy telephone consultation with our clients in Scotland, we were instructed to keep digging. Ours is not to reason why when clients make their decisions, so we continued with the investigation into outstanding lines of enquiry.

The Isle of Man

I had no contacts in the Isle of Man. I did not want to run the risk of wasting time (and our client's money) by making a personal trip over there, and I was lucky enough to be introduced by a friend to a retired UK CID police inspector, Kerry, who had apparently retired to live on the island. I spoke to him on the telephone. I needed confirmation of the trip taken by Frank, Gertie and Ann immediately before Gertie's death in August 1988: where they stayed; what they did; and anything else he could come up with. I gave him details of the registration numbers of the two cars that we knew about, the silver Mitsubishi and the Toyota Camry. We agreed a fee plus receipted expenses to be paid when I received his written report, and I wished him luck.

I know the Isle of Man is small but he was good, very good. Three days later, Kerry gave me an oral report, which was followed two days later by a written report.

Frank, Gertie, Ann and John, the chauffeur, had arrived in the Isle of Man by car ferry on 15 August 1988. Their first port of call was to the Isle of Man Steam Packet Company, where Frank booked and paid cash for the passage of a car and four passengers from Douglas to Dublin on 17 August. They had taken two rooms in the Empress Hotel in Douglas, Gertie and Ann in one and Frank and John in the other. The reservation had been made in Frank's name and he paid the hotel bill in cash.

Very little was seen of John on this trip. Frank, Gertie and Ann ate in the hotel restaurant each evening. The hotel staff thought that, apart from when she came down for dinner, Gertie remained in the hotel bedroom. Frank and Ann, on the other hand, spent most of their time in the hotel bar drinking brandy, and getting drunk. Their activities, or lack of them, were noticed by hotel staff, particularly as Ann was dressed in her 'nun's habit' and wearing make-up. As far as the staff were concerned, that was the extent of their activities. Apparently, they surmised that Frank and Ann were having a fling.

Kerry had spoken to the staff at the ferry port. They recalled the group that arrived at the ferry port on 17 August, Ann wearing her nun's habit, Gertie in her wheelchair, John, who appeared 'normal', and Frank, who was dressed as a Roman Catholic priest! They departed by the night ferry, arriving in Dublin on the morning of 18 August, leaving behind an unpaid restaurant bill, which was forwarded to the Castlerea address.

They were back on the Isle of Man on 18 September 1988. This time Frank and Ann were alone – Gertie had died in August, and there was no sign of a chauffeur. This time they stayed in the Grand Island Hotel in Ramsey. They had separate rooms and, once again, Frank settled the hotel bill in cash when they departed two days later.

Frank was driving a car, which had been hired from a company in Swinford, County Mayo. After leaving the Grand Island Hotel on 21 September, they moved to Douglas. Ann stayed in Derby Road, at a premises normally used for summer holiday flats, which are let by the day during the winter months. The accommodation was very basic. She stayed for two weeks and paid on arrival, in cash. She used the name Sister Marie Emmanuel.

Ann told the owner of these premises that she was on the Island on 'business' – but she didn't specify what this business might be. She also told the owner that her friend was a retired merchant seaman who dabbled in business. Frank, on the other hand, stayed in what was described as more luxurious accommodation – a private flat in Cleveland Court. Kerry didn't make any enquiries there, as there was a risk that any such enquiries could be reported back to Frank.

He did check with his former colleagues to see if anything was known about the pair, either in the Isle of Man or in the UK mainland. The only information he could come up with was that in 1986 Merseyside Police had carried out a preliminary investigation of Ann – under the name Sister Marie Emmanuel – arising from expenditure of over £30,000 sterling in one month on her American Express card, but as no offences were found, the file was closed. Based on collators' notes, Merseyside Police were then approached by Hertfordshire Police, seeking information on a Sister Marie Emmanuel and 'the identity of a man, disguised as a priest, who accompanies her'.

Apart from that one enquiry, Frank did not appear to have come to the notice of the UK police.

The information obtained by Kerry gave an excellent picture of the two trips to the Isle of Man. But there were no leads on the nature of the business, if any, that was being carried out by Ann and Frank on the island. This was yet another line of enquiry that had been followed and, yet again, there were no definite conclusions.

Maybe something would turn up when we checked out the 'passports' held by Frank. Remember, this was late 1988, before the peace process and the Good Friday Agreement. The Anglo-Irish Agreement was in its infancy, having been signed in 1985; Lord Justice and Lady Gibson had been murdered on the border with Northern Ireland in 1987; the 'Troubles', as we euphemistically called them, were still in progress.

I needed to clarify the matter of the possible duplicate passports held by Frank, and I thought the appropriate source would be the British Embassy, but I felt I couldn't simply walk up to the front door of the embassy, ring the bell and say, 'Hello, I need confirmation of some information please.' I wouldn't get anywhere near anyone who could help me.

This is my report on my visit to the British Embassy in October 1988.

The British Embassy, Dublin

The embassy is located on Merrion Road, Dublin. There is no parking and double yellow lines run along the entire frontage of the embassy grounds. There is only one way into the building and that is past a permanent garda checkpoint. After passing the garda officer, you enter what is in effect a tunnel. Midway along this tunnel, there is a security hatch on the left-hand side. When past that hatch, you enter the passport section of the embassy.

I wanted to talk to someone who might be able to clarify the position with regard to Frank's documents, and I knew that in order to avoid ending up in the passport office, I would have to pose, shall we say, an interesting question or proposition that would arouse the interest of the consular or diplomatic members of the embassy.

Sam drove me to Merrion Road and parked around the corner, so that he could pick me up when I left the embassy. This was a first-time scenario for me and I admit I was feeling a bit apprehensive. Maybe it was because I knew I would be attempting to deal with someone who was unlikely to exhibit the usual laid-back or 'ah sure' attitude we generally experienced in the course of our investigations.

I walked up to the gate of the embassy, went past the garda at the entrance, entered the tunnel and approached the security hatch, which was fronted by a type of glass that prevented you seeing the person on the other side clearly: I could just see a silhouette. I really hated performing 'dramatics', but I had to say something that would get me into the embassy proper.

The voice behind the glass said, 'Hello'.

'Hi, I'm an insurance investigator,' I replied. There was no response. I continued, 'During the course of a current investigation, I think I have come across a situation where someone may be holding two British passports. I need to talk to someone about this.' No response.

'I think this may be important,' I added, trying to keep my voice on an even keel.

'One moment, please,' replied the voice, deadpan, no emotion or interest apparent in his tone.

I don't know what went on at this point. I couldn't see the person behind the glass, nor could I hear anything that was being said. I glanced around and saw there were at least two CCTV cameras, one on the wall behind me, which would give a clear view of my back and anything I might be carrying; and the second mounted on the wall above the hatch, which obviously recorded 'facials'.

It seemed like ages later, but it was probably only a matter of minutes, when the voice said, 'Place your handbag, your mobile phone and the contents of your pockets in the hatch, please.'

I realised how thorough their security was, and I was glad that I had left the full investigation file in the car with Sam. I wanted to trade information: in other words I wanted to receive information in return for telling them what I knew. I had decided that a general approach, without specific details, would be best until I gauged their response.

'Please continue to the passport office and wait,' said the voice.

I went into the passport office. There was no one else there. I waited. Looking around, I noted more CCTV cameras. I also noted an alarm PIR unit on the wall and a smoke detector unit on the ceiling, which I half suspected also contained covert CCTV cameras. I had attended CCTV courses that had covered the installation and operation of overt and covert camera surveillance, and I would have been disappointed if I had not spotted the additional security cameras.

I was left standing in that room, alone, for ten minutes. Then a man entered who appeared to look me over before approaching me. I was nervous and on edge but so as not to be seen to back down, I eyeballed him. He looked pretty nondescript – an ordinary-looking guy in his mid-fifties, wearing a dark suit, white shirt and wine-coloured tie. You wouldn't pay any heed to him if you saw him on the street.

'How can I help you?' he asked.

I repeated like a mantra the opening I had given at the security hatch. I waited for his reply, feeling that his response would dictate the remainder of our conversation.

'So how can I help you?' he asked again.

I really do try to avoid swearing but, frankly, this guy, his demeanour and attitude, really pissed me off – pompous git, I thought.

'Let me explain,' I said, and gave him a general, non-specific description of the two 'passport' documents. 'If this man holds two passports,' I continued, 'I thought it might be of interest to you – but I need clarification as to the validity of the two documents.'

Because of his attitude, I decided not to give him the two passport reference numbers. If he could provide me with some clarification as to the source of the second 'passport' – the document with the Department of Trade logo on the cover – maybe then I would 'trade' him some specific reference numbers.

As an afterthought, I added. 'He claims diplomatic immunity and drives around in a car with CD plates.'

I waited for his response. The silence was deafening.

Finally he said, 'Okay, for a start will you give me his name?'

I replied 'Francis Gray, aka Francis Lloyd'.

He left the room and I waited. I didn't know what to expect but I half thought that no matter what he said, I would probably not believe him.

When he returned he said that neither of the names I had

mentioned, nor any combination of those names, was operating in Ireland, in any capacity, for the British government. Well, he was hardly going to admit that Gray was working undercover for the government, if that was indeed his role.

I asked him about the second passport-type document with the light blue cover and the Department of Trade logo. What was it? What did it signify? He left the room again.

When he returned he stated that he could not clarify this aspect without further details. He continued, 'It is possibly a discharge document issued by the Department of Trade to merchant seamen at the end of their service. Perhaps the Marine Office in Belfast might be able to help,' he added, as he walked towards the door. It was obvious that I was getting the brush-off.

I collected my belongings at the security hatch and walked back to the car. 'Got the bum's rush,' I said as I got in. 'But there is an office in Belfast that may be able to help with the blue book thing.'

Back at the office, I rang the Marine Office in Belfast, who in turn referred me to the General Registry of Merchant Shipping in Cardiff. The guy I spoke to in the Cardiff office was a little more forthcoming. He told me that before 1984, merchant seamen's identity books had been issued by the Department of Trade and did have a light blue cover. Since 1984 they had been issued by the Department of Transport. I gave him the reference number I had copied from Frank's book. He rang back the next day.

'I love Welshmen,' I said to Sam as I put down the phone. That lovely man had given me Frank's UK National Insurance number (a line of enquiry that my clients in Scotland would be able to follow), the date he was discharged from the Merchant Navy, and his date of birth.

'That's it,' I said to Sam. 'I can't do any more on this line of enquiry.'

Gertie

The only lead we had with regard to Gertie's background was the statement by both her and Ann that she was a member of the Lever family – Lever Brothers, the detergent manufacturing company. I ordered copies of the latest annual returns for this company from the UK Companies Registry. The only item that may have had some significance was the fact that the chairman of Lever Brothers was a Ronald George Gray, born in 1929. Frank was born in 1934, so could George be his older brother or otherwise related to Frank?

I decided to take the bull by the horns and telephoned Lever Brothers' head office in the UK, getting through to the chairman's secretary. I opened with the usual, 'I'm an insurance investigator . . .' Sticking as closely to the truth as possible, I told her that I was investigating the sudden death of Gertrude Gray in August 1988 (the implication being a claim under a life assurance policy), and that since it was reported that she was connected with the company, I was wondering if she was related to Mr Ronald Gray, the chairman. She thought not, but agreed to ask the chairman. I did tell her that the relationship could be by marriage, as Gertrude had been married to a Joseph Francis Gray, commonly known as Frank.

She rang me back within the hour. The chairman had never heard of either Gertie or Frank. She suggested I contact the company's chief archivist, Ronnie, who might have some information. I phoned Ronnie at the company's central London office and told him that the chairman's secretary had referred me to him. I have always found this type of approach helps when trying to get information: a referral usually makes people feel quite comfortable about giving information. It's as though they think, someone further up the chain of command says it's okay to talk to her. I gave Ronnie more or less the same story I had told the chairman's secretary.

When he rang back the next day, he confirmed that he had traced some records for Gertie. Yippee, I thought. Gertie had worked in the factory at Lever Brothers for a number of years. According to their records, she was formerly Mrs Gertrude Challinor. She was in receipt of a small company pension, and, no, they were not aware that she had died. Ronnie had also checked to see if Frank showed up anywhere in their records. There was no trace of him.

So, while Gertie and Ann had stated she was one of the Lever Brothers family, it turned out that she had merely worked in the factory. Perhaps their use of the word 'family' meant that all the factory workers at Lever Brothers were like one big family, but somehow I didn't think so. Given the context in which they had used the word 'family', I believe that they wanted to create the impression that Gertie was a very rich woman, and this supposition was somewhat supported by the fact that on Gertie's death certificate her occupation was described as 'stockbroker'.

Drink Driving Charges

Alan phoned me in the middle of November 1988. Frank had been arrested on a number of charges arising from one of the rare occasions when Frank drove himself. It was alleged that he had been very drunk, had hit a number of parked vehicles and had left the scene, after which he was chased by gardaí. In his attempt to escape, he drove across part of the fairways and a couple of the greens of the local golf course. He was arrested, charged, bailed to attend court at a later date, and released.

The next morning, Frank arrived at a garage in Castlerea, handed over the keys of the Camry and £5,000 sterling in cash. He gave instructions for the repairs to be made to the Camry, estimated to be IR£1,000, and the balance was to be used to repair the other cars that he had damaged.

Frank and Ann disappeared from Castlerea later that day. No one seemed to know their means of transport.

Two weeks later, Alan received a telephone call from a customs officer in Dublin Port. A young English lad driving the Camry had been stopped by customs as he was about to board the ferry. The lad had told the officers that he had been paid to transport the car from Castlerea to an address in the Wirral. They decided to check the facts before allowing the lad to board or, alternatively, taking the car apart. They obviously didn't like the look of this lad or were suspicious because either his age or his appearance didn't fit the usual profile of a driver of a top-of-the-range car. The background information was given to the customs officer and the lad was allowed to continue on his journey.

It was obvious that Frank and Ann had left the jurisdiction and now, with the car gone, they probably wouldn't be back.

It was very frustrating, to say the least. We had been working on this case periodically for five months. We had gathered various pieces of the jigsaw and put them together but there was a bloody big hole right in the middle. We would never get the full picture now.

I prepared my final report and sent it to Scotland.

———

In April 1989, I received a telephone call from Alan. He told me there was talk around Castlerea and in Cloonard that Frank had been killed in a road traffic accident in Switzerland. I rang my client and told him the news, and he asked me to go over to Castlerea as soon as possible.

Both Sam and I had found this case intriguing so off we went, quite happily, the following morning. If Frank was dead, I could be more direct in my approach to the former neighbours in Cloonard and they would probably be forthcoming.

The only change in the bungalow was that all the religious statues and icons were gone. I was going to 'play it by ear' so I knocked on the door. There was no reply. I went to the nearest cottage and knocked.

'I'm making enquiries about the bungalow down the road,' I said to the elderly man who had opened the door.

'I know nothing about it,' came the gruff reply. 'You can try Mrs M,' and he pointed to another cottage nearby.

'Would Mrs M be home?' I asked at the next cottage. An elderly gentleman had opened the door.

'She's not here,' he replied.

'Maybe you can help me? I've come all the way from Dublin. I hear Mrs M looks after the bungalow down the road.'

He invited me in and told me he was Mrs M's brother.

Patience is one of the virtues of a good PI. When trying to obtain information, particularly from an elderly person, you have to be prepared to let them talk at their own pace; let them tell the story in their own way. Sure, they may wander into extraneous details at times, but you bring them back on track by asking an appropriate question. Being officious or abrupt simply won't work.

This is the story Mrs M's brother told me over a cup of tea.

His sister had looked after the cottage for Ann during Ann and Frank's frequent absences. This had involved 'minding the house', lighting the fire and so on. At about ten thirty one night about two weeks earlier, he couldn't remember exactly when, his sister had received a telephone call from a man with an English accent who said his name was Andrew Mason and that he was a lawyer in the Isle of Man. Andrew Mason had told her that Frank had been killed in a road traffic accident and went on to explain that Frank and 'sister' (Ann) had purchased a villa in Switzerland and that Frank had been travelling from France to Switzerland when the accident occurred.

Ann was so distraught that she had taken herself off to a closed order of nuns in Italy. The lawyer told Mrs M that she could remove any of Frank's possessions, including 'the crystal chandelier'.

'But I thought they moved out last November,' I said.

'Sure,' he replied, 'but the rent is still being paid.'

Apparently, it was clear to Mrs M that the lawyer had extensive knowledge of the help Mrs M had given to Frank and Ann; and he thanked her on Ann's behalf. Because of this 'knowledge' Mrs M had no reason to doubt the validity of the call.

Her brother continued with the story. His sister asked the lawyer if Frank would be brought over to Knock to be buried with his wife. Mason avoided answering the question by saying that there were still a lot of arrangements to be made. The call concluded with Mason saying that he would write to Mrs M to confirm that she could empty the bungalow of the personal possessions.

As they had received no further communication from Mr Mason or Ann, they hadn't touched anything in the place.

I thanked him for the tea and the chat, and Sam and I returned to Dublin that evening.

I telephoned my client the following morning and gave him an oral report. My written report and bill followed. Once again, the files relating to this investigation were put away.

On Tuesday, 23 May 1989, Christine came into my office with the post as usual. She was always of a pleasant disposition, but that morning I noticed that she had a huge grin on her face.

'You'd better have a look at this,' she said, the grin getting bigger by the minute. There was a handwritten note from Castlerea and attached to it was a copy of an advertisement and a small piece that had appeared in the *Roscommon Herald* the previous Friday, 19 May.

'Bloody hell, it could only happen on this bloody job,' I said to Christine. I was grinning too – I couldn't help it.

I phoned Alan in Castlerea. 'Got your note, thanks,' I said. He started laughing.

'It's not bloody funny,' I said.

'It could only happen to you, Shirl,' he replied.

'I need to know if it's genuine. Do you know anyone in the *Roscommon Herald*?' I asked.

'Done that already,' came his reply.

When he saw the advertisement and the piece, Alan had rung a contact in the paper. They had received written instructions for the advertisement, accompanied by a sterling cheque drawn on the AIB Bank in the Isle of Man. The advertisement was so unusual that they telephoned the number specified and spoke to a man who stated he was Francis Grey and that the wording was correct. The advertising section mentioned it to the editor, who in turn called the number in the Isle of Man and interviewed the man who answered the phone. This resulted in the small editorial report in the newspaper.

I am being a bit circumspect here: this case had so many inconsistencies, twists and turns, illogical behaviour on the part of the subjects of our, who knows who was actually at the end of the phone line in the Isle of Man? I certainly couldn't say it was Frank.

The advertisement and the editor's piece are self-explanatory.

Re: HOAX TELEPHONE CALL

By an unknown English man re :

JOSEPH FRANCIS GRAY,

Formerly of Cloonard, Castlerea, Co. Roscommon, Eire

TO WHOM IT MAY CONCERN

Please take no notice of these calls — I am very much alive.

Signed : **J. F. GRAY.**

Any person with any information regarding these calls please contact :

J. F. GRAY, 3 Wesley Court, Lonan, Isle of Man.
Telephone 0624-781186.

Joseph is Alive and Well!!

An English businessman who, for a time, resided in Castlerea area, this week expressed his "utter disgust" at a hoax call to a friend in the town stating that he had died in a road traffic accident.

Speaking to the *Herald* on Tuesday from his Isle of Man home, Joseph Francis Gray explained that while he was on a recent business trip to Italy the hoax call from a person "with an English accent" came to Castlerea causing much upset and heartache. He added that words could not express his anger and hurt following the call, but he wished to assure his friends in the Castlerea area that he was very much alive and well.

Roscommon Herald, 19 May 1989

As Mark Twain said, 'The report of my death was an exaggeration.'

At this stage, I was getting quite fed up. Nothing about this case was making any sense. I like to be methodical in my work and I like it even more when there is a logical conclusion to an investigation.

I telephoned my client, told him of the latest developments and sent him a copy of the newspaper cuttings and a brief written report.

I didn't bother to make out a bill.

2008

While it was an interesting case, it was probably the most frustrating investigation I have ever carried out. It would have been easier to find the Holy Grail.

I kept all my files and records relating to this investigation and I also kept in touch with my client during the 1990s.

When last heard of, Frank had officially changed his surname to Grosvenor, nobody seems to know why. Ann married Frank, in or around 1998 we think. She is now looking to have the marriage dissolved or annulled or to get a divorce. When last heard of, she was living in Kharian city, in Gujarat District, north of Punjab Province, Pakistan.

Gertie is still in the cemetery in Knock. I couldn't resist going back to check on the grave. The twentieth anniversary of her death will be later this year. Her grave is overgrown with weeds. It hasn't been maintained in any way. It is unmarked, with no headstone, not even a cross marking the spot. There is a kerb around the perimeter of the grave, which suggests someone had intended to erect a headstone or do something with the grave, but according to the cemetery superintendent, this was not so. The local stonemason had mistaken Gertie's grave for another one elsewhere in the cemetery and had built the kerb before he realised his mistake.

'No one has set foot at the grave in twenty years,' he added.

Yet again, I stored away my files on this investigation. Maybe, just maybe, I will get another telephone call from Scotland and this saga will start all over again.

In a way, I hope so. As far as I am concerned it still remains unfinished business. And who knows, I might come out of retirement, get Sam, and go looking for some more jigsaw pieces . . .